UNITED NATIONS CONFERENCE ON TRADE AND DEVELOPMENT

PROCEEDINGS OF THE SECOND INTER-REGIONAL DEBT MANAGEMENT CONFERENCE

Geneva, 3–5 April 2000

UNITED NATIONS
NEW YORK AND GENEVA, 2001

NOTE

The designations employed and the presentation of the material in this publication do not imply the expression of any opinion whatsoever on the part of the Secretariat of the United Nations concerning the legal status of any country, territory, city or area, or of its authorities concerning the delimitation of its frontiers or boundaries. Further, the views expressed by the authors of the papers included in this publication do not represent the views of the Secretariat of the United Nations with regard to individual governments' policies, or positions on financial policy issues that form the subject of the discussions below.

UNCTAD/GDS/DMFAS/Misc.23

UNITED NATIONS PUBLICATION
Sales No. E.01.II.D.17
ISBN 92-1-112528-6

Executive summary

This document is a compilation of presentations made by debt management experts and professionals during UNCTAD's Second Inter-regional Debt Management Conference held in Geneva in April 2000. The conference addressed recent trends in the area of debt management, and, in particular, it aimed at highlighting the consequences recent developments have had, and will have in the future, for individual national debt offices and for the profession of debt management.

At the end of the twentieth century, the world's financial markets saw a number of dramatic events. The Asian and Russian debt crises sent shock waves not only through the economies of those regions, but also affected economies all over the globe. In spite of lessons learned in Asia, private sector debt continued to represent a problem. Eleven European countries decided to introduce the euro on 1 January 1999 and Ecuador defaulted on its Brady bonds in October the same year. These developments have had both short- and long-term consequences for debt managers. Amortization tables, risk management models and debt strategies have to be reconsidered.

At the same time, the institutional set-up for effective debt management continues to represent a problem for debt managers all over the world. A study undertaken by the World Bank showed that among the main obstacles and concerns that Governments face in debt management, no less than 51 per cent of the replies related to the institutional environment. In addition to this, important factors also include the rapid development in computer technology. Sophisticated integrated computer systems open up new possibilities and challenges that affect the institutions where they are used.

The aim of the conference was therefore to: analyse the implications that recent events in the financial markets have had and will continue to have for debt managers in the twenty-first century; analyse how institutions, procedures and financial instruments have to adapt to the new international financial architecture and the role of the debt manager in this process; discuss the general usefulness and impact of risk management; and analyse the new requirements for computerized debt management tools in changing environments.

Contents

Part 1: Debt management in today's economic environment

Part 2: Financial tools and risk management

Part 3: Financial management systems

CONTRIBUTORS

Mr. Yilmaz Akyüz

Officer-in-Charge
Division on Globalization and Development Strategies
UNCTAD
Geneva, Switzerland

Mr. Osvaldo N. Albano Landesa

International Financial Management Project
Ministry of Finance
Guatemala

Mr. Pål Borresen

Financial Economist
Debt and Development Finance Branch
UNCTAD
Geneva, Switzerland

Mr. Thomas P. Briggs

Senior Advisor
Office of Technical Assistance, U.S. Department of
Treasury
Washington DC, United States of America

Prof. Leonor Magtolis Briones

Treasurer
Treasury of Philippines
Philippines

Mr. László Buzas

Managing Director
Government Debt Management Agency, State Treasury
Hungary

Mr. Stijn Claessens

Lead Economist
World Bank
Washington DC, United States of America

Mr. Andrew Cornford

Senior Economic Affairs Officer
Macro-Economic and Development Policies Branch
UNCTAD
Geneva, Switzerland

Dr. Enrique Cosío-Pascal

Officer-in-Charge
Debt and Development Finance Branch
UNCTAD
Geneva, Switzerland

Mr. Andres de la Cruz

Partner Cleary, Gottlieb, Steen & Hamilton
New York, United States of America

Mr. Ettore Dorrucci

International Relations Officer
International Relations Division
European Central Bank
Frankfurt/Main, Germany

Mr. Luis Foncerrada

Former Director of the Mexican Debt Office
Mexico City, Mexico

Mr. Richard Fox

Director
Latin America, Fitch IBCA
London, United Kingdom

Ms. Julia Holz

Senior Control Officer
Asian Development Bank
Manila, Philippines

Mr. Zhao Jianping

Deputy Director-General
State Administration for Foreign Exchange
Beijing, People's Republic of China

Mr. Lars Kalderen

Chairman
DEVFIN Advisers AB
Stockholm, Sweden

Mr. Trevor de Kock

Manager
New Loan Products
African Development Bank
Abidjan, Côte d'Ivoire

Mr. Jerome Kreuser

Executive Director
RisKontrol Group GmbH
Bern, Switzerland

Ms. Aracelly Mendez

Director
Credito Publico
Ministry of Economy and Finance
Panama

Mr. Christian Michel

Financial Expert
Ministry of Foreign Affairs
Paris, France

Mr. Louis de Montpellier

Director
Strategy and Risk Management Debt Agency
Treasury of the Kingdom of Belgium
Brussels, Belgium

Mr. Emilio Nastry
Mr. Marcelo Tricarico

Ministry of Finance
Buenos Aires, Argentina

Ms. Christina Orbeta
Former Director
External Debt Department, Central Bank
Manila, Philippines

Mr. Rubens Ricupero
Secretary-General of UNCTAD
Geneva, Switzerland

Mr. Erkki Vehkamäki
Payment Systems Expert
Interbank Funds Transfer Project of the Central Bank of
Lithuania
Former Development Director of the CSD
Helsinki, Finland

Mr. Ziga Vodušek
Senior Economist
Inter-American Development Bank
Paris Office, France

Mr. Leonard P. Wales
Assistant Budget Director
Office of Management and Budget
Fairfax County, Virginia, United States of America

Mr. James P. Wesberry
Director
USAID Accountability/Anticorruption Project for Latin
America and the Caribbean
Virginia, U.S.A.
Consultant to the World Bank
Washington DC, United States of America

ABBREVIATIONS

ADAPS	Automated Debt Auction Processing System (Philippines)
ADB	Asian Development Bank
ADF	Asian Development Fund
ALM	asset/liability management
BCBS	Basel Committee on Banking Supervision
BIS	Bank for International Settlements
CABEI	Central American Bank for Economic Integration
CIP	Capital Improvement Program (Virginia, United States of America)
CIS	Commonwealth of Independent States
CSD	Central Securities Depository
DMFAS	Debt Management and Financial Analysis System
DSR	debt service ratio
DVP	delivery versus payment
ECB	European Central Bank
ECSDA	European Central Securities Depositories Association
EMI	European Monetary Institute
EMS	European Monetary System
EMU	European Monetary Union
ERM	Exchange Rate Mechanism (of the EU)
EU	European Union
FDI	foreign direct investment
FY	fiscal year
GDP	gross domestic product
GNP	gross national product
HIPC	heavily indebted poor countries
HLI	higly leveraged institution
IBRD	International Bank for Reconstruction and Development
IDA	International Development Association
IDB	Inter-American Development Bank
IFMS	integrated financial management systems
IMF	International Monetary Fund
ISD	investment service directive
IOSCO	International Organization of Securities Commissions
IT	information technology
LAC	Latin America and the Caribbean
LDC	least developed country
LIBOR	London Inter-Bank Offered Rate
MIS	management information system
NAFTA	North American Free Trade Area (or Agreement)
NCU	national currency units
NEDA – ICC	National Economic and Development Authority Investment Coordination Committee (the Philippines)
OCR	ordinary capital resources
ODA	official development assistance
OECD	Organisation for Economic Co-operation and Development

OPEC	Organization of Petroleum Exporting Countries
OTC	over-the-counter (market – for derivatives)
PDI	past due interest
RIG	rolling interest guarantee
SAFE	State administration of foreign exchange (People's Republic of China)
SAT	Tax Administration System (Guatemala)
SDDS	Special Data Dissemination Standard
SDR	Special Drawing Right
SEGEPLAN	General Planning Secretariat (Guatemala)
SIAD	Integrated Administrative Systems (Guatemala)
SIAF	Integrated Financial Management System (Guatemala)
SIDIF	Integrated Financial Information System (Argentina)
SIGEPRO	Project Management System (Guatemala)
SINARH	Human Resource Administration System (Guatemala)
SNDO	Swedish National Debt Office
SNIP	National Public Investment System (Guatemala)
UDAFs	Financial Management Units (Guatemala)
UDAIs	Internal Audit Units (Guatemala)
UNCTAD	United Nations Conference on Trade and Development
USAID	United States Agency for International Development
WADMO	World Association of Debt Management Offices
WAEMU	West African Economic and Monetary Union
WB	World Bank

OPENING STATEMENT

Rubens Ricupero

Distinguished participants, ladies and gentlemen,

It is a great pleasure to welcome you to United Nations Conference on Trade and Development's (UNCTAD) Second Interregional Debt Management Conference. Debt managers and experts gathering here today share one common endeavour: to manage a country's external and domestic debt. Around 200 government officials from more than 80 countries representing all regions of the world are here to listen to experts, participate in debates and meet with colleagues from different countries. This is a great opportunity for all of us, and UNCTAD is honoured to host such an important meeting.

Its objective is to take stock of the problems faced by debt managers in the twenty-first century and to propose appropriate solutions. Recent events, such as the Asian and Russian financial crises, the Heavily Indebted Poor Countries (HIPC) Initiative, the introduction of the euro and Ecuador's default on its Brady bonds, have both short-term and long-term consequences for debt managers. At the same time, the establishment of the institutional machinery for effective debt management continues to represent a challenge for debt managers all over the world. In addition, the development of sophisticated integrated computer systems opens up new possibilities and challenges that affect the institutions where they are used. Accordingly, the conference will address the various components of the debt management function in the current economic environment, particularly financial tools, risk management and financial management systems.

The experience gained in the area so far shows that debt management differs significantly among various groups of countries. Thus, debt managers face different challenges and approach their tasks from different situations, experiences and perspectives. For some, debt sustainability is at the forefront; for others, market access or risk management techniques are the major issue. Whatever these differences, it is critical for all countries to have a professional debt management function. Some experts believe that investment in a professional debt management office is one of the most important investments a country can make. After all, the senior debt management officials are the defenders of the Government's reputation in the international financial community and in the marketplace. Attracting and retaining qualified staff, establishing a debt management office with sufficient autonomy to do its job effectively and ensuring that it has the required information systems, authority and accountability to successfully implement strategies are key issues that need to be addressed.

As you know, UNCTAD is also organizing the constitutional General Assembly of the World Association of Debt Management Offices (WADMO), to be held on 6 April. UNCTAD has played a prominent role in the creation of the association, which will provide debt management professionals with a forum to discuss technical matters of common interest. The idea for such a grouping was first proposed by the Philippines in 1997 at the first Interregional Conference on Debt Management, where participants agreed that there was a considerable need for the regular exchange of experience, know-how and information on debt management at the international level.

Recently, UNCTAD X – held in Bangkok in February – underlined the importance of UNCTAD's technical cooperation and recommended that we should focus our work on activities that provide practical assistance to developing countries and countries with economies in transition. We were also requested to provide continued support for debt management. As a key component of UNCTAD's technical cooperation activities, the Debt Management and Financial Analysis System (DMFAS) Programme, is an excellent example of how the organization is assisting member countries through practical work at the country level. This is an issue directly relevant to the integration of developing countries and countries with economies in transition into the international economy.

The DMFAS Programme originated more than 15 years ago at the start of the so-called "debt crisis". It resulted from UNCTAD's participation in the Paris Club, as well as from its long experience in dealing with the debt problems of developing countries. UNCTAD's economists recognized the strengths and weaknesses of numerous national debt management systems. We therefore thought that enhancing the capacity of developing countries to manage their foreign debt would make a significant contribution to tackling some aspects of the debt problem. UNCTAD started by building a computer-based debt management information system, which is the origin of DMFAS. Since then, the DMFAS has been regularly upgraded in order to adapt it to the evolution of international finance and to rapid changes in information technology.

The DMFAS Programme is now one of the major providers of technical cooperation services in the area of debt management. Its software is the most widely used standard system for debt management in the world. The gains obtained from the DMFAS Programme by user countries are difficult to quantify, as the benefits of better information, analysis, negotiations and policy-making cannot easily be measured. However, it is generally accepted that these gains far exceed the cost of DMFAS country projects. At the very least, DMFAS pays for itself by making debt-servicing procedures more efficient and by checking inconsistencies in the claims of creditor agencies. Substantial savings can also be made by avoiding unnecessary costs such as overpayments to creditors or penalty interests due to poor bookkeeping. In Argentina, for example, where the DMFAS project cost around US\$ 1 million, the direct savings made during the three-year implementation phase of the project amounted to around US\$ 25 million. Today, the DMFAS client base consists of more than 50 developing countries and countries with economies in transition and the number of user countries is still rising. Taken together, the long-term and medium-term public and publicly guaranteed debt currently being managed or about to be taken under management by the DMFAS, represents around 30 per cent of the total outstanding debt in this category of debt of developing and transition countries. It amounts to close to US\$ 600 billion – a highly impressive figure, and an indication of the confidence placed in our organization by the countries concerned.

Finally, let me thank all of you for participating in this event; our special thanks are due to our donors, who have provided financial support to the DMFAS Programme for many years. I wish you a successful meeting and profitable deliberations.

Part 1

The debt management in today's economic environment

THE DEBATE ON THE INTERNATIONAL FINANCIAL ARCHITECTURE: REFORMING THE REFORMERS

Yilmaz Akyüz

This paper briefly surveys the progress made in various areas of reform of the international financial architecture since the outbreak of the East Asian crisis, and explains the principal technical and political obstacles encountered in carrying out fundamental changes needed for dealing with global and systemic instability. It ends with a brief discussion of what developing countries could do at the global, national and regional levels to establish defence mechanisms against financial instability and contagion.

1. Introduction

After the recent bouts of turbulence and instability in international currency and financial markets – including the 1992/93 European Monetary Union (EMU) crisis, large gyrations in the exchange rate of the dollar,[1] and the emerging-market crises in Brazil, East Asia, Mexico, and the Russian Federation – a consensus seemed to emerge that instability was global and systemic, that national efforts would not be sufficient to deal with the problem, and that there was a need to overhaul, and indeed, reconstruct the global financial architecture. The ensuing debate has concentrated mainly on the following areas:

(i)   Standards and transparency;
(ii)   Financial regulation and supervision;
(iii)   Management of the capital account;
(iv)   Exchange rate regimes;
(v)   Surveillance of national policies;
(vi)   Provision of international liquidity; and
(vii)   Orderly debt workouts.

Measures under these headings can help to prevent or manage financial crises, and sometimes serve both objectives simultaneously. Clearly, reforms in these areas generally imply significant changes in the operating procedures and governance of the Bretton Woods institutions, notably the International Monetary Fund (IMF). Indeed, these issues are often addressed in the context of the reform of these institutions, as does the recent Meltzer Commission Report commissioned by the United States Congress (International Financial Institution's Advisory Commission, 2000).

Since the Asian crisis, a number of proposals have been made in these areas by Governments, international organizations, private researchers and market participants. Some of these proposals have been discussed in international institutions such as the IMF, Bank for International Settlements (BIS) and the newly-established Financial Stability Forum. A close look at a recent IMF report reviewing the progress made so far shows that many of the proposals

---

[1] The dollar swung from 79 yen in the spring of 1995 to about 150 yen in 1997, coming back to some 100 yen at the end of the decade. During the past year it showed substantial gyrations against the yen, sometimes changing by 15–20 per cent within weeks.

and actions considered in these forums, have concentrated on marginal reform and incremental change rather than on the big ideas that emerged in the wake of the East Asian financial crisis.[2] More specifically, attention has focused on standards and transparency, and, to a lesser extent, on financial regulation and supervision. However, efforts have been piecemeal or absent in the more important areas that address systemic instability and its consequences. With stronger-than-expected recovery in East Asia, the containment of the damage in Brazil and the Russian Federation, and the rebound of Western stock markets, emphasis has increasingly shifted towards costly self-defence mechanisms and greater financial discipline in debtor countries. Developing countries are urged to adopt measures such as tight national prudential regulations to manage debt, higher stocks of international reserves and contingent credit lines as a safeguard against speculative attacks, and tight monetary and fiscal policies to secure market confidence while maintaining open capital account and convertibility. Big ideas for appropriate institutional arrangements at the international level for global regulation of capital flows, timely provision of adequate international liquidity with appropriate conditions, and internationally sanctioned arrangements for orderly debt workouts have not found favour among the big powers. Some "very big ideas" did not even make it to the agenda of the international community, as they were, presumably, found to be too radical to deserve official attention. These include:

(i)   A proposal by George Soros to establish an International Credit Insurance Corporation, designed to reduce the likelihood of excessive credit expansion;

(ii)   A proposal by Henry Kaufman to establish a board of overseers of major international institutions and markets with wide ranging powers for setting standards and for the oversight and regulation of commercial banking, securities business and insurance;

(iii)   A similar proposal for the creation of a global mega-agency or world financial authority for financial regulation and supervision, with responsibility for setting regulatory standards – for all financial enterprises – both offshore and onshore entities;

(iv)   A proposal to establish a genuine international lender-of-last-resort with discretion to create its own liquidity;

(v)   A proposal to create an international bankruptcy court in order to apply an international version of chapter 11 of the United States Bankruptcy Code for orderly debt workouts;

(vi)   A proposal to manage the exchange rates of the G-3 currencies through arrangements such as target zones, supported by George Soros and Paul Volcker; and

(vii)   A "Tobin tax" to curb short-term volatility of capital movements and exchange rates.

There are certainly conceptual and technical difficulties in designing reasonably effective global mechanisms for the prevention and management of financial instability and crises. Such difficulties are also encountered in designing national financial safety nets, and they explain why it is impossible to establish fail-safe systems. At the international level, there is the additional problem that any system of control and intervention would need to be reconciled with national sovereignty, diversity and conflicting interests. For all these reasons, it is not realistic to expect replication of national financial safety systems at the international level, involving global regulation, supervision and insurance mechanisms, or an international lender-of-last resort and international bankruptcy procedures.

However, political constraints and conflict of interest, rather than conceptual and technical problems, appear to be the main reason why the international community has not been able to achieve even a modest degree of real progress in setting up effective global arrangements

---

[2]For a summary of the proposals discussed and actions so far taken in the IMF (see IMF, 1999a).

for the prevention and management of financial crises. However, political disagreements are not only between industrial and developing countries; there have also been considerable differences among the G7 countries regarding the nature and direction of reforms. A number of proposals by various G7 members for regulation, control and intervention in the financial and currency markets have failed to achive consensus, in large part because of the opposition of the United States. By contrast, agreement among the G7, has been much easier to reach in areas aimed at disciplining the debtor developing countries.

It seems that the major industrial powers oppose a rules-based global financial system that explicitly defines the responsibilities of creditors and debtors, and the roles of the public and private sectors. They continue to favour a case-by-case approach because, *inter alia*, such an approach gives them considerable discretionary power due to their leverage in international financial institutions. However, it is not clear if such a system would be desirable from the point of view of smaller countries, particularly developing countries. It is not realistic to envisage that a rules-based global financial system could be established on the basis of a distribution of power markedly different from that of existing multilateral financial institutions. It would likely reflect the interests of larger and richer countries, rather than redressing the imbalance between international debtors and creditors. Such biases against developing countries exist even in the so-called rules-based trading system[3], where the North-South relationship is a great deal more symmetrical than in the sphere of finance, where developing countries are almost invariably debtors and industrial countries creditors.

Indeed, developing country Governments have not always been supportive of proposed measures for reform. In a sense, they have been ambivalent about the reform of the system, even though, because of their greater vulnerability, this is an issue deserving top priority for them. In many cases, this is motivated by their desire to retain policy autonomy. But they have also opposed measures, at national or global level, that would have the effect of lowering the volume of capital inflows and/or raising their cost, even when such measures could be expected to be effective in reducing instability and the frequency of crises in emerging markets:

(i)   A large majority of developing countries have been unwilling to impose controls on capital inflows during the boom phase of the financial cycle with the objective of moderating them and deterring short-term arbitrage flows.

(ii)   Emerging markets are generally unwilling to introduce bond covenants and collective action clauses, and expect industrial countries to take the lead in this respect.

(iii)   Again developing countries are generally opposed to differentiation among sovereign risks in the Basel capital requirements for international bank lending, a measure now being proposed as part of the new framework by the Basel Committee on Banking Supervision (BCBS) (Cornford, 2000).

Given these differences among various groups of countries and conflicts of interest, it should come as no surprise that so far very little progress has been made in the reform of the global financial architecture. The following section briefly goes through the main areas of reform and discusses the state of play and the difficulties encountered in the reform process.

---

[3] For a discussion of the asymmetries and biases against developing countries in the international trading system see UNCTAD (1999).

2. Progress in various areas of reform

2.1. Standards and transparency

It was generally agreed in the wake of the Asian crisis that prevention and better management of financial crises required greater transparency and disclosure of information regarding the activities of the public sector, financial markets and institutions and international financial institutions, particularly the IMF. This was thought to be necessary for markets to make prudent lending and investment decisions, for Governments to implement effective measures for regulation and supervision of financial institutions and activities, and for the IMF to improve its surveillance. While many observers argued that greater availability of information would not by itself be sufficient to prevent financial crises, it was, nevertheless, generally agreed that disclosure and transparency were necessary ingredients of an improved financial architecture.

Action in the international community has so far concentrated on setting standards for, and improving the timeliness and quality of, information concerning key macroeconomic variables and transparency of public sector activities, including fiscal, monetary and financial policies. Less progress has been made regarding the financial reporting of banks and other financial firms, and almost none in the case of highly leveraged institutions and offshore markets.

While the laissez-faire ideology has played some part in the slow progress in achieving transparency of financial institutions, there are also serious conceptual and structural problems. It is generally agreed that public disclosure of information submitted to supervisors could, in some circumstances, enhance, rather than diminish, instability. Nor is it clear what constitutes relevant information, since there is considerable variation among industrial countries in both the quantity and form of publicly disclosed information. Furthermore, the increased speed at which financial firms can now alter their balance sheets and off-balance sheets positions renders financial statements out of date almost before they can be prepared.

Even more contentious is the transparency of the IMF itself. New mechanisms have been introduced in the form of Public Information Notices following Article IV consultations and a pilot programme for voluntary release of Article IV staff reports. However, there are difficulties in attaining full transparency of the IMF since Governments often object to the disclosure of the confidential information they provide to the Fund. Moreover, owing to the political sensitivities involved as well as the questions regarding its track record in macroeconomic and financial diagnosis, temptations to turn the Fund into a fully-fledged credit rating agency are rightly resisted. Within these limits, however, there is scope to improve the transparency of the IMF. Its prescriptions could be subjected to independent review, for instance by a commission constituted by the United Nations.

2.2. Financial regulation and supervision

The official position here is to formulate global standards to be applied by national authorities, rather than to establish a global regulatory agency. In order to ensure that such standards be adopted and implemented by developing countries, IMF surveillance has now been extended to financial sector issues. However, it is generally agreed that the IMF itself should not become a global standard-setting authority in financial regulation and supervision, and that the BIS should not become a policeman of the international financial system.

Developments in the past few years have shown that the standards of the Basel Capital Accord are increasingly divorced from the credit risks actually faced by many banks, and are distorting incentives for banks regarding the capital maintained for a given level of risk. Moreover, while the short-term exposure of international banks has been a major feature of recent external debt crises, the Basel Capital Accord attributes a low-risk weight for the purpose of calculation of capital requirements on interbank claims. Again, in the case of the majority of countries, the same capital charge is assessed against a loan to a sovereign State with an investment-grade rating as to one with a junk-bond rating. These have led to pressure for regulatory changes, which would have the consequence of raising the cost to banks of such lending so that they better reflect its risks.

The new capital rules proposed in June 1999 include, *inter alia*, provision for risk weights for exposure to sovereign entities based on external assessment by rating agencies.[4] However, such an approach is highly contentious for two reasons. First, past record suggests that private rating agencies cannot be trusted for the assessment of country risk. Secondly, as noted above, developing countries generally resist such an approach on the grounds that the introduction of differentiated sovereign risk weights would lead many of them to increase their spreads and reduce the volume of lending.

There seems to be a consensus that tightened regulation and supervision should be extended to highly leveraged institutions (HLIs) – of which the most important examples are hedge funds – as well as to offshore centres (closely related, since HLIs are often incorporated in offshore centres). In the case of HLIs, this consensus reflects partly the realization (since the narrowly averted collapse of Long Term Capital Management in 1998), that such funds can be a source of systemic threat to financial stability. Thus the traditional argument for subjecting them to only light supervision, based on their restriction to wealthy investors capable of protecting their own interests, no longer suffices. Moreover, the consensus is also a response to evidence assembled by certain Asian Governments that such institutions, on occasion, contribute to the accentuation of volatility in the markets for currencies and other assets. However, so far little progress has been made in these areas. These issues are on the agenda of the Financial Stability Forum. Indirect control of HLIs (e.g. through their creditors, on the basis of enhanced transparency) appears to be the preferred option. The extent to which such institutions may eventually be subjected to direct control will depend on the effectiveness of the reforms so far proposed.

2.3.   Management of the capital account

The continuing incidence of financial instability and crises in industrial countries suggests that regulatory and supervisory reform and transparency are unlikely to provide fail-safe protection in this area. And if this statement is true even of countries with state-of-the-art financial reporting, regulation and supervision, it is likely to apply a fortiori to most developing economies. Thus, capital controls are increasingly seen as essential for greater stability.

There is broad agreement that the boom-bust cycle in private capital flows needs to be moderated, and this can be attained by controlling short-term, liquid capital inflows through market-based measures such as such as taxes or reserve requirements. Controls on inflows

---

[4] For an up-to-date account of the Basel Committee's proposals for revised standards, see Cornford (2000).

would also reduce the likelihood of a rapid exit. Nevertheless, as the Malaysian experience indicates, should a crisis occur, temporary controls on outflows, which constitute an essential complement of debt-standstills (see below), can also be very effective.

Given that developing countries have no international commitment regarding the capital account, the position of international financial institutions on such matters may be thought to have little practical consequence. However, without the IMF's unqualified recognition of the need for control over short-term capital flows, developing countries would generally be unwilling to apply such measures for fear of undermining market confidence and reducing their overall access to international finance. Indeed, only a few countries have so far resorted to such measures during the boom phase. Moreover, in order to effectively carry out its bilateral surveillance, IMF recommendations should include capital controls, particularly to countries where the financial system is not robust enough to withstand intermediate short-term inflows without leading to a build-up of excessive currency risk and fragility. While retaining autonomy with respect to capital account policies remains essential for developing countries (as often reaffirmed in G-24 communiqués), an official sanctioning of controls over certain types of capital flows would considerably strengthen their hand in managing their capital accounts.

However, there has been no agreement in the IMF Board on the use of capital controls. Some major shareholders still consider even moderate forms of control as exceptional and temporary, rather than essential components of capital account regimes in emerging markets. They seem to believe that sound macroeconomic policies and improved prudential regulations would do the trick. Thus, the IMF Progress Report states that the "Executive Board reached agreement on broad principles but differences remain on operational questions about the use and effectiveness of capital controls", and they put "stronger emphasis than was previously placed on the need for a case by case approach and on the adoption of prudential policies to manage the risks from international capital flows" (IMF, 1999a).

2.4. Exchange rate regimes

Recent debate on exchange rate policies in developing countries has concentrated on the question of connections between exchange rate regimes and financial crises. Pegged or fixed exchange rates have fallen out of favour on the grounds that financial and currency crises in emerging markets have often been associated with such regimes. Accordingly, developing countries are increasingly advised to choose one of the two extremes: either to float freely, or to lock in their exchange rates to one of the major currencies – often the United States dollar – through such arrangements as currency boards, or even simply to adopt the dollar as their national currency.[5]

However, there are strong doubts that under free mobility of capital, either of these extremes will provide better protection against currency instability and financial crisis than nominal pegs. Moreover, there is a danger that neither will allow the exchange rate to be tailored to the requirements of trade and competitiveness. Contrary to some perceptions, countries with flexible exchange rates are no less vulnerable to financial crises than those with pegged or fixed exchange rates. Differences among pegged, floating and fixed regimes lie less in their capacity to prevent damage to the real economy and more in the way damage is inflicted: for instance, in real term, Argentina and Hong Kong (China) – both economies with currency boards – have suffered as much, or even more, than their neighbours, experiencing sharp declines in their

---

[5] For a discussion of these alternatives see Eichengreen (1999: 103-109).

currencies. There now appears to be a growing consensus that better management of exchange rates in developing countries requires targeting real exchange rates in combination with the control and regulation of destabilizing capital flows. This is often seen to offer a viable alternative to free floating or to a complete ceding of monetary authority to a foreign central bank.[6]

Developing countries have resisted the proposal that adoption of a particular exchange rate regime should be part of the IMF conditionality for access to international liquidity. In any case, the IMF has not always kept to the newly emerging consensus among the mainstream economists to avoid pegged exchange rates. For instance, the Fund has been supporting an exchange-based stabilization programme in Turkey, put in place at the end of 1999, with a preannounced exchange rate to provide an anchor to inflationary expectations.

But perhaps more fundamentally, it is open to question whether emerging markets can attain exchange rate stability simply by adopting appropriate macroeconomic policies and exchange rate regimes when the currencies of the major industrial countries are subject to large gyrations. Indeed, many observers (including Paul Volcker and George Soros) have suggested that the global economy will not achieve greater systemic stability without some reform of the G-3 exchange rate regime, and that emerging markets remain vulnerable to currency crises as long as major reserve currencies remain highly unstable. However, various proposals for exchange rate coordination, including target zones for G-3 currencies (an idea briefly supported by Germany), have so far been opposed by the United States.

2.5.   Surveillance of national policies

A crucial area of reform concerns IMF surveillance over the policies of creditors as well debtors. In view of the growing size and integration of financial markets, every major financial crisis now has global ramifications. Consequently, preventing a crisis is a concern not only for the country immediately affected but also for other countries, which is why global surveillance of national policies is considered necessary. So far, however, IMF surveillance has not been successful in preventing international financial crises. This reflects, in part, belated, and so far only partial, adaptation of existing procedures to the problems posed by large private capital flows, and it is closely related to serious shortcomings in the existing governance of the IMF.

Traditionally, bilateral surveillance has concentrated on macroeconomic policies, with little attention to sustainability of capital inflows and financial sector weaknesses associated with surges in such inflows. After the Mexican crisis, IMF surveillance was extended to include the sustainability of private capital flows,[7] but this did not prevent the East Asian crisis. In April 1998, the Interim Committee again recognized the need for strengthening IMF surveillance when it agreed that the Fund "should intensify its surveillance of financial sector issues and capital flows".[8]   Clearly, to succeed, the IMF will need to pay greater attention to unsustainable exchange-rate and payment developments and, as already noted, its recommendations should include control over capital inflows. However, this would mean a major departure from the current official approach to capital account management.

But perhaps more fundamentally, the failure of IMF surveillance in preventing international financial crises is due to the unbalanced nature of these procedures, which give too

---

[6] For a detailed discussion of this issue see UNCTAD (1999, chapter VI).

[7] IMF Executive Board Decision No. 10950-(95/37) of 10 April 1995.

[8] Interim Committee Communiqué of 16 April 1998.

little recognition to the disproportionately large global impact of monetary policies in major industrial countries. Financial crises in emerging markets are not always home-grown; they are often connected with major shifts in exchange and interest rates in the major industrial countries. This was true not only for the debt crisis of the 1980s, but also for more recent booms and busts in capital flows to Latin America and East Asia.

Certainly, given the degree of global interdependence, a stable system of exchange rates and payments positions calls for a minimum degree of coherence among the macroeconomic policies of major industrial countries. But the existing modalities of IMF surveillance do not include ways of attaining such coherence or dealing with unidirectional impulses resulting from changes in the monetary and exchange rate policies of the United States and other countries of the Organisation for Economic Co-operation and Development (OECD). Other countries lack mechanisms under the existing system of global economic governance for redress or dispute settlement relating to these impulses. In this respect governance for macroeconomic and financial policies lags behind that for international trade, where such mechanisms are part of the regime of the World Trade Organization (WTO). But if such a function is to be performed effectively by multilateral financial institutions, it is necessary to reform not only the surveillance procedures, but also the governance of these institutions, including their voting structure and decision-making procedures, to give greater weight to the views of developing countries. However, so far the only significant reform in this respect has been to rename the Interim Committee (International Monetary and Financial Committee) and to reaffirm that after 25 years of existence it is no longer interim but permanent!

2.6. Provision of international liquidity

With the increased frequency of crises in emerging markets, a consensus has emerged on the need to provide contingency financing to countries experiencing payments difficulties linked to the capital account, in addition to the traditional role of the IMF to provide current account financing. However, the modalities regarding the provision of liquidity, its adequacy, the conditions attached to it, and its funding remain extremely ad hoc and are inadequate for addressing the problems associated with systemic instability.

The provision of liquidity to pre-empt large currency swings has not been the international policy response to currency crises in developing countries. Rather, assistance, coordinated by the IMF, has usually come after the collapse of the currency in the form of bailouts designed to meet the demands of creditors, maintain capital-account convertibility, and prevent default, thereby creating moral hazard for international lenders and investors, and putting the burden on debtors. Moreover, availability of such financing has been associated with policy conditionality, which, at times, has gone beyond macroeconomic adjustment, interfering "unnecessarily with the proper jurisdiction of sovereign government" (Feldstein, 1998: 26). Finally, provision of funds needed for bailouts has often depended on ad hoc arrangements with the IMF's large shareholders, which, as creditors, often have important interests to protect.

Efforts to redress these shortcomings in the provision of liquidity have been unsatisfactory. The IMF has taken several steps to strengthen its capacity to provide financing in crises. These include the creation of a Supplemental Reserve Facility, established in response to the deepening of the East Asian crisis, and, more recently, the creation of the Contingency Credit Line to provide a precautionary line of defence against financial contagion. However, neither of these facilities has resulted in additional money; instead, they have had to rely on the existing resources of the Fund. A proposal has been made to allow the IMF to issue a reversible Special

Drawing Right (SDR) to itself for use in the provision of international liquidity (Ezekiel, 1998; United Nations, 1999; Ahluwalia, 1999). But this would require an amendment of the Articles of Agreement and would face opposition from some major industrial countries.

The terms of access to such facilities continue to face a number of problems. Clearly, lending in unlimited amounts and without conditions, except for penalty rates, would require tightened global supervision over borrowers to ensure their solvency – an unlikely development. While automatic access would ensure a timely response to market pressures, it could also create moral hazard and considerable risk for the IMF. On the other hand, conditional withdrawal of funds would reduce the risk of moral hazard, but negotiations could cause long delays, perhaps leading to a deepening of the crisis. It could also lead to irrational and unnecessarily tough conditionality, since the countries facing attacks on their currencies would be too weak to resist such conditions.

Pre-qualification is proposed as a way of avoiding these problems.[9] In such an arrangement, countries meeting certain *ex ante* conditions would be eligible for lender-of-last-resort financing, with eligibility being determined during Article IV consultations. However, it would still be necessary constantly to monitor the fulfilment of the terms of the financing, adjusting them as necessary in response to changes in conditions. In these respects difficulties may emerge in relations between the Fund and the member concerned.

Such problems are exemplified by the recent Brazilian agreement with the IMF. The Brazilian package might be described as the first experiment with the provision of international lender-of-last-resort financing to an emerging market; it was intended to protect the economy against contagion, subject to a stringent fiscal adjustment and a gradual depreciation of the *real* throughout 1999. After a political struggle, the Brazilian Government succeeded in passing the legislation needed to meet the fiscal target. But when the attack started, the currency was allowed to collapse, and the Fund required additional and more stringent conditions regarding the fiscal balance in order to release the second tranche of the package.

2.7. Orderly debt workouts

The international community faces a major dilemma in formulating policies towards international capital flows. In the absence of capital controls, financial crises are likely to be more frequent, severe and widespread. When a crisis occurs, defaults are inevitable in the absence of bailouts. But bailouts are becoming increasingly problematic: not only do they create moral hazard, but more importantly, the funds required have been getting larger and are now reaching the limits of political acceptability. This is the main reason why the international community has been engaged in finding ways to "involve" or to "bail-in" the private sector in the resolution of currency and debt crises. However, in this area too no agreement has been reached, in large part because of the resistance of some major countries to involuntary mechanisms.

A way out of the dilemma would be recourse to the principles of orderly debt workouts along the lines of Chapter 11 of the United States Bankruptcy Code, first raised by UNCTAD in its 1986 *Trade and Development Report* (*TDR*) in the context of the debt crisis of the 1980s, and further elaborated in *TDR 1998*. These procedures are especially relevant to international currency and debt crises resulting from liquidity problems because they are designed primarily to

---

[9] This was first proposed by Fischer (1999) and more recently by the Meltzer Commission Report (International Financial Institutions Advisory Commission, 2000).

address financial restructuring rather than liquidation. They allow a temporary standstill on debt servicing in recognition of the fact that an asset-grab race by the creditors is detrimental to the debtor as well as to the creditors as a group. They provide the debtor with access to the working capital needed to carry out its operations while granting seniority status to new debt. Finally, they involve a reorganization of the assets and liabilities of the debtor, including extension of maturities, and, where needed, debt-equity conversion and debt write-off.

Naturally, the application of bankruptcy procedures to cross-border debt involves a number of complex issues. However, the principles are straightforward and can be applied without establishing fully-fledged international bankruptcy procedures. The most contentious issue is the standstill mechanism, since IMF now lends into arrears and it is heavily involved in debt workouts. Clearly, to have the desired effect on currency stability, debt standstills should be accompanied by temporary exchange controls over all capital-account transactions by residents and non-residents alike. According to one proposal, standstills would need to be sanctioned by the IMF. Canada has proposed an Emergency Standstill Clause to be mandated by IMF members.[10] There could also be other arrangements, including pre-qualification for unilateral standstill decision by the countries concerned, or empowering an independent panel to sanction such decisions, similar to the way in which WTO safeguard provisions allow countries to take emergency actions.

As noted by the IMF Progress Report, there has been no agreement over empowering the IMF to impose stays on creditor litigation: "Some Directors thought that amending Article VIII, Section 2(b) warranted further consideration; others did not see the need for, or feasibility of, such action" (IMF, 1999a). A number of G7 countries, including Canada and the United Kingdom, proposed to establish a rules-based system for crisis resolution, with explicit rules on the respective roles of the public and private sectors. However, private financial institutions have been opposed to an involuntary mechanism of standstill or rollover. The United States continues to defend a case-by-case approach for the reasons already mentioned.

This lack of agreement also means that a greater emphasis has been placed on voluntary mechanisms (Group of 22, 1998, section 4.4; IMF, 1999b). The dilemma here is that the need for mandatory provisions has arisen precisely because voluntary approaches have not worked in stemming debt runs. On the other hand, while a number of proposals have been made to introduce mechanisms to provide automatic triggers, such as comprehensive bond covenants, automatic debt rollover options or collective action clauses designed to enable debtors to suspend payments, these are unlikely to be introduced voluntarily and would need an international mandate.[11] Indeed, developing countries fear that such clauses would reduce their access to financial markets, and insist that they first be introduced in sovereign bonds of industrial countries, an objective which may require an international mandate.

---

[10] Department of Finance, *Canada's Six-point Plan to Restore Confidence and Sustain Growth*, September 1998.
[11] Concerning these difficulties see Eichengreen (1999: 66–69). For universal debt rollover options, see Buiter and Silbert,1999.

3. Conclusions

The discussion above suggests that, despite a proliferation of meetings and communiqués, as well as a multiplication of groups and forums, there remains a reluctance to accommodate the concerns of developing countries regarding international financial reform. Thus in the current political environment, the maximum feasible strategy for developing countries in their search for an effective reform at the global level would seem to be to press for internationally-agreed arrangements for debt standstills and lending into arrears to help them to better deal with financial crises when they occur. However, until systemic instability and risks are adequately dealt with through global action, the task of preventing such crises falls on Governments in developing countries, both at the national and regional level.

There can be little doubt that the developing countries now enjoy much less policy autonomy than at any time in the post-war period. This loss of autonomy has three origins. First, systemic pressures have increased on Governments as a result of the liberalization and integration of markets. This is most visible in the case of financial markets. As a result of the greater exit option enjoyed by capital, Governments' policies have now become hostage to financial markets, and the kind of discipline that these markets impose on Governments is not always conducive to rapid growth and development. Second, policies in developing countries are also subject to pressures from major industrial powers and multilateral institutions. Finally, a number of policy instruments are no longer available to some developing countries as a result of their international commitments as members of such groupings as the OECD or North American Free Trade Area (NAFTA).

Nevertheless, there is much greater scope for domestic policies for regulating and controlling capital flows than has been exploited by many developing countries. There is no global agreement that forces the developing countries to open up their financial markets. There is indeed considerable variation within the South in the extent to which policy autonomy has been used in the domain of finance. For instance, while China and India have pursued a gradual and cautious approach to international capital flows, many countries in Latin America have rapidly opened up their capital account and financial sector. Again, a comparison between the policies adopted by Malaysia and its neighbouring countries in response to the East Asian financial crisis shows that policy options, even under crisis conditions, are not as narrow as is generally assumed. If developing countries are to avoid costly financial crises, it is essential that their autonomy in managing capital flows and choosing whatever capital account regime they deem appropriate should not be constrained by international agreements on capital-account convertibility or trade in financial services, and that they should effectively exploit the room for manoeuvre that they have for these purposes.

There is also much that could be done at the regional level, particularly among like-minded Governments who are prepared to establish collective regional defence mechanisms against systemic instability and contagion. In this respect, the experience of Europe with monetary and financial cooperation and the Exchange Rate Mechanism (ERM), introduced in response to the breakdown of the Bretton Woods system, holds useful lessons. Regional monetary and financial cooperation among developing countries, including exchange rate arrangements, macroeconomic policy coordination, regional surveillance, common rules and regulations over capital flows, and regional mechanisms for the provision of international liquidity, could be a viable and more easily attainable alternative to global mechanisms, designed to attain greater stability.

References

AKYÜZ Y and CORNFORD A (1999). Capital flows to developing countries and the reform of the international financial system. Paper prepared as part of the WIDER Project, New Roles and Functions for the UN and the Bretton Woods Institutions, *UNCTAD Discussion Paper*, No. 143. Geneva, UNCTAD, November.

AHLUWALIA MS (1999). The IMF and the World Bank: Are overlapping roles a problem? *International Monetary and Financial Issues for the 1990s, Vol. XI.* United Nations publication, sales no. E.99.II.D.25. New York and Geneva, UNCTAD.

BUITER W and SILBERT A (1999). UDROP a contribution to the new international financial architecture. *International Finance*, July.

CORNFORD A (2000). *The Basle Committee's Proposals for Revised Capital Standards: Rationale, Design and Possible Incidence.* G-24 Paper. Geneva, UNCTAD: 48.

EICHENGREEN B (1999). *Toward a New International Financial Architecture.* Washington DC, Institute of International Economics.

EZEKIEL H (1998). The role of special drawing rights in the international monetary system. *International Monetary and Financial Issues for the 1990s – Vol. IX.* United Nations publication, sales no. E.98-II-D.3, New York and Geneva, UNCTAD.

FELDSTEIN M (1998). Refocusing the IMF. *Foreign Affairs,* 77 (2), March/April.

FISCHER S (1999). On the need for an international lender of last resort (mimeo). Washington DC, International Monetary Fund.

GROUP OF 22 (1998). *Report of the Working Group on International Financial Crises* (mimeo). Washington DC.

INTERNATIONAL FINANCIAL INSTITUTIONS ADVISORY COMMISSION (IFIC) (2000). Report ("Melzer Report"), WashingtonDC, March.

IMF (1999a). Report of the Managing Director to the Interim Committee on Progress in Strengthening the Architecture of the International Financial System. Washington DC, September.

IMF (1999b). *Involving the Private Sector in Forestalling and Resolving Financial Crises.* Washington DC.

United Nations (1999). *Towards a New International Financial Architecture.* Report of the Task Force of the United Nations Executive Committee of Economic and Social Affairs. New York, January.

UNCTAD (1999). *Trade and Development Report, 1999* (chapter VI). United Nations publication, sales no. E.99.II.D.1, New York and Geneva.

HAS 1999 CHANGED ANYTHING (FOR ECUADOR AND OTHERS)? THE NEW INTERNATIONAL FINANCIAL ARCHITECTURE

Andrés de la Cruz

1. Introduction

This paper aims to discuss how 1999 has influenced the views of the legal community when advising sovereign Governments on debt management issues. In a sense, in 1999 the international financial community had more time than in previous years to think about structural "architectural" issues. Although recession continued to affect several of the large developing countries, there were no major crises that required coordinated efforts from the international financial institutions and industrialized country Governments to bail out developing countries. This pause gave players time to reflect and come up with new ideas as to how "debt management" issues should be approached in the future.

It was in the context of the debate on the new international financial architecture that Ecuador, Pakistan, and Ukraine had to confront official and private sector creditors as well as the IMF. While the external debt of these countries was not significant enough to affect the international financial system, it soon became clear that their particular situation would be discussed in the light of this ongoing debate. While it is still too early to draw lessons of general applicability from the way in which those three countries approached their creditors in 1999, it is useful to summarize the issues raised by each of them. Also, it is worthwhile to focus on the recently announced deal between the Russian Federation and its London Club creditors.

This presentation focuses on "legal aspects" and discusses some of the most significant issues recently encountered by sovereign borrowers that have had to restructure foreign debt, a significant portion of which consists of bonds. This presentation will concentrate on questions likely to be confronted not by the policy-makers, but rather by those government officials responsible for debt management, who often need to reconcile policy decisions with contractual obligations. It is they who have to be in contact with foreign lawyers, and need to understand and appraise the risk of litigation and advise accordingly.

Discussions during 1999 focused mainly on three questions:

- What does burden sharing or comparability of treatment imply for a sovereign borrower that runs into difficulties servicing its external debt obligations or negotiating a programme with the IMF or a rescheduling with the Paris Club?
- Should the financial community as a whole accept the notion that sovereign bonds may need to be restructured? How should it go about such restructuring?
- What contractual and legal problems do legal advisers and debt management teams need to address to permit sovereign bond restructurings?

The first section of this paper compares briefly the cases of Ecuador, Pakistan and Ukraine and highlights certain features of the Russian Federation's arrangement with the London Club. The second section examines the history of debt management in order to identify aspects that, to some extent, have a bearing on our approach to sovereign bond restructurings today.

With these recent cases in mind and the historical context, the subsequent section turns back to 1999 and reviews the legal issues involved in sovereign bond restructurings.

2. Pakistan, Ecuador, Ukraine and the Russian Federation

Pakistan had significant principal amounts coming due under its Eurobonds in December 1999. According to press reports, the Paris Club made it clear that Pakistan would need to implement comparable treatment between official sector creditors and the holders of its bonds if it planned to have its bilateral debt rescheduled. Short of making funds available to Pakistan to ensure the continued servicing of its Eurobonds, official creditors reportedly questioned the wisdom of a Paris Club rescheduling without a comparable rescheduling of the Eurobonds; there would be no bailing out unless bondholders were bailed in.

Pakistan approached some of its largest bondholders informally, several of whom reportedly were Pakistan nationals, and discussed with them the principal components of a possible restructuring. The Government subsequently made a unilateral offer to exchange its existing Eurobonds at par for its US dollar 10 per cent bonds due in 2002/2005, which was accepted by more than 90 per cent of the bondholders.

Ecuador became the focus of attention during the summer of 1999: as the August 1999 interest payment date on its Discount Bonds due in 2025 and Past Due Interest (PDI) Bonds due in 2015 approached, it became apparent that the country would have difficulties finding the resources to make the interest payment. Noticeably, while Pakistan and, as discussed below, Ukraine, were troubled by inpending principal payments due under their Eurobonds, Ecuador could not continue servicing interest on its Brady bonds. Rolling over maturities was not a solution. Ecuador took advantage of the 30-day grace period for interest payments on its bonds, while the authorities considered alternatives. On expiry of this grace period, the authorities made the interest payment on the PDI Bonds, which had no interest collateral, but not on the Discount Bonds, which had 12-months of interest collateral. The authorities asked holders of the Discount Bonds to draw upon the interest collateral and thereby "cure" the interest payment default. In doing so, the Discount Bond holders would avoid causing a cross default to all of Ecuador's other bonds, while Ecuador initiated discussion to develop an overall solution to its debt problems. Bondholders reacted adversely to Ecuador's request and, rather than drawing on the interest collateral, they voted to accelerate the Discount Bonds thereby formally opening the doors to litigation. This decision can be interpreted as a response by private holders of sovereign debt to the burden-sharing speeches that were being made by official and multilateral lenders. Ecuador subsequently failed to make interest payments on the remaining categories of its Brady bonds as well as on its US$ 500 million worth of outstanding Eurobonds. Having failed to bring about a restructuring of its bonds prior to defaulting on its interest payment obligations for all categories of bonds, Ecuador will now need to work out a solution subject to the inflexibilities of sovereign bond documentation. It will also have to assess very carefully the risks created by bondholders who choose to challenge any restructuring proposal it elects to put forward.

With a view to engaging bondholders in a constructive dialogue intended to ultimately lead to an exchange offer, Ecuador has invited eight of the larger institutional holders of its bonds to participate in a consultative group. The purpose of this group, as announced by Ecuador, is not to "negotiate" the terms of an exchange offer, but rather, to provide a formal mechanism through which the Government can communicate with the bondholder community and receive feedback on issues considered relevant to a possible exchange offer. The process has been overshadowed by domestic developments on the political front. To date, Ecuador has not submitted to its bondholders specific terms for any exchange offer. Unlike Pakistan, Ecuador must find a solution that is acceptable to a broad and diverse base of apparently mainly foreign holders of approximately US$6 worth of Brady bonds and US$ 500 million worth of Eurobonds.

Ukraine faced the issue of bond restructuring in the context of its discussions over disbursements by the IMF under a line of credit included in its IMF-approved economic programme, which had been suspended by the IMF for a number of reasons. Between the years 2000 and 2001, five series of bonds were scheduled to mature, which would have depleted the country's currency reserves. After considering several proposals that involved some degree of debt relief, Ukraine offered to exchange approximately US$ 2.7 billion aggregate principal amount of bonds, at par for the series of bonds maturing in 2000 and 2001, and at an 11 per cent discount for the so-called "Gazprom bonds" amortizing through 2007. Participants were offered a choice of a 10 per cent Euro-denominated bond or an 11 per cent US dollar-denominated bond. In either case the new bonds amortize over six years, after a one-year grace period, that is, they have a 4.5-year average life (as in Pakistan). In addition, Ukraine agreed to come current on certain missed interest payments under the old bonds, but only to participants tendering bonds in the exchange offer. According to market sources, the offer made by Ukraine was "market-friendly" insofar as on a mark-to-market basis investors received at least as much value under the new package (including the cash payment) as they held in the bonds they tendered. One of the interesting aspects of Ukraine's exchange offer was the challenge presented by the need to reach and entice a largely disseminated German retail holding of its deutche mark-denominated bonds to participate in the exchange offer. Ukraine announced, during the last week of March 2000, that it had attained the 85 per cent critical mass required for the transaction to close. Essentially, as in the case of Pakistan, Ukraine managed, through the exchange offer, to stretch out its principal maturities. The debt relief component of Ukraine's package was not significant.

Regarding the *Russian Federation's* recent agreement with its London Club creditors, the deal announced in 2000 amounts to a restructuring of a 1997 rescheduling agreement according to which a State-owned bank (but not the Russian Federation itself) had assumed the debt of the former Soviet Union. That rescheduling agreement (essentially a loan document) included an obligation to pay the principal and an exchange of past interest owing accrued through 1997 on the rescheduled debt for Luxembourg-listed "interest notes", which were functionally bonds. In 1999, Russia reconstituted the London Club advisory committee, replacing some members who no longer held significant positions in the debt with institutions active in the secondary market trading of the paper, and began negotiations to restructure the debt, including the interest notes. The agreement announced includes a 37 per cent reduction in the principal amount of the outstanding debt (a write-off of approximately US$ 10 billion), stretching out maturities to 30 years, and a reduction in the interest coupons. Two aspects of the transaction deserve special attention in connection with the issue of sovereign bond restructurings. First, holders of the old debt formally incurred by a State-owned bank with practically no payment capacity will receive bonds to be issued by the Russian Federation, a different debtor, which, to date, has punctually honoured its payment obligations under all of its Eurobonds issued after the demise of the former Soviet Union. Second, the Russian Federation has obtained a significant amount of debt relief from its private creditors prior to its next round of Paris Club negotiations. According to press reports, the official sector may see the principle of burden sharing a boomerang: the Russian Federation has allegedly tabled a request for debt forgiveness by its official creditors comparable to that obtained from its London Club creditors. This amounts to reverse comparability and is expected to attract the attention of other sovereign Governments.

A review of the historical evolution of debt reschedulings provides helpful insights from the past that shed light on the present discussion.

3. A summary review of sovereign debt restructuring

3.1.   Development finance: 1945-1970

In the years following the Second World War, sovereign States primarily called upon other sovereign States and multilateral financial institutions for financing. Private sources of capital, whether in the form of bank loans or bonds, had no significant role in the financing of developing countries during this period.

Soon enough, official sector lenders learned that "restructuring" was part of the lending experience, and the Paris Club came into existence. From the outset, the Paris Club acted in close coordination with the multilateral institutions. Indeed, having an IMF-assisted programme was a pre-condition for a Paris Club restructuring. Furthermore, Paris Club lenders were not bothered by the idea that their sovereign borrowers would at all times religiously service their debt to multilateral lenders. This implied "seniority" never became an issue. While the general rule was that debts were "rescheduled" (not reduced), since terms were already preferential, the Paris Club was an ideal forum for the implementation of politically-driven initiatives on debt matters, which, in several instances, resulted in debt forgiveness programmes for the least developed countries.

3.2.   The "Petro-70s"

The world of sovereign borrowing and debt management, changed significantly in the 1970s. The arrival of petrodollars and the eagerness of commercial banks to lend to developing countries, even at negative interest rates, had a profound impact on the world's financial architecture. The public sector both – borrowers and lenders – welcomed the arrival of commercial bankers to the scene of sovereign lending. It was only several years later, in the early 1980s, that the players realized how the horizon of sovereign borrowing had permanently changed.

What were the salient features of this period in terms of debt management?

(i)   Lenders were primarily commercial banks;
(ii)   Loans were extended primarily to sovereign States and State-controlled entities; and
(iii)   The form chosen was the "syndicated bank loan contract" not a bond or other form of publicly-traded security.

In sum, the international financial architecture of the time was intended for a small number of players that made business on an ongoing basis pursuant to agreements generally governed by a law foreign to the borrower.

Debt management during the 1970s was primarily concerned with incurring debt. However, during these years eurocurrency loan documentation evolved, which changed the form of dealing with disruptions and developments in the allocation of risks and costs between borrowers and lenders (Buchheit, 2000).

Between 1973 and 1979, the architecture managed to make billions of dollars available to developing country borrowers, primarily through syndicated loans. The syndicated euro-dollar loan, however, contained a "Trojan horse." The euro-dollar market and the euro-dollar loans used to effect transactions in that market were based on the principle of matched funding: the lender's short-term cost of funding was automatically transferred to the borrower through the floating interest rate formula. Borrowers paid an interest rate which included a spread or margin payable to the lender in addition to the lender's cost of funding. The spread was determined the borrower's credit quality and represented the lender's revenue. Large or small, the spread was the fixed component of the formula. A bank's short-term cost of Euro-dollar funding, instead, was directly dependent upon movements in the US dollar interest rate. Hence, after Mr Volcker made his appearance on the scene in 1979, and used, among other tools, step-ups in the United States Federal Reserve's interest rates to reverse inflationary trends in the United States, developing countries immediately had to pick up the tab, as the rate at which the vast majority of their external debt accrued interest floated steadily upwards. The London Inter-Bank Offered Rate (LIBOR - the cost of funding) climbed from approximately 8.7 per cent in 1978 to 16.5 per cent by 1981.

Although the flow of capital between industrialized and developing countries began to change in 1979, and banks gradually ceased making new money available to refinance existing debt, the international financial community was, nevertheless, caught off guard in August 1982, when Mexico announced a moratorium on the repayment of its external debt. By the end of 1982, all major Latin American borrowers and a good number of other developing countries were in arrears on their external debt payments (Madrid,1990). And the international financial machinery all of a sudden came to a screeching halt. Although lenders had diversified their risk exposure by lending to many developing nations, the Mexican crisis triggered a reaction that recognized few, if any, distinctions between developing borrowers. That was the first expression of the phenomenon known as "contagion," which currently merits many lines of disclosure in securities offerings by emerging-market issuers.

3.3. Rescheduling

Once creditors managed to get organized, the sovereign borrowers' loan rescheduling process began. The guiding principle, driven primarily by the way commercial banks were required to treat assets for accounting purposes under the regulatory framework, was to keep sovereign borrowers current on their interest payments.

What did "debt management" amount to for a sovereign borrower in that environment? In a nutshell, sovereign debt reschedulings proceeded during the 1980s as follows:

- The banks formed advisory committees typically composed of representatives of banks, selected primarily on the basis of exposure to the borrower and, in certain circumstances, on geographic criteria.
- The purpose of the committees was to represent the banking community in the negotiations with the borrower. In doing so, they operated by unanimous consent, with a view to achieving maximum support for the package negotiated with the borrower.
- From the borrower's perspective, the unanimous consent method translated into always being negotiated down to the minimum common denominator, one acceptable to all members of the committee based on consultation with their respective constituencies. Thus, one bank had the ability to prevent an entire package from being adopted if it disagreed with any one of its features.

During the first years, the rescheduling process was relatively dynamic. Debtors had practically no experience; there was a general expectation that the crisis, perceived as a liquidity crisis, would pass, and that better times lay ahead, and banks were generally able to arrange reasonably attractive packages.

Multilateral institutions and the official sector in the industrialized nations also made resources available to heavily indebted developing countries. The sovereign borrowers used a significant portion of those proceeds, together with new money raised as part of the rescheduling process, to remain current on interest payments. Burden sharing did not form part of the rescheduling jargon in those days. Flows from the official sector, on a net basis, were favourable to the borrowers. Ultimately, the continued assistance of the industrialized countries through the rescheduling process could be viewed as a hidden subsidy to their own banking institutions, many of which could otherwise have collapsed, creating serious problems for those Governments on the domestic front. Industrialized country Governments occasionally exerted pressure on banks to participate in the reschedulings and to show flexibility to the heavily indebted sovereign borrowers by continuing to transfer capital to the borrowers and allowing (and in some instances even requiring) the sovereign borrowers to apply the proceeds of loans made by the official sector to service their external debt with the private sector. However, taxpayers in the industrialized countries shouldered a significant portion of the losses attributable, at least in part, to bad lending decisions taken by private banks flush with capital gained in the 1970s.

The rescheduling dynamic ultimately avoided an across- the-board default by developing country borrowers, which would have had devastating consequences for the global financial system. As time went by, however, and the economic crisis continued to deepen in the developing countries, with negative economic growth in many cases, fatigue crept into the rescheduling process. Borrowers became increasingly sceptical about taking on additional debt to pay interest only, and began stiffening their negotiating positions, demanding greater concessions from the lenders. The ability of the advisory committees to summon support for the next rescheduling package, which always involved new money for an ever growing mass of interest payments, eroded, especially as mid-sized and regional United States banks balked at the idea of putting more money into developing countries. In fact, as soon as they had created sufficient provisions, many of those banks began selling their developing country loan portfolios into the secondary market, which became increasingly dynamic. Lenders sought to monetize their bad loan portfolios and thus, even if at a loss, did away with the problem altogether.

While many argued that the international community was confronting a solvency and not a liquidity crisis, under the rescheduling model there was practically no debt forgiveness and no room for concessionary (non-market) terms. The Baker Plan (1985-88) fell short of debt relief measures and ultimately, by late 1987 and early 1988, the borrowers' debt management initiatives turned back to default and moratorium. Interestingly, though, overall, there were few instances of creditors litigating against borrowers during this period. These are some possible explanations for this:

- An expectation that the problem was transient, a liquidity crisis likely to pass;
- A willingness to maintain friendly relations between debtors and creditors in anticipation of future business;
- Discrete discouragement by industrial country Governments through bank regulators;
- The chilling effect of the sharing clause included in the standard eurocurrency loan documentation; and
- The difficulty of enforcing judgments against foreign Governments and their central banks.

Under the Baker Plan, sovereign debtors continued to increase their stock of debt only to remain current on their interest payments, but not to improve their repayment capacity generally. In fact, the economic condition had continued to deteriorate in many countries, making them ever more dependent on foreign financing to repay their debt. Large banks gradually lost their ability to align mid-size and smaller banks behind "new money" initiatives. In 1989, sovereign debtors made clear their unwillingness to continue managing their foreign debt under the terms of the Baker initiative.

Perhaps encouraged by the absence of litigation, debtors decided to tighten the screws and, once again, the officers responsible for debt management entertained the idea of a default on interest payment: Ecuador in 1987, Argentina and other small and medium-sized countries in 1989, and Brazil in 1990. The banks responded with legal actions: Citicorp seized $80 million in funds that Ecuador held with the bank to offset an overdue loan; action was brought against Peru in New York in 1990, to recover $1.2 billion in loans. Clearly, things had changed, and a new approach was needed to keep the international financial community from falling apart.

3.4. The Brady Plan (1989-1990)

In March 1989, United States Treasury Secretary, Nicholas Brady, announced his Government's decision to favour debt, or debt service, reduction for sovereign debtors. The debt reduction was in the form of a discount on the principal amount (the discount bonds) or the acceptance of concessionary (non-market) interest rates (the par bonds). Under the Brady Plan, commercial banks agreed to extend debt relief, on the condition, that billions of dollars of commercial bank debt be exchanged for bonds, the principal payments of which were backed by United States Treasury bonds. The loan concept thus exited from the scene of developing country debt.

Brady bonds blended United States Government risk with respect to payment of principal at maturity with developing country debtor risk with respect to interest payments during the life of the instrument. In exchange for the debt reduction granted, the banks received a security that could be resold to a wider variety of investors than the banking community. Later on it became clear that this "blended" instrument is not favoured by bond investors. But, at the time, banks were guided in the negotiations by the need to satisfy regulatory ratios which favoured isolating "principal" payment risk so as to book the instruments as a United States Government risk asset.

While the Brady initiative represented a breath of fresh air, it came at a time when the mood at the debt negotiation table had turned sour. It was in this increasingly hostile environment that the negotiations for Brady restructurings took place. And they were far from smooth, as debt negotiators still recall. The "unanimous consent" principle followed by the advisory committees, in an increasingly hostile environment, caused enormous tension not only between the debtors and their creditors but also among creditors. Furthermore, the United States Government exercised pressure over the parties to force accords, extracting concessions from debtors as well as from the banks.

3.5. The "good" post-Brady years (1993-1994)

No matter how painful the Brady process may have been, as with all things in life, one day it ended, and sovereign borrowers awoke to a new "financial landscape" (Buchheit, 1999). Indeed, the commercial banks no longer visited the offices of the ministries of finance or public credit to offer loans. They had been substituted by a new breed of suppliers of capital: the investment banks.

The damage caused in the 1980s to the reputation of developing countries as borrowers had not reached that corner of the financial system represented by the bond markets. Indeed, sovereign debtors had not made significant incursions into the bond market since the nineteenth century, and those that did issue bonds during the 1970s and early 1980s generally honoured their payment obligations while their larger, more significant commercial bank debt was being first rescheduled and later restructured. Moreover, as a result of the Brady Plan, suddenly billions of dollars of developing country bonds fed the trading floors of the financial centres and became available for institutional fixed-income investors seeking higher returns than those available in the United States market, in an environment characterized by falling interest rates.

Debt management, therefore, turned away from commercial bank loans and restructuring and moved towards the capital markets – first the Euromarkets and later the United States institutional and public markets. One after the other, developing countries, until recently, chastised by the community, re-entered the financial markets under the guise of glossy prospectuses, offering, first hundreds, and then billions of dollars of bonds.

What were the implications of this new financial landscape in terms of debt management?

(i)   The lenders are no longer the good old friendly, or at least familiar, "commercial banks." Bondholders are generally anonymous and include a wide variety of institutional investors and occasionally individuals. Bonds are generally issued in "global book-entry" form, and sometimes in bearer form. In either case, unless the beneficial owner of the bond elects to identify itself, the borrower (now more commonly referred to as "issuer") has no way of knowing who its creditors are. Bond documentation includes nothing comparable to assignment provisions in loans, requiring the assignee to be identified and notices to be sent to the agent and the borrower.

(ii)   The form chosen to represent the obligation was the bond, an instrument that lended itself readily to trading in the secondary markets and was attractive to the wider community of emerging-market investors.

(iii)   The philosophy of the creditors also changed: sovereign borrowers would no longer deal with lenders, who see loans as revenue generation instruments through interest accruals. The new players are investors, who seek to realize profit, either by selling the bonds at a gain or through interest payments. While there are investors dedicated to emerging markets, they do not have the same kind of relationship with the issuers as commercial banks had with their sovereign clients. They generally have no local branches to protect, and by trading in these bonds they are able to enter and exit a country's financial scene as often as they want (albeit sometimes at a not insignificant loss), responding to variations in yields and their perception of country risk.

3.6.   The "bad" post-Brady years (1995-1998)

Between 1992 and 1995, this new breed of investors directing capital at Latin America was once again welcomed by the official sector. However, the Mexican devaluation in December 1994, and the pull-back by emerging-market investors that followed showed that sovereign borrowers as well as their industrialized nation creditors and multilateral financial institutions were now dealing with a new reality. In a world free of foreign exchange restrictions and adverse to imposing restrictions on capital flows, there is little a country can do if the market perception of risk, justifiably or not, turns against it. At the slightest indication of trouble ahead, bondholders can turn to the secondary market and monetize their position, thus staying away from that area until their perception changes. And once bond prices start to drop, the so-called "vultures", that are determined to deal with a troubled debtor – sovereign or corporate – on their terms, step in.

Thus, between 1995 and 1998, multilateral financial institutions and the Governments of the industrialized nations were called upon to act following the devaluation of the Mexican peso in December 1994, the Asian crises and the devaluation of the Russian rouble in 1997, and the devaluation of the Brazilian *real* in 1998. In all of those instances, with capital markets practically closed to emerging-market issuers and no commercial loans available to bridge the liquidity gap, developing nations once again turned to the IMF and the official sector for capital. The situation was far too complex and the stakes too significant for the official sector not to assume an active lending role.

The idea behind the bailouts in the 1990s was deterrence: massive standby lines of credit were arranged by multilateral and bilateral creditors primarily with the expectation that they would induce private sector investors to continue lending to the troubled borrowers. And countries would ultimately not need to draw under the standby facilities because the market, psychologically soothed by the standby arrangements, would have worked its way out of the crisis.

Major rescue packages were put in place. Once again taxpayer money from the United States and other industrialized nations was diverted to developing economies facing liquidity crises. The approach described above worked reasonably well in Mexico and in the Republic of Korea, but showed its weakness when the bailouts for Indonesia and Thailand failed to arrest contagion elsewhere in the region (Buchheit, 1999). And again, as in the past, when the model failed, private sources of financing dried up. The spreads at which emerging-economies' bonds traded in the secondary market increased and the ability of major sovereign countries to raise funds from the bond markets to continue servicing their debts came dangerously close to a halt.

4. The grounds for a new international financial architecture

Despite certain important cases of disruption to the financial system, the measures taken served the purpose of controlling damage, and a global financial crisis was once again averted. This time, however, Governments in the industrialized world and the multilateral financial institutions came under greater scrutiny by their constituencies. In the United States, particularly, prominent members of Congress questioned the use of taxpayer money ultimately to protect private bondholders from suffering the adverse consequences of the risks they had bought into. Needless to say, the authorities had difficulties justifying the transfers, especially where the recipient Governments failed to abide by the IMF programmes, allowed economic conditions to deteriorate, and ultimately resulting in a loss of the funds provided by the industrialized countries. The more aggressive stance favoured denying any kind of public sector assistance (whether from multilateral lending agencies or Paris Club lenders) to borrowers that failed to obtain significant concessions from their private sector creditors. It was in this context that the debate over a new financial architecture acquired prominence.

Proponents of the "new financial architecture" seek:

(i)   Management of private sector capital flows to emerging markets to avoid the boom/bust pattern;

(ii)   Promotion of dissemination of information to investors to encourage prudent investment decisions;

(iii) Development of mechanisms to permit countries to endure temporary economic or financial disruptions and resist speculative attacks on their currencies; and

(iv)   Prompt and orderly workouts when crises do occur, with losses being shared by all who made investment decisions.

But this is easier said than done. Sovereign borrowers confronted with the burden-sharing theory posed the following questions:

- Will bondholders be as prepared as commercial banks were in the 1980s to participate in a restructuring?
- Is it not likely that the bond markets, which were so carefully shielded during the 1980s, will punish a country that forces upon bondholders a restructuring by denying future access?
- Will contagion adversely affect the ability of all developing country borrowers to use the bond markets as an effective source of financing?
- If the bond markets end up closed to a sovereign borrower, where else can it seek financing?

And finally the bondholders responded to the promoters of the burden-sharing theory with the following thoughts:

- Bondholders are lenders of first resort; they are not prepared to bail out countries.
- Bondholders mark to market, and are punished far in advance of a payment default.
- Brady bondholders already received a "hair cut" when the Brady bonds were first issued. Only in the case of Poland did Paris Club lenders agree to significant write-offs.
- Long- and medium-term bonds are not responsible for the emerging-market crises. Rather, "hot" money, which flows in and out overnight for speculative purposes, is to blame. If the international financial architecture were designed to repress those flows, the crises could be avoided. It is not appropriate to impose a "stay" on payments on long- and medium-term obligations when the problem is caused by short-term capital constraints.
- There is no amount of plastic surgery that will remove the scars that a sovereign borrower will create by forcing a restructuring on its bondholders. Furthermore, a sovereign borrower's failure to punctually honour its external debt payment obligation will close the doors of international capital for that country's entire private sector.

That is how the players had positioned themselves towards the end of 1998 in the academic debate on burden sharing.

Bringing bondholders into the world of sovereign borrower restructurings: 1999

This final section focuses on the narrower problem of dealing with bondholders in the context of a sovereign debtor restructuring. Although Ecuador's current difficulties, and any solution found to address them, will not necessarily constitute a precedent generally applicable to sovereign borrowers in need of a workout, given the predominance of Brady bonds in the composition of Ecuador's external debt, it is certainly useful to illustrate some of the dynamics and pitfalls involved in the process.

The international financial community is debating ways of bringing bondholders into the picture of sovereign debt restructuring in a manner that minimizes the damage. Unless the official sector and commercial banks are willing to assume the entire burden of financing developing countries, which, for the time being, does not appear to be the case, any intelligent solution will have to preserve future access to the bond market for sovereign borrowers. While bondholders claiming absolute seniority may adopt an unreasonable stand when it is clear that a debtor does not have the capacity to service its debt, forcing a solution that leaves profound scars on the bondholder community would be foolish and most counterproductive in the long term.

Ecuador's current situation clearly calls for a compromise between a debtor and its creditors and among the various categories of creditors that recognizes the new reality. While public sector creditors may push for burden sharing, it is unlikely that a restructuring of Ecuador's external bond debt will succeed unless the proposal is received favourably; in other words perceived as market friendly by a significant majority of Ecuador's bondholders.

The following seven questions introduce some of the principal conditions affecting a restructuring of bonds issued by sovereign borrowers.

(i)   Why is restructuring bondholders' debt more troublesome in the context of a sovereign State than in the case of a corporate entity?

The simple answer is that sovereign debtors cannot be subject to insolvency and bankruptcy proceedings. In the United States, as in most industrialized countries, a corporate entity that engages in a "reorganization" procedure is in a position to force upon a minority group within a class of creditors a solution approved by the majority of that class. Thus, when it comes to changing payment terms of a debt instrument in the context of bankruptcy or insolvency proceedings, holdouts are overruled and there is no room for free riders. For better or for worse, no such rules apply to sovereign States.

(ii)   Are there legal impediments to the restructuring of bonds?

Most sovereign bonds have been issued in the international capital markets under the laws of the state of New York in the United States, or the United Kingdom. With few exceptions, bonds governed by New York law will not permit subsequent amendments to the payment terms of the instrument (amounts and dates) without the consent of each affected bondholder. In this respect, bonds and loans are similar. While this is not required under the law of the United States for a sovereign issuer, the market practice has been to include that feature in practically all bonds placed in the United States market. Bonds governed by English law are somewhat more flexible and permit amendments, even of payment terms, if approved by a qualified majority of bondholders (two thirds or 75 per cent).

In any case, if a sovereign Government wishes to avoid any uncertainty over whether it will gather the unanimous or qualified majority support required to amend the payment terms of an existing bond as a means of restructuring or rescheduling its debt obligations, it is more likely to use the exchange offer as an alternative restructuring technique. This amounts to making an offer to exchange its existing bonds (with payment terms that presumably can no longer be honoured) for new bonds, reflecting the financial terms of the restructuring. Those that accept the offer are, as stated by Lee Buchheit, "lifted out of the old bond without amending the payment terms of that instrument."(Buchheit, 2000).

(iii)   What does a sovereign debtor do with the non-participating holders, who are left with their old bonds and continue to enjoy the full legal rights and remedies under those instruments?

While an exchange offer approach may overcome the "unanimity" or "qualified majority" voting requirement, it leaves the sovereign saddled with the holdouts or "free riders." Indeed, because the participating bondholders have exited the instrument and can no longer block any attempt by an unfriendly group of bondholders to accelerate the bonds and open the doors to litigation, an exchange offer may actually enhance the bargaining position of hostile creditors. Sovereign issuers must, therefore, be prepared to deal with them in the aftermath of an exchange.

Litigation, however, is unappealing for both sides, and a holdout creditor will have to weigh its chances of success in litigation, particularly in terms of enforcing a judgement against a sovereign in any jurisdiction where assets can be found, against the odds of being left holding an illiquid security with no trading value. While the sharing clause was a deterrent to litigation by commercial bank lenders party to a syndicated loan (IFL Review, 1990), the mark-to-market accounting practice of new investors may induce many to accept the terms of a reasonably market friendly exchange offer.

(iv)   Once a sovereign has decided that a restructuring of its bond indebtedness cannot be avoided, how should it approach the process?

As described above, resort to the use of bank advisory committees was the procedure followed to reschedule first, and later to restructure, commercial bank debt during the 1980s and early 1990s.

Prior to the Second World War, in the 1930s, the world experienced a period of widespread defaults by sovereign borrowers on their bond obligations. In response to those defaults a number of variations of "bondholder protective committees" were set up to assist bondholders in dealing with their sovereign debtors. During that period, the United States and other nations recognized and enforced the doctrine of absolute sovereign immunity. Thus, while the financial aspects of a sovereign default in the 1930s may have been comparable to those in the 1990s, in those days bondholders were precluded from suing a sovereign in a United States or English (or any other foreign) court without the sovereign's consent. The reality today is entirely different: not only do nations no longer recognize the doctrine of absolute sovereign immunity, sovereign issuers are asked to expressly waive such immunity, through a waiver included as part of the terms and conditions of the bonds. Bondholder protective committees are therefore not useful precedents.

Was the bank advisory committee process workable for a bond restructuring?

It was not, mainly for three reasons. First, because it allowed negotiations to progress only to the extent that all banks sitting on the committee agreed with each and every aspect of the proposed transaction. This veto power of each member of the committee caused, in various instances, serious delays in the negotiations with the borrowers. Second, even after the sovereign debtor and the committee reached agreement, there was no certainty that the broader banking community would accept it. Frequently, banking regulators were asked informally to intervene to help convince non-committee banks under their jurisdiction of the benefits of the package.

There is clearly no comparable mechanism for persuading uncooperative bondholders. Finally, bondholders will generally want to remain at all times free to trade in the securities of the distressed borrower. Providing for a set-up that grants certain bondholders access to more or better information than others is unlikely to be viewed favourably by the market and raises important legal issues regarding privileged information.

Bondholders are generally believed to have little patience for lengthy negotiations and to be not easily influenced by any regulators. Furthermore, in the context of commercial bank lending, members of the committee tended to be representative of the banking community as a whole (a "commonality of interest"); however, such an assumption is no longer possible, given the different types of bondholders and the heterogeneous nature of their interests. A sovereign issuer in need of restructuring its bond debt may spend numerous hours discussing and even agreeing on a proposal with a group of bondholders, only to discover later that many others, who were not present, approach the restructuring from an entirely different perspective and arrive at a completely different conclusion. Even if certain institutions invoke "representativity" of the community of bondholders at large, sovereigns should not take such statements seriously. In fact, a sovereign debtor will most likely not be in a position to determine on its own, with certainty, whether the entity with which it is in discussion beneficially owns any of its bonds.

In sum, while a means of communicating with the bondholder community should be developed, the form chosen will most likely depend upon the composition of the bondholder group, the degree of concern for the legal issues raised by the process, and the extent to which the issuer and its advisers consider that the proposal they intend to submit needs preparatory "persuasion". The "friendlier" the terms, the less important will be the need for communications with the investors prior to launching a restructuring proposal.

(v)   Should a sovereign seek to negotiate with its bondholders or design a package unilaterally and present it to its bondholders as a take-it-or-leave-it option?

Once again, the answer to this question is likely to be tied to the sovereign's perception of the composition of its bondholder community. The tighter the community, the easier it should be for the sovereign to engage in informal consultations and to proceed to design an offer known prior to launching to be acceptable to a broad majority of the bondholders. This, apparently, was possible in the case of Pakistan's exchange offer. Direct negotiations with bondholders, if successful, have the clear advantage of enhancing the likelihood of success for the package. However, they may prove time consuming, and engaging in a negotiation process requires careful consideration of issues of confidentiality and insider trading. Also, deciding who to invite to sit on the committee raises the "representation" issue mentioned earlier.

Ecuador, with US$ 6 billion worth of Brady bonds to restructure that were owned by a broad and unidentified community of holders, considered it best to organize a "consultative group" and provide for a formal mechanism of communication with the bondholder community. This included broad dissemination of information prior to and after any meeting with the consultative group and an open line of communication (through e-mail) with bondholders who wished to make their thoughts known to the authorities. Ukraine, with respect to its DM-denominated bonds, faced a similar communications challenge in terms of communicating with its bondholders. The Russian federation, which was essentially restructuring a loan facility, adhered to the old-style bank-advisory committee process.

(vi)   In what other ways are bondholders likely to approach the restructuring process differently from commercial banks?

Because bondholders will be looking to the secondary market to determine the value of their restructured claim, the following factors are likely to be more significant than in the past.

- Any restructuring proposal will have to be part of a comprehensive package and be supported by credible economic information;

- The proposal will need to be perceived as causing no party, neither the creditors nor the debtor, to leave money on the table;

- Given the significance of burden sharing in the debate, bondholders may expect every category of creditors to make, or at least be asked by the debtor to make, comparable concessions. This does not necessarily mean that each category of creditors should extend the same measure of debt relief, but bondholders may have to be persuaded that other creditors, including domestic debt holders, are being asked to make comparable sacrifices;

- Because of the mark-to-market accounting practice, bondholders will generally expect the restructured debt to trade at least as well as, or even better than, the old debt (based on pre-default prices, of course). In this respect, sovereigns may more readily satisfy bondholders than their old commercial bank creditors, who focused on the stream of payments due under the debt instrument. A bondholder may be happy taking a paper which on its face is worth much less either in principal or coupon or both, than the old debt, if the market, taking into account all aspects of the programme, values the restructured debt more favourably.

- What changes could be made to bond documentation to make sovereign workouts less complicated?

Four ideas have been proposed and discussed although so far there appears to be no consensus within financial community as to whether they should be implemented.

- Include collective representation clauses expressly authorizing fiscal agents or trustees to join with representatives of other creditors in a sovereign debtor workout and make the outcome of the discussion binding upon the bondholders;

- Replace the unanimous consent approach with majority action clauses in New York law-governed bonds, to deal with the holdout creditors and to avoid the need for an exchange offer;

- Include sharing clauses in bond documentation to deter maverick litigation; and

- Combine exchange offers with exit consents to amend the non-payment terms of the bonds and make them less palatable to remaining bondholders.

6. Conclusion

Finding a way out of Ecuador's current external debt problems requires addressing the three questions posed at the beginning of this presentation. Bondholders will need to be persuaded that the burden sharing doctrine is not causing Ecuador to expect from them a sacrifice that is relatively more significant than the one being made by the other categories of creditors. Bondholders, however, will need to accept that their instruments need to be redesigned. Ecuador's cash flow limitations have become so severe that it clearly cannot be expected to continue servicing its external debt obligations on their original terms. Given that bonds constitute the bulk of Ecuador's external debt to the private sector, the country cannot even approach its external debt restructuring problem without involving its bondholders. Finally, the country/Government will need to design its restructuring proposal within the framework of its existing bond documentation, taking into account its lack of flexibility in terms of amending payment terms.

Debt management teams at the finance ministries of developing countries have an advantage vis-à-vis their predecessors in the 1970s: the bond markets constitute one additional, and probably the largest, source of potential financing for their countries. But by the same token, this category of lenders has to be managed with care, especially when a restructuring of the obligations cannot be avoided. The new international financial architecture, which is developing, in part, through the initiatives of the public sector, and in part, simply force of circumstances affecting countries such as Ecuador, appears to be gradually building the structures needed to make bond investors long-term participants.

References

Buchheit LC (2000). *How to negotiate Eurocurrency loan agreements* 16, 2000.

Madrid RL (1990). *Over-exposed,United States' Banks Confront the Third World Debt Crisis 79.*

Buchheit LC. A lawyer's perspective on the new international architecture. *14. Journal of International Banking Law 225.*

Buchheit LC (2000). Sovereign debtors and their bondholders, Jan.14 (unpublished manuscript, on file with author).

See IFL Review, The Sharing Clause as a Litigation Shield, Oct. 1990.

ROLE AND ORGANIZATION OF A DEBT OFFICE

Pål Borresen and Enrique Cosio-Pascal[1]

1. Introduction

The debt crisis contributed heavily to the social and economic crisis in most developing countries in the 1980s, and its impact on the poorer developing countries continued through the 1990s, affecting their macroeconomic stability and international creditworthiness. The debt overhang stunted investment, growth and world trade, and debt payments crowded out public expenditure on education, health and other social needs. An important contributing factor to the debt crisis was the neglect by many countries of the basic elements of debt management:

Active management of public debt is a relatively recent phenomenon in most countries. Before the debt crisis of the 1980s it hardly existed. In the early 1980s, UNCTAD's Debt Management and Financial Analysis System (DMFAS) started its technical cooperation activities in this field and this paper attempts to present the experiences of the Programme over the years. .

It examines the role, the organization and the location of a public debt office, the regulatory framework and institutional memory of debt management, involving the creation of procedure manuals for the inter- and intra-institutions' tasks and information flows, as well as the location and the degree of autonomy of a debt office.

The negative impact of neglecting debt management has been widely recognised by now. As a result of this, many countries have sought to improve the basic infrastructure and analytical capacity for debt management, starting with implementation of the best organizational set-up for a national debt office.

2. The role of a debt office

The role of a debt office depends on the debt management functions, such as the duties that the laws and regulations assign to it, the strategy it chooses to adopt and the means placed at its disposal to achieve its goals. This section deals with these aspects.

2.1. Debt management functions

The execution of the different functions involved in debt management at the national level is described in figure 1 below. Each function is represented by a separate unit, although in reality, the same organizational unit may be responsible for several of the described functions. The figure also attempts to organize the different functions by categorizing them as executive or

---

[1] The authors are grateful to their colleagues in the DMFAS Programme, especially Mr. Fernando Archondo and Ms. Hélène Fabiani, for helpful discussions and comments. The authors would also like to thank all the DMFAS users all over the world, who for many years have contributed to the material presented in this paper. However, mistakes and conclusions remain exclusively those of the authors.

operational functions of effective debt management (UNCTAD, 1993)[2] while at the same time following the loan through its different phases within the sequential framework.

Figure 1

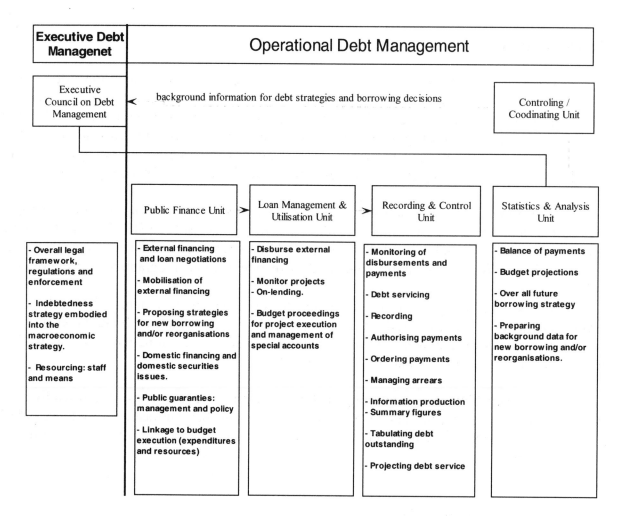

The arrows from the Public Finance unit to the Loan Management and Utilization Unit and to the Recording and Control Units represent the historical path of the loan from negotiation through to full repayment; they show which units are responsible for the different phases of operational debt management. The National Debt Office will normally be directly responsible for the functions on the Operational Debt Management side, and will provide substantial feedback to the executive functions in order to enable adjustment of the strategy and/or the legal framework in response to the latest developments. Another classification in figure 1 would be that the *Recording and Control Unit,* together with the *Loan Management and Utilization Unit,* constitute the *"back office"*; the *Statistical and Analysis Unit,* the *"middle office"*, and the *Public Finance Unit* and the *Controlling/Coordinating Unit,* the *"front office"*.

The institutional responsibilities of public debt management are allocated to the appropriate units, giving them the mandate and resources to accomplish their mission and coordinate their activities. The Debt Office could be an integrated office for all aspects of active

---

[2] See UNCTAD (1993).

– and passive – debt management (UNCTAD,1993)[3] or it could be a coordinating body for all agencies involved in debt management.

2.1.1. Executive debt management

Executive debt management might be viewed as the establishment of the "rules of the game" by the highest levels of government. This is represented in figure 1 as the Executive Council on Debt Management[4]. It thus gives direction and organization to the whole through its *Policy, Regulatory* and *Resourcing* functions. The executive management functions have an overall macroeconomic and macro-administrative dimension.

The *regulatory function* involves the establishment of a well-defined legal environment to provide for good coordination of recording, analysis, controlling and operation, supported by efficient information flows. The major output of this function is the establishment and continuous review of the administrative and legal framework of organizational responsibilities, rules and procedures among the units involved, and of the legal reporting requirements. In figure 1, this is the first item of the box, Executive Debt Management: *Overall legal framework, regulations and enforcement, and it provides* the organizational setting of the *legal, rules and regulations* structure. This function defines the *degree of control* exercised and the data which need to be recorded and monitored.

The *policy function* involves the formulation of national debt policies and strategies in coordination with the agencies that have prime responsibility for the economic management of a country. Broad policy considerations determine a country's sustainable level of external borrowing, such as deciding on what sectors should have access to external financing and on what terms, as well as fixing borrowing ceilings by creditor category. External debt policy, through foreign borrowings, affects national planning, balance of payments and budget management, and it also affects all government agencies that determine the type of investment undertaken in a country. The major output of this function is a well defined and feasible national indebtedness and external debt *strategy.* In figure 1 this is referred to as *Indebtedness strategy embodied into the macroeconomic strategy.*

The *resourcing function* involves recruiting, hiring, motivating, training and retaining staff[5]. At times, it might involve the hiring and supervision of outside consultants to provide specialized technical expertise in the area of external debt management (such as computerization, debt audits and preparation for rescheduling negotiations). This function must also be interpreted very broadly to include the provision of adequate material resources (e.g office space

---

[3] See UNCTAD (1993) *Op. Cit.*

[4] This is normally the Board of Ministers or a sub-set of it, including the governor of the central bank and, sometimes, senior officials of some large key parastatals, such as the domestic development banks, whose major activity is to borrow abroad in order to on-lend domestically.

[5] The major obstacle to the success of debt offices' operations was found to be the rotation of qualified staff. This was already pointed out empirically by UNDP (1988). Efforts should be made to retain qualified personnel in the public debt offices. The profile needed to manage the public debt is very similar to that of a banker or a financial manager of a multilateral organization. If the debt office does not offer competitive wages and good career development prospects, its staff will seek to work either with private financial institutions or with multilateral organizations. Indeed, one of the main motivations behind the creation of independent debt offices or agencies in developed countries was to be able to escape from the straitjacket of the public sector wage structure in order to retain personnel.

or communication equipment). The main output might be termed *staffing and means*, as labelled in figure 1.

2.1.2. *Operational debt management*

At the operational level of debt management, the responsibilities of a debt office will include recording, analysis and coordinating/monitoring. These functions take two forms: *passive* and *active*. This distinction is not always easy to make, but it is necessary for a better understanding of debt management. The operational debt management functions have a micro-administrative level (disaggregated level), but they also produce a synthesis of information at the macro-level (aggregated level), both levels requiring a feedback to the executive debt management functions for evaluation and decision-making. The *recording and analytical functions* are regarded as *passive functions*, in the sense that their performance does not imply a change in the debt profile. This is in contrast to the *operating and controlling functions,* the immediate effect of which would be a modification of the debt profile and would thus be regarded as *active functions*.

The *recording function* records information. In spite of the apparent simplicity of this function, it is often the source of bad debt management. Indeed good debt management requires accurate and up-to-date information. Prompt updating of debt data files necessitates a well-organized and efficient system of information flow to the office in charge of the registering function. This information flow is necessary at all levels, including new loans, transactions, disbursements and arrears created. This function is part of what is sometimes referred to as "back office" activities. The efficiency with which this function is performed depends upon the good implementation of the overall legal framework, regulations and their enforcement. This function also needs good information management (computerized) support. In figure 1, the Recording and Controlling Unit performs this function.

The *analytical function* provides elements for analysis and decision-making. It utilizes the information provided by the Recording Unit. At the aggregate level, it involves macroeconomic analysis to explore the various options available, given economic and market conditions, and the future structure of the external debt. It is necessary to constantly review the impact of various debt management options on the balance of payments and on the national budget and to help with assessing such matters as the appropriate terms for new borrowing. At the disaggregated level, the analytical function would look at such matters as the various borrowing instruments or the choice of maturities. It could also assist in the analysis of new financial techniques such as hedging, swaps and risk management. If the debt office has benchmarks to comply with, this function will also measure the accomplishment of the office in regard to those benchmarks. The output here, of course, is *analysis*. This function is part of what is sometimes called *"middle office"* activities, which in figure 1 are performed by the Statistics and Analysis Unit.

The *operating function* is divided into three different phases: *negotiating, utilization of loan proceeds* and *servicing*. The activities or actions involved in each phase will be different depending on the type of borrowing involved (bilateral and multilateral concessional loans, Eurocredits, etc.), but also these activities could be different in their nature. *Utilization of loan proceeds and servicing* are closer to the monitoring of projects and budget execution. In figure 1, they are performed by the Loan Management and Utilization Unit, and they are sometimes called *"back office"* activities. *Negotiating*, in broad terms, is external financing negotiations, including new borrowing and eventual rescheduling of operations. The negotiating activity decides on micro-financial strategic issues and fixes benchmarks based on the output of the analytical function. It also applies the executive debt management function's decisions to public guarantees. These activities are sometimes called *"front office"* activities, and, in figure 1, they are located in the Public Finance Unit.

The *controlling function* is the function of debt management which is the most difficult to define separately. Indeed, control is intrinsic to a debt management system. While the recording, analytical and operating functions are described here in their "pure form"; it might be correctly argued that control is embedded in those functions. However, separating the controlling function enriches the conceptual approach undertaken here and underlines better the central role of this function.

At the transaction (e.g. *disaggregated)* level, the *controlling/monitoring* function is more concerned with specific operations, utilization and service. It must ensure, among other things, that the amount and terms of new borrowings fall within current guidelines, that funds are being utilized on time and appropriately, and that repayments are made according to schedule within the budget allocations. In practice, the degree of *control* can vary widely (according to the different classes or types of debt and debt operations, the different public or private borrowing entities involved, etc.) ranging from close control to coordination and monitoring. This function is performed in different ways by all the units in figure 1.

At the *aggregated* level, the *controlling/coordinating* function is essential to ensure that operational debt management conforms with executive debt management. A strategy may, for instance, impose statutory limits or overall guidelines on how much borrowing can be done by the public sector and/or by the country as a whole. In this case, *controlling/coordinating* must ensure that borrowing is kept within the prescribed limits. Another important activity of this function is to serve as the information interface between the operational debt management functions and the executive ones. This makes the whole system dynamic, in that the feedback of this function to the executive level will allow it to modify the strategy in line with what is happening at the operational level and to reflect this back, through this function, to the units performing the operational functions. In figure 1, the Controlling/Coordinating Unit performs this function and its place in the figure shows its key strategical position, interfacing the operational with the executive functions (i.e. the Executive Council on Debt Management). In fact, the Controlling/Coordinating Unit is a kind of technical secretariat to the Executive Council. These activities could also be among those of the *"front office"*.

2.2.   Performing effective debt management

There are two basic elements for effective debt management: the organizational structure of the debt office and its management information systems.

2.2.1. *Organization of the debt office*

The debt office should have clearly defined functions as well as the skills required to do the work. It is useful to review the organizational set-up of the debt office on a regular basis to identify the functions that the office should be carrying out and to check them against the skills required for fulfilling its responsibilities. The outcome of this study should be compared to the functions being performed and the skills of the existing staff, to determine what new staff and/or what training programme(s) might be required. The result should be a list of the required new staff or training requirements, with corresponding job descriptions and training terms of reference[6].

The organizational study should also help to produce the basic managerial documents that are essential for the efficient functioning of the debt office:

- A **functions manual** with a detailed description of the various responsibilities and functions of the debt office;
- A **procedures manual** with a detailed description of information flows;
- An **organizational chart** for the debt office; and
- A **job description** for each officer.

The functions manual should specifically describe the role, functions and responsibilities of the debt office, in accordance with existing legal provisions, rules and regulations. The functions manual would set out the organizational structure – including supervision at senior, intermediate and operational levels, and a description of the debt office – with enough precision to enable the debt office to execute all the operations under its responsibility.

The procedures manual should establish the flow and composition of the information in the operational cycle of the debt office, including the frequency in receiving documentation and a detailed description of information of internal and external financing, how to register this information in the database, and the steps to follow for the registry of disbursements and public debt service. It should determine the flows of information and the functional groups involved in the process. The manual should also describe the outgoing information flows from the debt office to other bodies of the government, private entities and international organizations, including its regularity and the description of the information that it should contain. The procedures manual will thus link the operative activities with the structure and functions established by the functions manual. Both manuals should constitute the organizational and functional framework of the unit, indispensable for guaranteeing efficient executive and operational management. The functions and procedures manuals need to be supplemented with a chart of the debt office and a detailed job description for each staff member.

The *resourcing function* is of basic importance in order to have specialized staff with the necessary training. Attracting and retaining qualified staff requires that the salary scale and career opportunities in the debt office be fully competitive with other job opportunities in the public and private sectors. Attention should be given to training, including training abroad, when appropriate. High staff turnover can pose a serious threat to the prospects of success of a debt office and, as mentioned earlier, has been observed as one of the most common causes of failure of performance.

It is necessary to evaluate the office space and equipment requirements. Space is a basic need for effective performance of daily duties. Also, the staff should have at their disposal the required hardware and software with e-mail and Internet facilities as well as facsimile and long distance telephone services.

---

[6] If management planning and analysis in the debt office are limited, the task of developing an organizational plan and associated staffing policies may be best assigned to an external consultant with experience in the organization of debt offices, such as UNCTAD or the Commonwealth Secretariat.

The debt office should also have appropriate legal support and effective data collection mechanisms to do its job. If these legal and administrative elements are weak, debt data will be late, incomplete and/or inaccurate, and the debt office will produce poor results.

2.2.2. *Debt Management Information Systems*

Computers bring flexibility and rapidity to the debt data processing, and thereby allow debt managers to review the information in ways that are not otherwise practicable. Within minutes, computer systems can compute the current balances of hundreds of loans, sum them up and print reports organized by lender, borrower, currency and so forth. Even more important, computers allow the debt manager to answer "what-if" questions about the profile of future payments if interest rates and or exchange rates rise or fall, and thus rapidly analyse the changes in the country's debt burden resulting from hypothetical changes in financial markets. In the same way, a computerized system can allow the debt managers to check the debt data against the real economy's macroeconomic variables so that projections of financing needs to close the balance-of-payments and/or the national budget deficit are obtained. For these reasons, today it is impossible to effectively manage the national debt without a computerized system. In addition, if the system is decentralized, as explained in the previous paragraph, modern technology is required for the different actors to communicate quickly and efficiently. This is why the involvement of management information systems (MIS) is so vital for debt managers.

The tendency now, is to recommend installing a software package, available from the major suppliers of technical assistance in this field. At present, there are at least two well-tested debt management software packages available[7]. Compared to designing, programming and maintaining an entirely new system, the packages are relatively inexpensive. Their designers and users have debugged the available systems to the point where they are likely to have fewer operating problems than custom-made systems. They can be implemented quickly and the maintenance is centralized, creating economies of scale. The maintenance of a system is of vital importance: it has been proven that the personnel turnover in the MIS department makes domestically developed systems very vulnerable. All these direct and indirect cost factors should be analysed carefully in selecting a debt software package.

In a computerized environment, it is of paramount importance that the senior officials make clear their support for the information management needs of the debt office. The most important manifestation of this support is the assignment of competent individuals to staff the debt office and to operate the computerized debt management system. This involves a strategic decision to define the debt office's relationship with the MIS department, to make sure that the debt management system receives the necessary support in all its daily computerized activities. This means that the debt office needs to allocate computer specialists with well-defined terms of reference, defined by the MIS department, in order to provide regular daily services, including resolving eventual technical problems[8].

---

[7] The UNCTAD/DMFAS and the Commonwealth Secretariat CS-DRMS. These two systems can be considered as "back office" systems, but both of them are linked to a "middle-front office" software package, the DSM+ that was developed by the World Bank. The three institutions have a partnership agreement to maintain and distribute this software.

[8] It must not be forgotten in the budgetary planning process for computerization, that the debt office will need a regular supply of paper, computer maintenance and hardware spare parts. In some countries, work at the debt office has come to a standstill because of this.

3. The duties of a national debt office

In theory, the duties of a debt office are, or should be, quite simple, namely to conduct activities that it has been mandated to undertake under existing laws and regulations concerning public indebtedness policies. Any sovereign borrower should have such laws and regulations in place. In practice, however, this is often not as straightforward as it might seem. Several institutions are usually involved in the debt management process, and, depending on the strengths and weaknesses of individual units, it is not unusual to find a de facto debt office in an institution that does not have the corresponding mandate.

Furthermore, the role of a debt office is not static. As a country advances as a borrower, the role of the debt office will change, and accordingly, the organizational set-up will need to be adjusted. Sovereign borrowers fall into different categories, each having its own specific requirements for the execution of the debt management functions. The category determines the sources of external funding to which a country will have access. For this purpose, we can distinguish between the following four categories[9]:

(i)	Countries, members of the International Development Association (IDA) – "IDA only" countries;

(ii)	Other low-income countries;

(iii)	Middle-income countries; and

(iv)	High- income countries.

The main sources of financing for "IDA only" countries are bilateral and multilateral creditors with concessional funds. These countries deal mainly with international institutions. Bilateral funds are mostly in the form of official development assistance (ODA), rather than commercial loans. Some low-income countries have access to commercial sources of money, including suppliers' credits and foreign private banks – through buyers' credits – in addition to the bilateral and multilateral institutions. Middle-income countries and countries with economies in transition have some degree of access to international capital markets, but they still depend, to a large extent, on suppliers' credits, bilateral and multilateral funding. High-income countries obtain funding almost exclusively in domestic and international capital markets.

A debt office needs to be organized and staffed taking into consideration the type of lenders it will be dealing with. While international development agencies are coordinated and driven by development objectives and political decisions, the players in the international financial markets are international banks driven by competition and the profit motive. In any environment, the organizational challenge lies in pragmatic and firm decisions concerning which units will hold what data for what purpose, how these units will exchange information, and which unit will be responsible for what part of the effective debt management function. These functions must be made known to all the institutions involved.

The first decision to make regarding a national debt office is to define the scope of coverage of its activities. As already mentioned, the national debt office could be an integrated entity covering all aspect of debt management, or it could play more of a coordinating role where the debt management functions are distributed between several units. In IDA countries and other low-income countries, a debt office would focus on the relationship with international

---

[9] All categories of countries fund themselves to a smaller or larger extent in their domestic markets.

organizations and bilateral donors. Most financing to these countries is either for balance-of-payments/public budget support or for projects. In terms of coverage a national debt office will either be directly or indirectly involved with:

- External debt and foreign grants
- government debt
- government-guaranteed debt
- public enterprises debt
- short-term debt
- private non-guaranteed debt
- grants
- On-lending agreements
- Monitoring of project execution
- Domestic debt

Some countries choose to give their debt offices monitoring responsibilities for all these sources of financing, while others limit their offices' role to external debt only. Middle-income countries are "mixed" borrowers, and therefore, also oriented towards the international capital markets. The debt office of these countries may therefore need a specialized department dealing with international market operations. The debt offices of high-income countries are mainly market oriented and organized accordingly. Certain national debt offices even go beyond the borrowing functions, as the example of the Swedish National Debt Office (figure 2) shows.

The debt office of a country will, as a minimum, be responsible for monitoring the government debt. Other management functions related to debt will variy considerably from country to country: the Swedish Debt Office exercises a wide range of management functions; however, in other countries the management functions are often distributed among several different offices. The more integrated the Government's financial management system the more actively the debt will have to be managed, and the more active the debt office will normally be in the terms of overall public debt management, including budgeting, public accounting, cash flow and strategic decision-making.

A monitoring or management role for the debt office will be a decision that each country will have to evaluate, depending on the importance of the external debt within the national economy. One of the issues to be taken into account concerns the availability of skilled management resources, and whether management of currencies, exchange rates and interest rates is a priority use of these resources. Experience shows, that there is a tendency towards a more management-oriented debt office than in the past.

Also, the scope of the monitoring tasks may vary considerably, depending on what type of borrower a country is. Low- and middle-income countries are often charged with the monitoring of on-lending agreements, parastatal and private sector non-guaranteed debt, as well as grant flows and project execution. Debt offices of high-income countries do not have these monitoring responsibilities.

4. Location and Level of Autonomy of the debt office

Figure 2 [10]

```
                    SWEDISH NATIONAL DEBT OFFICE
    Manages the State debt as cost-effectively as possible by borrowing:
            - in the money and bond market mainly through
                            - Treasury notes
                            - Treasury bills
            - in the private market through
                            - Lottery bonds
                            - Savings certificates
                            - the national savings account
                            - the national debt account
            - in foreign markets mainly through
                            - bonds in the Euromarket and national markets
                            - Treasury bill programmes in foreign currency
                            - modern debt management techniques
                              (swaps, forward contracts, etc.)
            - from State authorities and funds in the form of
                            - deposits
    Grants credit to State corporations
    Issues guarantees on behalf of the State
    Coordinates State guarantee operations and loans to industry and trad, and
    monitors cost thereof
    Determines rates of interest for the National Savings Account and the Young
    People's Housing Saving System
    Makes forecasts for payments to and from the State and ensures that these
      transactions are managed as cost-effectively as possible.
```

The debt office's physical location in the national organizational set-up is of course closely linked to its role, responsibilities and mandate. This section looks at the location of the debt office in the overall organizational structure of the national debt management framework, and the interaction between this unit and other institutions in the national set-up. The debt office's links to other units will depend on the distribution of functions, delegation of authority and configuration of responsibilities among various government ministries and agencies.

The unit responsible for monitoring central government debt should logically be located in the ministry of finance, with close links to the budget office. This is because the process of monitoring central government direct debt is tied to the budgetary process: both in budget preparation and its execution[11]. However, in some countries these responsibilities may be distributed between several different institutions, depending on the organization of government services and historic precedent.

4.1. Centralized organization

The ministry of finance or the central bank have, historically, been the institutions in which the debt management function has been centralized. Below, models that have been implemented by different countries, are described.

4.1.1. Office at the ministry of finance

As mentioned above, this is logically where a central unit should be located. Loan negotiations are often coordinated by a team representing both the ministry of finance and the

---

[10]The Swedish National Debt Office (1990/1991).

[11] It is at the level of budget implementation where, normally, the formal accounting operations of debt management are performed.

central bank, while monitoring of payments is done by either the debt office, the budget office, the treasury department, the accountant general's office and/or the central bank. The debt unit at the ministry of finance monitors, as a general rule, only the government debt and publicly guaranteed debt, including that of the parastatals. A common problem facing ministries of finance, however, is that they often operate within restrictions imposed by the government budget and government personnel policies, which often prevent them from offering the salaries, training and other facilities necessary for attracting qualified staff and for retaining trained and experienced officers. The central bank performs the role of financial agent of the Government and manages the payments and the treasury accounts. The central bank is also in charge of managing the foreign reserves and provides a link to the debt service.

4.1.2. *Office at the central bank*

If the country is monitoring private sector non-guaranteed debt, in many cases this will be the responsibility of the central bank. Some countries have, for this reason among others, chosen the option of establishing their debt office at the central bank. As foreign currency for debt service payments is monitored by the central bank, this institution is in the best position to capture the total debt situation of the country. Occasionally, other considerations may also influence this decision. Central banks operate on a budget which reflects their own earnings, and therefore, they usually have a more generous administrative budget and more room for extra-budgetary expenses than a ministry of finance. The pragmatic solution is thus to establish the unit in the central bank because it is likely to have better facilities, and qualified personnel and salary levels. All these factors will, of course, influence the motivation of the personnel involved and will make it easier to retain trained staff. Locating the registering function in the central bank does not preclude the ministry of finances from having direct access to the database and from performing other operational functions such as implementation of the budget.

4.1.3 *Autonomous debt office (agency)*

An alternative to establishing the debt office either at the ministry of finance or at the central bank is to establish an autonomous unit, as has been done by the Irish and Portuguese Governments, for example. This model requires a very efficient and well-organized structure for information flows. The problem with this choice is that it appears not to work as intended in countries where poor organizational structures exist within the Government, a situation which often arises due to lack of resources. As an example, a number of French-speaking countries in Africa have applied this model without major success because of lack of institutional strength[12]. The autonomous unit may, in those cases, face problems with data collection due to lack of coordination between the different institutions involved in debt management. The attraction of this solution is that the unit may be independent of the government payroll system, permitting the remuneration system to resemble that of the private sector, for instance, employing a system of bonuses based on performance, and thereby attracting and retaining better-qualified personnel. In some instances, specific tax or other public revenues (i.e. lotteries) may be allocated directly to this office. In an autonomous unit or agency, the minister may execute control through regular meetings with its chief executive. In the Irish National Treasury Management Agency, for example, the chief executive clears the budget once a year with the Minister of Finance. In addition, the chief executive appears before Parliament once a year in the discussions concerning

---

[12] For example, the Caisse nationale d'Amortissement de la Dette Publique was very popular in the countries of French-speaking West Africa in the 1980s. However, this model has been gradually abandoned and the responsibilities transferred to the ministries of finance.

the budget execution. In any case, the establishment of such a debt office represents a high investment to start with.

Generally, the sole purpose of an agency is to fund the budget deficit at the optimal combination of cost and risk[13]. It is therefore a set up for the purpose of managing risk. The agency, however, is only needed if there is a budget deficit to be financed. If the budget deficit decreases, as occured in Ireland,[14] the need for this institution will diminish. It therefore makes sense for an agency to have its staff on relatively short contracts (e.g. fiscal year by fiscal year). This is also an argument thet can be used to justify paying the staff higher salaries than those offered within the government structure.

Debt offices in countries where the main source of financing is the capital markets generally have an organizational structure that incorporates the back, middle and front offices. The back office processes (and makes) payments, settles accounts, does the registering and accounting, as well as the debt reporting and statistics; the middle office does risk management and performance assessment by fixing benchmarks, and, finally, the front office devises the strategies and conducts the borrowing in capital markets, including negotiating with the lenders.

The trend in developed countries during the 1990s has been to move in the direction of an agency type of debt office. The model they have often considered is the National Treasury Management Agency of Ireland, which again took inspiration from the Swedish Debt Office. Before concluding that this is a model that may be implemented in any environment, however, it is important to understand its purpose and limitations.

- This model is generally designed for floating government securities, not for bilateral and multilateral borrowing, although some countries, such as Hungary, manage this type of financing in the same agency. This is reflected in the organizational set-up, the type of staff employed and the risk management model used. These countries have a full range of choices of financial instruments, and therefore, tap the capital markets that provide the greatest flexibility at a reasonable cost.

- The countries using this model generally have very little foreign debt: the loans are practically all in domestic currency. For example, Belgium has less than 2 per cent of foreign currency debt in its portfolio;[15] and the debt office of the Danish central bank does not even include the foreign debt stock in its risk management models.

- The use of the funds is not an issue for most agencies, as they are merely the executing arm for the budget. They therefore do not perform the executive functions of debt management. Thus, the model has generally been chosen in order to separate the debt management (funding) function from fiscal and monetary policy. It may therefore be regarded as a "funding machine" for the government budget. However, as mentioned earlier, it is important to bear in mind that if the institutional structure otherwise does not function, it is not possible to set up an agency where one function, namely funding, is pulled out and operates on its own.

---

[13] The IMF and the World Bank have recently issued a paper, *Draft Guidelines for Public Debt Management*, August 2000, Washington, that takes this approach; it defines the objectives of debt management as being "..to ensure that the government's financing needs and its payments obligations are met at the lowest possible cost over the medium to long run, consistent with a prudent degree of risk."

[14] As of November 1999

[15] As of November 1999

This type or organization, entails the risk of lack of coordination of public debt management with the treasury and budget systems. Under the modern concept of government financial management it becomes necessary to have the public debt module as a subsystem of an Integrated Financial Management System (IFMS). An IFMS contains the treasury, cash flow, budget operations and public accounting of the central Government. Thus, if an IFMS is implemented in a country, it is more efficient to have the debt office at the ministry of finance[16].

As already noted, the establishment of such a debt office represents a high investment to begin with. In addition to this, an agency of this type needs a well-organized secondary market for the different debt instruments that are issued in order to function efficiently.

4.1.4. Other Cases[17]

The former Soviet Union

The governmental structure of the former Soviet Union had a cabinet of ministers, directly supporting the President, where important decisions were made, and the central bank and various ministries, including the Ministry of Finance, played a relatively modest role compared to what is usual in other countries. This, of course, had important implications for the debt management functions. The generally accepted "rule of thumb" for where the debt office should be located no longer applies. For historical reasons, the State Bank of Foreign Trade, the *Veneshkombank*, had, until now, a paramount role in the management of the external debt of the Commonwealth of Independent States (CIS) – a fact that these now independent countries can no longer ignore. In the particular case of the Russian Federation, the *Veneshkombank* manages not only the country's external debt, but also the debt owed to it by third countries. The Russian Federation and some CIS countries have retained this structure and it will take some time to replace it.

Contracting a commercial bank

For special bond issues, in particular retail bonds, a sovereign borrower may consider the possibility of contracting the issue to a commercial bank. The debt office would retain the overall policy responsibility for the issue, but may sub-contract the commercial bank on a performance contract. Contracting the entire sovereign debt management function of a country to a commercial bank, however, is generally not considered an option because it does not permit a sufficient degree of control. Besides, a commercial bank probably would not have the expertise in monitoring loans linked to projects from multilateral organizations. The minister of finance will, in any case, carry full responsibility for public debt management, but would, in this case, lack some of the control mechanisms available within the government structure.

4.2. Decentralized organization

It is clear that control/monitoring or control/coordinating functions are better assumed by the ministry of finance and by the central bank. Nevertheless, other functions can be well handled by other actors, because they have the historical know-how. Many countries therefore decide on some kind of decentralized organization with shared responsibilities. As mentioned

---

[16] For instance, the DMFAS is integrated with budget and treasury systems in Argentina and Guatemala and is being integrated in Bolivia, El Salvador, Paraguay and Venezuela. In all these countries, the debt office is located at the ministries of finance.

[17] Useful material on other cases can also be found in Klein (1994).

above, the decision on the actual location of the unit should be considered in the context of the specific functions of external debt management of each institution, rather than on the staffing and means at their disposal. A recent trend, in countries where public debt traditionally has been managed by the *Veneshkombank*-type institution or by the central bank, is to transfer the responsibility to the ministry of finance. However, in many of these cases, the role of financial agent is left to the central bank and, in some cases, also the responsibility for monitoring non-guaranteed private debt. A more formal linkage of public debt management with budget execution and fiscal policy, has led to this transfer of responsibility to the ministry of finance and to a change in the formal status of the central bank (i.e. it has been made autonomous). In most cases, however, the changes take place as a result of the current trend of central banks reverting to "core" central banking functions. Recording of central government debt is not necessarily considered a core function of a central bank.

Decentralization of operations will only work provided the information flows and legal framework are in place. Otherwise, a central statistical office may not be able to collect the required data to compile management reports. To quote Kalderen (1986):

> "It may not be feasible to combine all functions and responsibilities and centralise them in one Debt Office. The more pragmatic approach is to establish a centralised statistical office that co-ordinates and integrates the data gathered by the various decentralised participants of the system and prepares a comprehensive report for the high-level policy committee".

Decentralization of the different functions must not jeopardize the principle of central control. Thus in a decentralized system, a long range of control/coordination problems will need to be resolved concerning: the collection and recording of data; who should be responsible for compiling data on the country's total debt; who will analyse the data; and who will have the main responsibility for dealing with and reporting to international organizations and foreign creditors.

The choice of agency responsible for collecting and recording data on government debt, public enterprise debt, private sector debt and short-term debt partly entails a consideration of primary responsibility of the institution and its access to the primary data sources. The location of the debt office would be influenced by historical precedent in the concerned country, since certain data collection procedures will already be in place. Nevertheless, in a computerized environment this may not be a decisive factor, because with modern telecommunication networks two recording units can be connected through a wide area network, facilitating the specialization of the different institutions concerned. It has to be kept in mind that the size of the debt being monitored is also very important, not in value terms, but in the volume of instruments and transactions. Complexity in the terms of instruments may necessitate the splitting of responsibilities for data collection and recording between different units, and better coordination.

The unit responsible for compiling data on the total debt situation of the country, analysing this data and reporting to different national and international institutions will need a strong mandate for this task in order to secure the necessary data flows. In a decentralized environment it would be important to avoid constant overlapping data in different institutions to avoid the risk of different institutions reporting different figures on the same debt. If this were to occur, the central statistical unit as well as international organizations compiling debt statistics, such as the IMF and the World Bank, would have the unnecessary task of verification. This is why specialization of the different institutions involved is of paramount importance. For instance, the ministry of finance could specialize in public and publicly-guaranteed debt, and the central bank, in non-guaranteed private debt. With good coordination, both institutions could exchange information on a regular basis so that both of them would have access to the whole database. When the treasury and or the accountant general are not formally part of the ministry of finance they also will have to be linked to the computerized information system.

A recent trend is the privatization of State enterprises, the contraction of the non-government public sector and a relaxation of exchange control regimes. This has resulted in increased borrowing by the private sector and a reduced ability of the public sector to monitor private borrowing, since the private sector now gets foreign currency directly from the banking system. At the same time, many Governments extend the scope of their monitoring activities and move into monitoring of short-, medium- and long-term private sector external debt, in addition to short-term external debt, public domestic debt, aid-grants and project linkages, on-lending and foreign loans to local governments. This trend enforces the need for integrated systems, because more than one debt recording office might be involved. Also, there is a need to interface with other financial management systems, such as budget, aid management and on-lending.

5. Organizational models

The organizational model that will be applied to the debt office will depend on several factors: the historical background, the legal division of responsibility between different government bodies, and the importance of external debt in the overall public indebtedness, as well as the volume of data and its complexity. However, the organizational structure of the debt office should be oriented towards a more global and efficient debt management approach capable of responding to all needs and responsibilities.

The debt office is frequently organized on the basis of geographical or institutional lines, where officers are responsible for all actions taken on their assigned set of loans. However,this is not the only possible way of organizing the office. If the required expertise exists in the debt office, it would be ideal to have different officers specialize in different types of financing[18] rather than divide the loan files along geographical or institutional lines.

5.1. Geographical organization

Many debt offices have applied division of work according to geographical regions, where each officer is responsible for all creditors within his or her assigned country or region. In addition, some staff are usually responsible for multilateral organizations, which are treated as a country or region. This is a better approach than giving the same desk officer responsibility for multilateral organizations as well as for creditors from a given region. The rationale behind this organizational structure seldom goes beyond the intention to distribute the workload evenly between the desk officers. The organizational chart for this type of organization is shown in Figure 3.

---

[18] In such an organizational set-up, at least one officer should specialize in loans from institutions using currency pooling. These loans are not a special type of financing as such, but with regard to accounting and monitoring, they represent a very particular problem.

Figure 3
Organizational chart for a geographical set-up

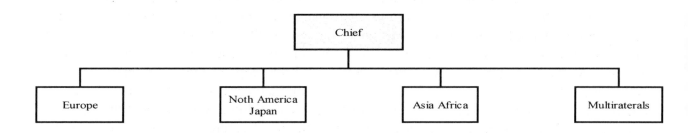

An alternative to the geographical organization is the loan source or type of financing organization or an organization according to transaction type, which may, in some cases, be more effective. The following section describes how the work in the debt office may be organized on the basis of the type of activity undertaken. This organizational model generally falls into two broad categories, and, for the sake of classification, they could be called **creditor-oriented organizations** and **task-oriented organizations**.

5.2.   Creditor-oriented organization

It has been suggested that a country's external debt management should be organized according to the types of loans (Kalderen, 1986) (i.e. bilateral loans, multilateral loans, export credits and private banks loans). The reasoning behind this is that these different types of financing have different characteristics, especially in the way they are negotiated and monitored. If a country follows this model (see figure 4.) it should have experts specializing in the different types of loans: bilateral Paris Club, bilateral non-Paris Club, multilateral, private banks, suppliers, and bonds.

Figure 4
Organizational chart for a creditor-oriented set-up

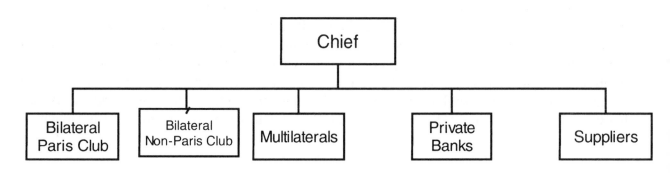

However, this organizational structure needs a well-established information flows network. If this requirement is not satisfied, this structure might not be efficient.

5.3. Task-oriented organization

Task-oriented data collection may be particularly useful in cases where adequate information flows are not very well established or in cases where data has to be collected by visiting different beneficiaries, ministries and institutions. An example of this type of organization, still valid in many countries, is shown in figure 5. It is organized according to four main tasks: -handling disbursements information; handling payments information; handling contract information; and reporting

Figure 5
Organizational chart for a task-oriented set-up

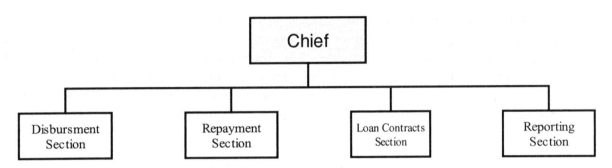

This type of organization may be needed in countries where the information is located in different institutions and ministries. However, interventions by different staff of the debt office would should not result in their visiting the same ministry or parastatal during the same week to collect similar information. It is necessary to assign a specific task force with the job of collecting all information regarding transactions. However, it is imperative to establish procedures so that the debt office automatically receives copies of all needed information on a regular basis.

Another example of a task-oriented organization was developed by UNCTAD/DMFAS in connection with the release of version 5.0 of the DMFAS software. This organizational structure, however, is more dependent on well-established information flows than the previous example. The model has its foundation in the different phases in the lifetime of a loan in relation to the Effective Debt Management Functions. It is reflected in the Main Menu of the versions of DMFAS from 5.0 onwards, as illustrated in figure 6.

Figure 6

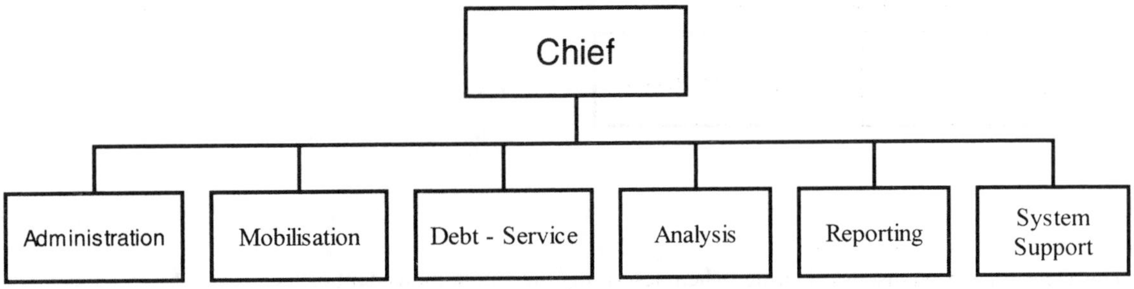

```
                              ┌──────────┐
                              │  Chief   │
                              └──────────┘
   ┌──────────────┬──────────────┬──────────────┬──────────────┬──────────────┐
┌────────────┐ ┌────────────┐ ┌────────────┐ ┌──────────┐ ┌──────────┐ ┌────────────┐
│Administration│ │Mobilisation│ │Debt-Service│ │ Analysis │ │Reporting │ │  System    │
│            │ │            │ │            │ │          │ │          │ │  Support   │
└────────────┘ └────────────┘ └────────────┘ └──────────┘ └──────────┘ └────────────┘
```

Under this type of structure, there is the risk of a dispersion of responsibilities between the registration of information of new borrowing and the execution of its operations. The separation of disbursements and debt service can also create excessive specialization, which might undermine the possibilities for training, rotation of personnel and knowledge of the whole process of debt management. The problem often seen with this form of organization is the bottlenecks that can be created in each unit as result of inefficiency. The separation of responsibilities might create bottlenecks in terms of flow of information, since the payment order cannot be processed if the information on the disbursement was not entered in time by the unit in charge of that function. All these reasons may suggest that an efficient model should integrate all the operative processes in a more vertical manner.

5.4. Organization of large debt offices

In debt offices where the mandate goes beyond external debt, more complex organizational structures will be required. The higher level structure could then be organized according to categories of debt, for example. The lower level organizational structure for data collection, however, would probably still follow one of the models previously presented in this section. This paper will not go into the details apart from showing two examples of more complex organizational structures; one of them hypothetical, in figure 7, the other from real life, in figure 8.

Debt offices in countries where capital markets are the main source of financing generally have an organizational structure that incorporates the back, middle and front offices[19]. This is not always the case in developing countries, where some of them perform only certain back office functions that are limited to the processing and recording of payments. Sweden offers a typical example of a debt office having all these functions. This type of debt office, in general, also has its own information technology unit operating from either the middle or the back office, as well as an internal auditor reporting directly to the chief executive, as shown in figure 8.

Figure 7

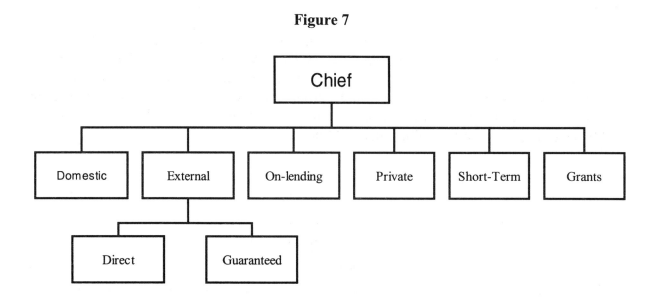

---

[19] This aspect has been discussed earlier when describing the autonomous debt office.

Figure 8[20]
Organizational Chart of the Swedish National Debt Office (1991)

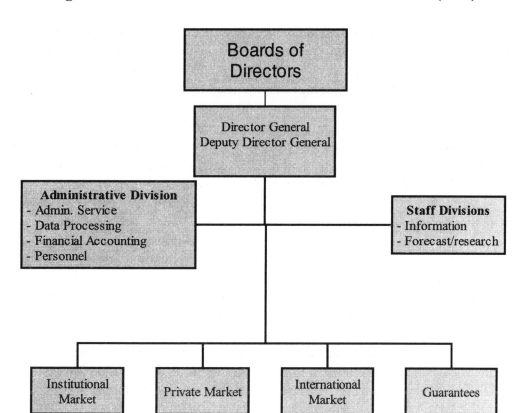

In some developing countries, it is quite usual for middle office functions to be missing completely, often because they are considered unnecessary. Most developing countries borrow from concessional multilateral or bilateral sources, where the rules of the game have been defined in advance and the negotiations primarily concern the use of funds, rather than the terms. Interest rates and repayment terms are therefore, not much of an issue which explains the perception of a reduced need for a middle office. Nevertheless, this perception is changing and there are some developing countries that are implementing middle office functions, very often in conjunction with assets and reserves management. This is because the elements of risk management and organizational structures applied in developed countries are potentially useful for developing countries. However, they cannot be transferred to developing countries without proper adaptation.

Regarding the front office function, it is important to point out that it is quite different in a developing country from that of Ireland or Sweden. While the front office in a developed country spends its time conceiving strategies for how best to tap capital markets, the front office of a developing country is involved in negotiating with the IMF and multilateral development banks. A developing country debt office also devotes considerable effort to developing the domestic capital market. Therefore the skill requirements and the profile of the staff of a front office of a developing country are, needless to say, different from those of the front office of the Irish debt agency, for example. The front office of a developing country requires people with decision-making power at the national policy level.

---

[20]The Swedish National Debt Office, 1990/1991.

6. Conclusions

- Countries at different levels of development will need different organizational structures for their debt office. For a developed country market borrower, it may be desirable to separate the debt management (funding) function from fiscal and monitory policy, while in a country with a "mixed" source of funding, it may be important to integrate the two.

- Irrespective of the country's level of development, it should, one way or another, organize its debt management office according to the type of sources of financing to which it has access. This is in line with Kalderen's suggestion (1986) that a country's external debt office should be organized according to the type of funding[21].

- A well-organized structure will improve information flows, the quality of information produced, the productivity of its personnel and the handling of responsibilities. Therefore, the structure should be organized with a distribution of operations that clearly defines and establishes the sources of financing and the coordination and monitoring functions of public debt management. An efficient model of debt management for a debt office integrates all the operative and monitoring processes in a vertical manner.

- Computerization is an essential tool for debt managers, and a careful choice has to be made in the different trade-offs between developing a system or taking one already available in the market. The development of an "in-house" computerized system can be far more expensive and risky than taking one already developed and available in the market.

- The autonomous debt office can have serious drawbacks in spite of it flexibility: it is designed for floating government securities, not for bilateral and multilateral borrowing. The countries using this model generally have very little foreign debt, and nearly all their loans are in their domestic currency. The use of the funds is not an issue for most agencies – they are merely the executing arm for the budget. Therefore, they do not perform the executive functions of debt management. This type or organization is more prone to a lack of coordination of the public debt management function with the treasury and budget systems. And last but not least, the establishment of this model of debt office represents a high investment to start with and needs a well-organized secondary market for the different debt instruments that are issued in order to function in an efficient way.

- Nevertheless, whatever the organizational set-up that a country chooses, it is important for it to have a good regulatory and legal framework. It is also well advised to have effective debt management functions in place, both at the executive and operational levels.

---

[21]Lars Kalderen , (1986) *Op. cit.*

Bibliography

IMF and World Bank (2000). *Draft Guidelines for Public Debt Management*, Washington DC, August.

Kalderen Lars (1986). *Institutional Aspects of Debt Management.* Working Paper No. M1986-03, World Bank, Washington DC, October.

Klein Thomas (1994). *External Debt Management: An Introduction.* Technical Paper Number 245, World Bank, Washington DC, June.

The Swedish National Debt Office (1990/1991*). Annual Report 1990/1991.*

UNCTAD (1993). *Effective Debt Management* UNCTAD/GID/DMS/15, Geneva, November.

UNDP (1989). *Debt Management and the Developing Countries: A report to the UNDP by an Independent Group of Experts.* UNDP, New York, July.

CAN CRISES BE PREVENTED?

Luis Foncerrada

1. Introduction

Can crises be prevented? The answer is that they can and this paper presents a very simple approach. *What is a crisis? Where does it come from? How does it develop?*

As outsiders, we view a crisis in terms of an inability to continue the usual transactions with other countries, including difficulties in importing, exporting, paying the debt and other obligations, and obviously, difficulties in borrowing new funds. That is to say, a country in crisis lacks foreign currency to meet its international obligations and to undertake international trade. Interest payments on public debt, are probably the first to stop, followed by any principal payments falling due in the same period. If there is a very critical lack of foreign currency, not even the private sector is able to meet its financial obligations. Then, any pending disbursements of loans due are usually interrupted, and letters of credit are immediately suspended, which worsens the situation, following which even the flow of goods and services becomes seriously disrupted.

What follows is well known. Emergency, and usually desperate, measures are taken, beginning with the introduction of exchange controls and/or multiple exchange rates in order to attempt an emergency allocation of the scarce reserves.

What happens to the domestic economy?

Depending on the size and importance of the external sector, there could be a big devaluation, capital flight – if any resources are still left – a deep recession, unemployment, social unrest, political activity, and eventually, a transition to a new government, sometimes through a very violent process.

There appear to be three main causes of a crisis, discussed below.

(i) Elements external to an economy

An external variable, or external shock, can change or affect the equilibrium of the balance of payments, and eventually, all domestic variables: interest rates, prices of exports, prices of imports, capital flows and domestic prices, among others.

When the external variables are out of control, there is not much that can be done about them.

(ii) Natural disasters and political problems

Natural disasters are generally impossible to foresee, and political problems, even when predictable, are very difficult to prevent. In any case, there is not much that can be done to prevent them.

(iii)   Economic policy and debt management

It is this third issue that forms the subject of our analysis. We all know, and have often seen, how crises are initiated or caused by mistakes in economic policy, and/or by poor management of foreign resources, including foreign debt.

The common problems in this area are:

a) Above all, a lack of understanding of the importance of good and sound monetary and fiscal policies, and a lack of understanding of the implications of some wrong policies. Thus, often crises stem from an absence of fiscal and monetary discipline. The lack of training and of a thorough understanding of the economy and lack of basic necessities for the people make a dangerous combination.

b) A high rotation of the technical teams in both the policy and management areas.

c) A lack of knowledge and a failure to understand the importance of timing. An early negotiation with, or a "previous" approach to, institutions and creditors can help to avert a crisis, or at least diminish its impact.

d) A lack of information about newly available instruments and about past experiences of other countries.

e) A lack of understanding of the importance of voluntary lending, and consequently, of the importance of market-oriented solutions for the private creditors, or at least quasi-market solutions.

f) Another problem is that we human beings, are not entirely rational, and are ready to believe in magic.

The urgent needs of the people in most of the countries, combined with a lack of experience and understanding, are a fertile field for non-orthodox practices, and this can easily trigger a decision to experiment with a faster, and supposedly less costly, approach: a magic solution. This search for the "magic solution " is not difficult to understand. when officials of a Government, who are responsible for their country's well-being, are under intense pressure to solve the problem of enormous scarcities faced by their people. This urgency to provide for people's needs, often combined with personal and political goals, is a factor that induces Governments to step away from certain basic principles. The urgent needs easily push presidents, governors and officials to cut corners. Politically, time is a tough enemy.

The search for rapid results hardly allows individuals, even those with lucid mind, to stick to orthodoxy. Probably, they are even less likely to pursue orthodox practices when adjustments seem to take an eternity and results do not seem encouraging. With resources continuing to be scarce, external variables do not help and internal savings are just not there. And last, but certainly a key issue: foreign financing, balance of payments, monetary policy and fiscal policy are all different aspects of the same phenomenon. In many cases, there is not even a minimum understanding of these links, even among key officials. Macro-links are not clear to decision-making teams.

2. A proposal

Let us, as in medical science, examine the preventive medicine concept. In this sense, the mechanism of the prevention of a crisis should go far beyond a system of red lights and horns. The basics of what I shall call, a "preventive economy', are nothing more than the sound administration of the economy. Obvious as this may sound, it is far from being widely accepted or even understood, and certainly it is not practised. Even countries with educated officials have experienced problems during the last decade. We should not, therefore, underestimate this issue.

The solution proposed is therefore nothing more than the logical consequence of the stated premises:

- Training and education; and
- Supervision and monitoring.

2.1. Training and education

This is necessary in two main areas: (a) monetary and fiscal policy; and (b) foreign financing and debt management.

a) *Monetary and fiscal policy*

Not academic courses, but "practical", well-targeted short programmes. And let me insist that I do not know of any university which ever offered, or could ever offer something like this. It is not a university field, it is a practical task for us to solve. I can think of some courses:

- Use and design of accounting models;
- Use and design of monetary and financial programmes;
- Foreign currency "budgets";
- Sound fiscal concepts and practices;
- Sound public deficit financing practices;
- Budgeting: priorities and resources;
- Fiscal strategies;
- Domestic savings: instruments and strategies;
- Other countries' experiences;

b) *Foreign financing and debt management*

Again, practical, short, targeted courses that would cover the following subjects:

- Improving negotiating capacity and assistance to acquire a good understanding of the financial markets;
- Internal savings instruments and foreign investors;
- Training programmes to update technical teams on the new instruments and new practices in the international financial markets;
- Courses and/or information sessions on other countries' experiences: failures and successes; new administrative practices; non-orthodox practices: successes and failures;
- Institutional environment in Asia, Europe, Japan, the United States and others;
- International trends in trade, financing, legal and institutional changes;
- Improving understanding of the different roles of banks, investment banks and brokers; issuers and investors versus borrowers and lenders;
- Understanding of the importance of a secondary market for the nation's debt; the importance of building and monitoring the markets: role of agents; and

- Finally, an understanding of the vital importance of having access to voluntary loans, and market placements – market oriented solutions.

2.2. Establish a comprehensive system to monitor the country

This is the second and complementary element of the solution; it should, ideally, include the following:

- Establish internal monitoring teams;
- Establish cross checking systems;
- Set quarterly and monthly targets;
- Define the critical variables: targets and limits;
- Internal cross-checking teams; and
- External monitoring.

3. Who are the responsible actors, and/or participants?

- The country;
- The creditors (not investors); and
- The multinational institutions: IMF/ WB/ development agencies/ other banks/ UNCTAD.

No doubt, each of the different participants has developed a different role. Monitoring has probably been the most important of the tasks, but the training aspect – the development of human resources – has not yet been addressed in accordance with its critical and key importance.

Will these two measures end crises? Probably not, but they will definitely help to solve them, and they would certainly be a step in the right direction. There is no doubt that it is difficult to prevent crises, but not necessarily impossible to foresee them. This fact is a very important one, since it might at least help to reduce surprises and uncertainty, which are the most disrupting elements in the financial markets.

TRANSPARENCY, DISCLOSURE AND EARLY WARNING

Mr. Andrew Cornford & Yilmaz Akyüz

The Asian crisis has accelerated initiatives to improve the timeliness and quality of information on key macroeconomic variables as well as the financial reporting of banks and non-financial firms.[1] These are viewed as essential for better decision-taking by private lenders and investors, greater market discipline, more effective policy surveillance by multilateral financial institutions, and strengthened financial regulation and supervision.

Regarding key macroeconomic variables, after the Mexican crisis, the IMF established the Special Data Dissemination Standard (SDDS) in April 1996 to guide member countries in the public dissemination of economic and financial information in the context of seeking or maintaining access to international financial markets. At the time, it was hoped that the new, more stringent rules associated with the SDDS would serve as an early warning system that would help to prevent future financial crises. However, in the event, the rules did not serve this purpose in the case of the East Asian crisis. In April 1998, the Interim Committee proposed a broadening of the SDDS – clearly inspired, in part, by what it considered to be the role of informational deficiencies in the East Asian crisis – so that the system would also cover additional financial data such as net reserves (after allowance for central banks' liabilities under forward or derivative transactions), private debt (in particular, the short maturities type), and other indicators having a bearing on the stability of the financial sector. At the same time, the Interim Committee also asked the IMF to examine the desirability of a code of good practice on transparency with respect to monetary and financial policies, which was completed in July 1999 and adopted in September 1999 by the Interim Committee.[2] The code identifies practices designed to enhance the transparency, accountability and integrity of the institutions or agencies responsible for the conduct of monetary policy, for financial regulation and supervision, and for oversight of payments systems. Moreover initiatives are under way in the Committee on the Global Financial System to explore ways of improving disclosure by the financial intermediaries involved in international capital flows.

While such initiatives are useful, their impact is likely to be gradual, since it will depend to a substantial extent, on their success in shaping standards and norms not only of official bodies, but also of financial firms; and changes in standards and norms, especially those related to private business operations, generally require considerable lengths of time. Moreover, the potential of such initiatives for preventing financial crises should not be overemphasized. Emphasis on inadequate information as the major reason for failure to forecast the East Asian crisis, for example, appears exaggerated. Although there were some important gaps in information, data were generally available concerning key variables in the countries concerned, such as their balance of payments, both their short- and longer-term external debt and external assets (in particular in the periodic reports of the Bank of International Settlements (BIS) concerning international bank lending), their capital inflows, the exposure of banks and other

---

[1] See, for example, Group of 22 (1998b).

[2] This code is to complement one of good practice on fiscal transparency aimed at strengthening the credibility and public understanding of macroeconomic policies and choices regarding fiscal policies. For a summary of the main features of the code of good practices on transparency in monetary and financial policies and discussion of other current initiatives to strengthen the international financial system, see Drage and Mann (1999: 44-45).

financial firms to different sectors or categories of economic activity, and the problems in the property sector. What was missing was adequate evaluation, by both multilateral financial institutions and market participants, of the implications of available information on countries' ability to continue to obtain funding from the international financial markets. A similar unwillingness to be influenced by available data was evident during the crisis in the Russian Federation. Much of the increase in the external financial exposure to the Russian Federation took place during a period when information was widely available concerning the shortcomings of that country's macroeconomic policy, the weaknesses of its banks, and the underdeveloped state of its legal and regulatory framework and of its system of corporate governance. Moreover, most of the capital inflows into the Russian Federation took place when the country was carrying out IMF stabilization programmes.

The implicit assumption here appears to be that the deterioration in a debtor country's external payments, net external assets, the growth of domestic credit, and so on will trigger a gradual response and adjustment in the behaviour of lenders and investors, thereby avoiding sudden breaks and panics. But the reality is often that the initial deterioration has little or no effect. Indeed, despite the existence of data and information on such variables, currencies and financial asset prices continue to overshoot their sustainable levels. While the emergence of such misalignments is often a gradual process, spread over a relatively long period of time, their correction is usually compressed into a very short period, and is associated with overshooting in the other direction. Indeed, once the rush to exit has begun, the process itself will lead to a rapid worsening of key indicators, and in these circumstances, transparency may simply accelerate it.[3]

The East Asian crisis has also focused attention on standards of accounting and financial reporting, particularly those of financial firms. At first sight, recommendations for greater transparency on the part of financial firms have an almost self-evident quality, and the value of improvements in this area seems incontrovertible. Yet, on closer scrutiny, the issues become less simple. The quality of information made available to financial supervisors has an important bearing on the effectiveness of their work. However, there is less consensus as to the benefits of disclosure to market participants. Public disclosure of information submitted to supervisors is typically subject to limits resulting from a belief that it could undermine the confidence in the financial system that regulation is intended to promote, complicate the task of banking supervisors in handling the problems of banks in difficulty,[4] and enhance, rather than diminish, the likelihood of increased volatility and instability confronted by financial firms more generally.[5] Indeed, the Basel Committee on Banking Supervision (BCBS) itself has acknowledged that "there are certain types of information that should be held confidential by banking supervisors" and that "the types of information considered sensitive vary from country to country" (BCBS, 1997: 37).

---

[3] The question may be asked, for example, whether disclosure during the spring of 1997 of the accumulation by the Central Bank of Thailand of a large part of the forward-exchange liabilities that depleted its net foreign exchange reserves would have fostered more orderly adjustment, or simply have accelerated its currency crisis.

[4] Even in the United States, where the banking sector is required to meet relatively high standards of disclosure, and where there are growing arguments for increased reliance on disclosure in vetting and disciplining banks, historically "the objective of the bank regulatory agencies has been to preserve the soundness of individual institutions and the integrity of the banking system as a whole. This objective influenced their approach in requiring compliance with disclosure requirements. Generally, the agencies preferred to allow institutions time to resolve financial difficulties. This approach clearly is antithetical to the theory of a marketplace governed by the intense glare of full disclosure" (Arista, 1998: 340).

[5] See, for example, Caouette et al. (1998: 409).

Despite widespread acknowledgement of the problems which full disclosure by financial firms may cause, there remains an important school of thought among financial regulators which supports the idea that full disclosure's favourable effects, through its strengthening of market discipline, outweigh its costs. Indeed, according to this view, during periods of financial stress, lack of information about a bank's exposures to credit and market risks can create a situation in which rumours restrict the willingness of its creditors and counterparties to deal with it, thus threatening not only its survival but, possibly, also that of other banks, which, often, also because of inadequate disclosure, appear similar to outsiders (BIS, 1994: para. 2.4).

As with macroeconomic information concerning debtor countries, an implicit assumption of this argument would appear to be that disclosure would make possible the exercise of market discipline in an orderly way, avoiding herd-like or panic-stricken reactions on the part of creditors and other counterparties. Such a scenario will undoubtedly apply in some cases. But the outcome will depend on the reactions of different categories of counterparties, some of which have greater access to direct information about a debtor than others, and on different national legal rules and norms. Here too, experience shows there is a danger that initial indications of something amiss may have, at most, a limited effect. But once the climate of opinion among creditors changes, disclosure will simply intensify the debtor's difficulties, thus exacerbating the supervisory problems already mentioned (and possibly posing a threat of broader financial destabilization).

Arguments for full disclosure also raise the question of the value of information made available by financial firms for decisions by supervisors as well as by creditors and other counterparties. Financial liberalization and innovation have greatly increased the speed at which financial firms in many countries can now alter the assets and liabilities on their balance sheets as well as their scope for taking off-balance sheet positions of an opaque nature, thereby changing the risks they face in ways which can be difficult for outsiders to identify. For example, William McDonough, President of the Federal Reserve Bank of New York and current chairman of the Basel Committee on Banking Supervision, has made this point in surprisingly strong terms: " formerly, you could look at the balance sheet of a financial institution and quickly get a sense of exposure and risks. Today balance-sheet information is clearly inadequate for this purpose ... the fast pace of activity in today's market renders financial statements stale almost before they can be prepared" (Leach et al., 1993: 15-16). These considerations are especially pertinent to banks with substantial trading operations, an increasingly common feature of financial firms.

These limitations of accounting information would apply even if financial firms were fulfilling the requirements of best practice in this area. But in fact there is considerable variation even among industrial countries in both the quantity and form of publicly disclosed information: while arrangements for its provision are widely being strengthened, they frequently fall well short of levels corresponding to what is now considered to be best practice.[6] This observation emerges from recent surveys of regimes for financial reporting and the regulatory treatment of loan losses.[7] The information in these surveys, some of which is summarized in the table, is not necessarily fully up-to-date, but although the divergence between accepted best practice and national legal regimes may have narrowed since they were undertaken, in many areas it is still

---

[6] For recommendations as to best practice see BCBS; (1998).

[7] Ernst and Young (1993), which covers 17 industrial economies as well as Bahrain, Hong Kong (China), Saudi Arabia, Singapore, South Africa and the United Arab Emirates; and *Price Waterhouse Survey of Bank Provisioning* (1995), reproduced as Appendix A of Beattie et al. (1995), which covers 14 industrial countries. The period to which these surveys relate is 1992-1994.

likely to be substantial.[8] Moreover, with regard to the topical subject of banks' trading and derivatives activities, the Basel Committee on Banking Supervision and the International Organization of Securities Commissions (IOSCO) have concluded, on the basis of a series of surveys of the annual reports of a selection of major banks and securities firms, that, "Despite ... improvements, there remain significant disparities as regards the type and usefulness of the information disclosed some institutions continue to disclose little, generally, about key aspects of their trading and derivatives activities" (BCBS and IOSCO, 1998: para. 18).

The potential value of the information associated with fuller disclosure for improved surveillance has been a stimulus to econometric analysis of the determinants of currency and banking crises. One of the objectives of this work is the development of leading indicators. Analyses of country risk have long been standard features of the operations of firms and other institutions involved in cross-border lending and investment.[9] The new econometric work on currency crises represents an attempt to identify more systematically the relations between, and the relative importance of, variables traditionally included in analyses of country risk (but often evaluated more informally, for example, on the basis of scoring systems). Work so far[10] has served to clarify certain issues in the international discussions on financial crises, but it seems more likely to supplement (or serve as an additional input to) pre-existing methods of analysing country risk, which, owing to their operational role, must often rely on preliminary, tentative estimates of key variables and inevitably incorporate qualitative evaluation that is specific to particular cases but has an important bearing on the likely actual outbreak of crises. The contribution of econometric work on banking crises can be expected to be similar. Here too the discussion of certain issues can be clarified, but it is difficult to foresee a situation where such work replaces first-hand (and sometimes confidential) information about the financial sector that is available to supervisors (and in some cases also to financial firms), and the rapidly proliferating techniques used by both to analyse different types of financial risk. While efforts to develop early warning indicators of financial crises – such as financial firms' and supervisors' techniques for identifying financial risks – are capable of improving policies towards financial crises, there are limits to their effectiveness partly owing to shortcomings in the methods eeeeinvolved and to the information on which they depend,[11] and also because of limitations of financial regulation and supervision (to which analysis of financial risk is closely connected).

---

[8] In some countries there may also be divergence between the enunciated standards of the regime for accounting and financial reporting and the actual practice of several financial firms.

[9] See, for example, Krayenbuehl (1988: Parts Two and Three); and Caouette et al. (1998: chap. 22).

[10] For brief surveys, see Goldstein (1998), and Eichengreen and Rose (1998/99).

[11] A harsh assessment of efforts to develop early warning indicators of currency and banking crises has been made by one well-known economist as follows: "(Concerns over the adverse impact of financial crises on financial liberalization) have encouraged the official community to invest in early-warning indicators of currency and banking crises in the hope that they will see what is coming. Unfortunately, these models will have about as much success in predicting financial crises as geologists' models have in predicting earthquakes. Earthquakes and financial crises are products of complex nonlinear systems, whose parts interact in unpredictable ways. Consider the following entirely realistic example. The government will devalue the currency only if it fears that the interest rate increases required to defend it will irreparably damage a weak banking system. But the banking system will weaken to this point only if investors withdraw their deposits from the country because they anticipate a devaluation ... Whether speculators attack depends not only on the weakness of a country's banking system but on how much a government cares about further aggravating this problem when deciding whether to defend the currency. And the only thing more difficult to measure than a government's resolve is investors' assessment of it." (Eichengreen,1999: 13).

Table 1
Features of financial reporting and supervision for banks in selected economies, 1992[a] and 1994[a]

Features (column headings):

- I. Consolidated accounts required
- II. Accounting standards fixed by law
- III. Exemptions from disclosure obligations for banks
- IV. Direct communication between auditors and supervisors in prescribed circumstances
- V. Segmental reporting required
- VI. Criteria for establishment of general loan loss provisions
- VII. Criteria for establishment of specific loan loss provisions
- VIII. Levels of specific loan loss provisions
- IX. Levels of general loan loss provisions
- X. Valuation of collateral

Country	I	II	III	IV	V	VI	VII	VIII	IX	X
United States	Yes	Yes	No	No	Yes	MD	ORh	ORh	MDh	OR
United Kingdom	Yes	No	No	No	Yes	MD	MD	MD	MD	MD
United Arab Emirates	Yes	No	No	No	..	..	..	..	ORjk	..
Switzerland	Yes	No	No	Yes	No	OR	MD	MD	ORjk	MD
Spain	Yes	Yes	No	Yes	No	OR	MD	OR	ORj	OR
South Africa	Yes	No	Yes	Yes	No	..	..	..	..	..
Singapore	Yesb	No	Yes	Yes	Yes	..	..	..	..	..
Saudi Arabia	Yes	Yes	No	No	Yes	..	..	..	..	..
Portugal	No	Yes	No	No	No	..	..	..	..	..
Netherlands	Yes	No	No	Yes	Yes	MD	OR	MD	ORj	MD
Luxembourg	No	No	No	Yes	Yes	MD	OR	MD	ORkl	MD
Japan	Yes	Yes	No	No	Yes	MDg	OR	ORi	ORl	MDm
Italy	Yes	Yes	Yesc	No	No	MDf	MD	MD	ORi	MD
Ireland	Yes	No	Yes	Yes	No	..	..	..	..	..
Hong Kong (China)	Yes	No	No	No	No	..	..	..	..	..
Germany	Yes	Yes	No	Yes	Nod	MDe	MD	MD	ORk	MD
France	Yes	Yes	No	No	No	MDe	MD	MDi	ORj	MD
Denmark	Yes	Yes	No	Yes	Yes	MD	OR	MD	OR	MD
Canada	Yes	No	No	Yes	Yes	MD	OR	MD	ORj	MD
Belgium	Yes	No	Yes	Yes	Yes	MD	MD	MD	ORj	MD
Bahrain	Yes	No	..	Yes	Yes	..	..	..	MD	MD
Austria	Yes	Yes	..	Yes	No	..	..	..	..	..
Australia	No	Yes	Yes	Yes	Yes	MD	MD	MD	MD	MD

Sources:

I, II, III, IV and V: Ernst & Young, *International Bank Accounting*, 3rd edition (London: Euromoney Publications, 1993); VI, VII, VIII, IX and X: Price Waterhouse Survey of Bank Provisioning, reproduced as appendix A of V. A. Beattie, P.D. Casson, R.S. Dale, G.W. McKenzie, C.M.S. Sutcliffe and M.J. Turner, *Banks and Bad Debts: Accounting for Loan Losses in International Banking* (Chichester: John Wiley, 1995).

- *a* 1992: 23 economies (17 industrial, 6 developing); 1994: 14 industrial economies.
- *b* Subject to exemptions for non-banking subsidiaries.
- *c* Reflecting flexibility regarding presentation of accounts.
- *d* Some breakdown of assets and liabilities required.
- *e* Subject to some guidelines of the French Banking Commission.
- *f* Subject to general regulatory guidance.
- *g* Subject to approval of Ministry of Finance.
- *h* Without distinction between specific and general loan loss provisions.
- *i* Subject to official guidance as to minimum levels for different categories of loan.
- *j* For country risk.
- *k* Including rules for hidden reserves.
- *l* including rules set by tax authorities.
- *m* In consultation with Ministry of Finance.
- **MD:** Management's discretion.
- **OR:** Official rules.
- *..* Not available.

References

BCBS (1997). Core Principles for Effective Banking Supervision. BCBS Compendium of Documents. Vol. 1, Basic Supervisory Methods.

BCBS (1998). Framework for Supervisory Information about Derivatives and Trading Activities. BCBS Compendium of Documents. Vol. 2, Advanced Supervisory Methods.

BCBS AND IOSCO (1998). Framework for Supervisory Information about Derivatives and Trading Activities, September.

CAOUETTE ET AL (1988). Managing Credit Risk: The Next Great Financial Challenge (Wiley Frontiers in Finance).

D'ARISTA JW (1994). The evolution of U.S. Finance. *Volume II: Restructuring Institutions and Markets* (Armonk, N.Y.: M.E. Sharpe).

DRAGE J. AND MANN F. (1999). Improving the Stability of the International Financial System. *Financial Stability Review* , Issue No 6, June.

EICHENGREEN B (1999). *Toward a New International Financial Architecture*. Washington DC, Institute of International Economics.

EICHENGREEN B and ROSE AK (1998/1999). The empirics of currency and banking crises, NBER Reporter, Winter.

GOLDSTEIN M (1998). Early warning indicators of currency and banking crises in emerging economies in *Financial Crises and Asia*, CEPR Conference Report No. 6 (London: Centre for Economic PolicyResearch).

GROUP OF 22 (1988b). *Report of the Working Group on Transparency and Accountability* (mimeo). Washington DC.

KRAYENBUEHL T (1988). Country Risk: Assessment and Monitoring. Cambridge: Woodhead-Faulkner.

CRISIS PREVENTION
AND THE INTER-AMERICAN DEVELOPMENT BANK

Žiga Vodušek

1. Introduction

Since the outbreak of the Asian crisis in 1997 and the Russian crisis in 1998, the economies of Latin America have experienced difficult times. As a result of adverse external conditions, the terms of trade for many countries continued to decline, and capital inflows contracted. By 1998, growth throughout Latin America had dropped to a meager 2.3 per cent compared with 5.3 per cent the previous year. Growth in 1999 only reached an estimated 0.3 per cent. The combination of low international prices for basic export commodities and the decrease in the supply of financing implied a doubly severe adjustment for many countries in the region. This highlighted their vulnerability, associated with a dependence on basic commodities and external savings.

2. Policy responses to crises

In many countries, the domestic policy response to the external shocks began with the decision to significantly increase interest rates, so as to prevent a drop in international reserves or a depreciation of the currency. In a second phase, the typical policy response was to launch a fiscal adjustment programme, either through spending cuts, or by approving measures to strengthen tax revenues. The third component of the adjustment process consisted of an exchange rate correction by many countries. Macroeconomic stability was, however, largely maintained. All these policy responses produced rapid results, and most of the economies affected by the crises are now in the recovery stage. This is expected to be reflected in a 3-4 per cent growth rate for the region as a whole in 2000.

The policy responses and economic recovery do not mean, however, that the region has become immune to what is called the boom-and-bust cycle. External conditions will continue to be crucial for Latin America because the fiscal, financial and exchange rate policies in the countries of the region have not yet built up a line of defence against external shocks.

And it is in this context that it is necessary to look at crisis prevention and mitigation. We have been hearing of different "types" of crises – crises of confidence, liquidity crises, solvency crises, currency crises and so on. I would also like to mention two specific aspects of crises, or one could say, realities, which are of particular relevance to Latin America at this juncture, and which can be looked at in relation to financial crises. The first aspect is linked to natural disasters, and the second to the social dimension.

A series of natural disasters have recently struck the region: the El Niño phenomenon, hurricanes Mitch and George, the earthquake in Colombia and flooding in Venezuela, to name the most devastating ones. The Inter-American Development Bank (IDB) had to respond swiftly to these emergencies – by approving new loans and by redirecting existing ones. The social aspect of crises – or in a broader sense, the social crisis itself – requires more than just providing safety nets at times of financial crisis. It is more than just a short-term phenomenon linked to the economic cycle; it is primarily a structural one that can be overcome by the reduction of poverty and inequality. Viewed in this context, the concept of crisis prevention acquires a broader dimension.

Crisis prevention can be looked at from two distinct perspectives. One is the level at which it is undertaken – this can be at the international level (that of regulations); at the national level, (that of policy makers); and at the level of private lenders. Another level of action that should be given more consideration is that at the subregional level. This can refer to actions in the economic and financial area or, in the case of Central America, for example, in the area of disaster prevention as well.

The other perspective is that of the level of development of the developing countries – whether they are middle-income countries or low-income countries. It is the middle-income countries that have been the main recipients of official liquidity financing, particularly a few large borrowers. In terms of a new financial infrastructure, however, more attention should also be devoted to the low-income countries. This refers to the need to reverse declines in official development assistance (ODA) flows, implement the Heavily Indebted Poor Countries (HIPC) Initiative, increase multilateral lending, and facilitate the access of this group of countries to foreign direct investment (FDI) inflows.

3. Activities of the Inter-American Development Bank

Concerning the activities of the Inter-American Development Bank, looking at internationally coordinated emergency financing, the Bank approved US$ 3 billion in emergency loans in 1998, and US$ 4.6 billion in 1999, bringing the total to US$ 7.6 billion in emergency lending for the 1998-1999 period.

These loans have a five-year maturity with a three-year grace period; the annual interest rate charged is equivalent to the six-month US dollar London Inter-Bank Offered Rate (LIBOR), reset semi-annually, plus a loan spread of 400 basis points. Disbursements are carried out over a significantly shorter period than ordinary loans, and are not longer than 18 months. In the case of contingent loans, funds are disbursed at the discretion of the borrowers once certain conditions have been met. Emergency loans have thus been approved for Argentina, Brazil, Colombia and Ecuador.

The loan to Brazil, for example, was approved in March 1999, for a total of US$ 3.4 billion. The goal of this form of financing is to enhance confidence in Brazil's capital markets, while shielding urgent social spending during the country's economic downturn. Funds are being released in three tranches based on progress in implementing measures aimed at monetary discipline, macroeconomic stability, and reforms in the health, education, labour and social welfare sectors. With the view to minimizing the social cost of fiscal adjustment, the programme has been set to ensure that Brazil's 1999 and 2000 budgets maintain financing and delivery levels for a social safety net that protects children and the elderly, the indispensable social service for the poorest of the poor, and innovative services with a high distributional impact.

In the area of prevention and reconstruction from natural disasters, IDB has, up to now, approved a total of US$ 1.5 billion. At the subregional level, looking at Central America, the Bank's contribution is estimated at US$ 3.5 billion over the next four to five years, in the form of both concessional and regular loans. The Bank is coordinating the process of assistance at the international level through the Consultative Group for the Reconstruction and Transformation of Central America, which it chairs.

Within the process of debt relief as part of the HIPC Initiative, the Bank has provided support for Bolivia and Guyana, and will extend it to Nicaragua, as well as Honduras. This process of debt reduction is linked to undertaking poverty reduction strategies in the beneficiary countries.

Finally, there is the regular process of loans to the borrowing countries in the region, which supports economic policy and institutions, with the aim of enhancing financial crisis prevention. Activities linked to the development and deepening of local capital markets are of particular importance.

EXTERNAL DEBT CRISIS PREVENTION FROM A POLICY PERSPECTIVE

Zhao Jianping

1. Policy options for debt crisis prevention: Self-reliance, self-discipline and self-confidence.

The best way to prevent a debt crisis is through efficient use of domestic savings rather than by incurring foreign debt (self-reliance). This is the goal that China should aim to accomplish in the future. China has maintained one of the highest savings ratios (more than 30 per cent) in the world. At present, the country has a relatively underdeveloped capital market, financial system and corporate management, as well as low efficiency in allocating capital resources relative to its high savings. The ultimate way to solving China's funding shortage is by developing the country's domestic financial market, with the aim of improving efficiency in the allocation of domestic funds. Inefficient use of excessive external borrowings will ultimately lead to international payments crisis, even though it might boost growth in the short run. Therefore, such factors as incentives and demonstration effects for the domestic financial and corporate sector should be taken into account when using foreign funds.

The second choice is to aim at borrowing less while maintaining a sound capacity for refinancing or holding "secondary reserves" (self-discipline). The country needs to establish the necessary arrangements or channels through which it can easily make external borrowings when needed at a relatively low cost in case of emergency. The use of foreign debt means that a country consumes its resources ahead of schedule and has to repay the debt with its future foreign exchange earnings. Therefore the following factors should be taken into account when formulating polices concerning the use of foreign funds:

(1)   The volume of required foreign funds is related not only to domestic funding shortages, but also to a country's debt service capability. Therefore, external borrowing should be made according to a plan defining borrowing limits.

(2)   The investment of borrowed funds should be coordinated in a way that encourages the introduction of advanced technologies, management expertises and export capability, in order to improve the country's overall capacity for earning foreign exchange, and to achieve short- and long-term balance of payments. The annual plan for external borrowings and the appropriate ceiling on the balance of external debt, will be determined by China's economic situation or its overall strength, including such parameters as political objectives, balance of payments and capacity to make payments with foreign exchange, as well as by the international market environment. External funds should be directed to productive uses and high-tech industries via project approvals to improve China's industrial structure as well as its debt service capacity.

An important consideration concerns the creditors' involvement in determining the debt volume. In seeking external funds, a country should not have to rely entirely on creditors' assessment of that country's credibility. Creditors' willingness to lend money may not be a good thing, and empirical evidence shows that creditors' judgement may not always be correct. The arbitrary optimism of creditors and the absence of self-discipline on the part of borrowers usually result in default in the debt obligation, causing harms to both lenders and borrowers. For example, many creditors mistakenly believed that the Guangdong International Trust and Investment Company (GITIC) was "too big to fail". The Government's decision not to bail out the GITIC serves as a reminder to foreign creditors of the moral hazard problem, both on the side of borrower. from the lender and the borrower..

2. Lessons from crises

We draw the following conclusions from those countries that have experienced deep crisis:

(1)   The pace at which the domestic markets are opened to the outside world should be determined by the progress in domestic structural reforms, in order to avoid chaos, moral hazard and capital flight.

(2)   An open small-size economy, in contrast to international "hot money", that adopts a fixed exchange rate regime, may exhaust its foreign reserves. When the country adopts a floating exchange rate policy, the domestic economy may fluctuate or may lose its independence in policy-making.

(3)   A transitional economy may cause greater moral hazards to creditors, borrowers and the Government. (The issue of ownership is not a problem.)

China's experience shows that:

(1)   Capital markets or capital account should be opened gradually.

(2)   Self-control should be exercised with regard to the volume of the external debt.

(3)   An equilibrium of current account transactions should be sought.

(4)   Prudential and stable reserve and exchange rate policies are effective in adjusting domestic savings, allocating resources and boosting national competitiveness. These policies can effectively safeguard the long-term equilibrium of international payments (and hence long-term stability in the value of the domestic currency), enhance foreign investors' confidence and benefits, and prevent the occurrence of crises or their contagion effect. China's experience also implies that the convertibility of the current account has been conducive to the expansion of foreign trade and economic exchange, but it has also provided an exit for illegal capital outflow. Therefore, verification of current account transactions is important when a nation introduces convertibility while still maintaining controls on capital transactions.

3. Unequal values of different kind of foreign funds

Foreign funds may be classified into three categories: foreign direct investment, portfolio investment and external debt. Depending on their relative importance to the domestic economy, assuming US$1 of the nominal value of external debt is equal to US$1 of real value received, then US$1 nominal direct investment may be equal to US$1.2 of real value received, given its additional values stemming from management, technology and the export market; by the same token, the real value of US$1 nominal portfolio investment may only equal US$ 0.8, adjusted for the short-term liquidity risk associated with it. The inflow of foreign funds should therefore be treated with prudence; it is important to determine the following:

(i) The appropriate size of external debt, which achieves the optimal combination of risk (political or economic) and return (economic and social);
(ii) Structure (composition of direct investment, external debt and portfolio investment);
(iii) Timing and sequence of opening to the outside (corresponding to domestic structural reforms); and
(iv) Management (e.g. complete data collection and effective regulation). China has adopted a prudent approach to the management of external debt, while restricting portfolio investment and encouraging FDI, especially those investments that bring in management and technology and boost exports.

4. Comprehensive management of external liabilities

- A comprehensive management of external liabilities should cover the following areas:
- On-sheet and off-sheet (contingent) liabilities;
- External borrowings both by domestic institutions and their overseas companies;
- External debt and FDI (contingent liability); and
- Conditions of balance of payments based on the size and composition of the foreign exchange reserves.

Thus, the best policy is to manage a country's external assets and liabilities as well as its cash flows. As an example, it appears that imports have nothing to do with external debt. But the determination of the size of the external debt and the control of debt risk may be linked to the elasticity or substitutability of imports, or the extent to which a country's imports can be reduced during times of payments difficulties due to debt service payments.

China's State Administration of Foreign Exchange (SAFE) is responsible for:

(1) Statistics, monitoring and regulation of spot international payments and foreign exchange transactions;
(2) Registration, monitoring or regulation of foreign direct investment, external debt and other forms of liability (which may have an impact on international payment flows in the long run); and
(3) Management of foreign reserves to ensure a reasonable size and structure compatible with the status of balance of payments, external debt and foreign investment. The concentration of responsibilities in a single government agency for monitoring external payment risk will help prevent a potential external debt crisis.

5. Management of external debt at three levels

At the macro level, China imposes controls on the size of the external debt and an annual plan covers the maturity, currency, interest rates and use of the funds. To enable the Government to control different economic variables and the ratios between those variables, the plan takes into consideration the country's external assets and liabilities, balance of payments, size of foreign reserves, investments and external debt. The State Development and Planning Commission and the Ministry of Finance are responsible for controlling the size of the external debt at a macro level while SAFE is responsible for registration, repayment verification and statistics.

Concerning the use of foreign funds, an industrial policy and priority guidelines have been stipulated to direct medium- and long-term funds to industries designated or encouraged by the State. Currently, these include infrastructure, such as energy and transportation, advanced technology, export-oriented industries and technical transformation in State-owned companies.

As for the maturity structure, the internationally accepted safety standard of 20 per cent is applied to the ratio between short-term debt and the total debt, and the ratio has long been strictly held below 15 per cent. The currency structure of the external debt was determined with reference to the structure of China's export earnings and foreign exchange assets, so that currencies may be roughly matched to each other with regard to external debt, foreign exchange receipts and foreign currency assets. Since opening up to the outside world, China has had a good record of debt service and liquidity and a reasonable size of external debt. The economic stability achieved in the midst of regional debt or financial crises after the 1980s has been mainly attributed to China's effective macro-management of its external debt.

The Government has also been required to improve its regulations concerning the external debt at a macro-level. Nowadays, the unprecedented degree of world economic integration, international capital movement and financial innovations have presented a challenge to the Government's regulatory methods. It is imperative for the supervisor to introduce the advanced electronic system to monitor and set up a data bank for capital inflows and outflows, and to conduct risk surveillance and "stress tests". Special attention should be given to the negative impact of the inflow of international "hot money" and the operation of foreign speculators in domestic markets. Currently, China is developing a foreign exchange management information system (MIS), with the purpose of enhancing the accuracy of balance-of-payments statistics, and improving the efficiency of regulatory practices. The MIS has been designed to set up a reporting system of international payments, and a verification mechanism between exchange control data and banks' foreign exchange operation records, foreign exchange payments and the customs' trade flow data. A surveillance system on China's international payments will be established using the MIS.

At the medium level, China seeks to prevent market chaos and irrational economic behaviours – such as rapid, large-scale capital inflows and outflows – and operations motivated by strong expectations of exchange-rate trends. China's foreign exchange sale system and its control on capital account transactions have discouraged companies from seeking speculative profits out of exchange rate fluctuations, and have facilitated the normalization of markets and the achievement of exchange-rate stability. The increase in the debt obligation of China's borrowers has been avoided due to the absence of a rapid depreciation in the value of the domestic currency. China's current exchange control policies have ensured that the Government could enhance its capacity for adjustment of the external sector of the economy and, hence, the ability to prevent an external debt crisis.

At the micro level, lenders and borrowers have been diversified to reduce risk. China's outstanding external debts total US$150 billion, or 20,000 loans amounting, on average, to US$ 7.5 million, and the matured debt repayments are spread rather evenly over the next few years. Foreign direct investments total about US$ 300 billion, with about 300,000 foreign-funded companies operating in China. They are diversified in a wide range of industries, and there is a low probability of withdrawals on a large scale. China has imposed some administrative controls on domestic borrowers, such as a strict ceiling on public debt, regulations governing asset and liability ratios for the State-owned commercial banks on external borrowings, quota of external debt for other domestic commercial banks, individual approval of external borrowings by China-funded companies, and a strict control on the issuing of debt securities and the debt-equity ratios applied to foreign-funded companies. China has diversified its debt portfolio either by geographic regions or by the type of creditors. Geographically, the country has raised funds from diverse economies or regions, such as Canada, France, Germany, Hong Kong (China), Macao, the United Kingdom and the United States. As of the end of June 1999, 16 per cent of the debt balance came from government loans, 15.9 per cent from international financial institutions, 37.8 per cent from financial intermediaries, 13.4 per cent from corporations, 8.3 per cent from private individuals and 8.6 per cent from other sources.

6. The registration of capital account transactions

All the external borrowings, including foreign exchange guarantees and other forms of contingent liabilities made by domestic institutions, should be registered with SAFE. Only registered debts are regarded as legal and may be repaid with foreign exchange bought from banks. China's external debt consists of not only sovereign debt, but also borrowings made by financial institutions, State-owned enterprises and foreign-funded companies. The integrity and authority of debt statistics have been ensured by China's verification system covering capital outflows, such as verification of debt repayments and honouring of surety obligations among others. The registration system has provided a legal foundation for China's comprehensive management of external debt. Under this system, the Government can not only control payments, but it can also make a relatively accurate forecast of future cash flows. Nonetheless, a comprehensive statistical database does not necessarily lead to the prevention of debt crises; but without it, crisis prevention is out of the question.

Table 1. China's External Debt, 1994-1998 (in US$ 100 millions)

Year	Out-standing balance	Short-term balance	Debt balance/ export earnings (%)	Repayment / export earnings (%)	Debt balance GDP (%)	Short-term debt / total balance (%)	Reserves / short -term debt %
1994	928.1	104.2	78	9.1	17.1	11.2	495
1995	1065.9	119.1	72.4	7.6	15.2	11.2	618
1996	1162.8	141.1	67.7	6.0	14.2	12.1	744
1997	1309.7	181.4	63.2	7.3	14.5	13.9	771
1998	1460.4	173.4	70.4	10.9	15.2	11.9	836
1999.6	1487.7	171.1	NA	NA	NA	11.5	859

DEBT MANAGEMENT AND CRISIS PREVENTION: THE PHILIPPINE EXPERIENCE

Cristina Orbeta

1. Introduction

The Philippines was spared the foreign debt servicing problems experienced by its neighbours during the Asian financial crisis that erupted in 1999. The magnitude of its commercial loans maturing during that time was small compared to other South-East Asian countries. This is due to the fact that the Philippines was just starting to benefit from an inflow of foreign capital when the crisis hit. From 1983 to 1992, when the Philippines was in rescheduling mode, it had to rely mainly on official and bilateral credits, while other Asian countries experienced a surge in capital inflows. It was only in 1993, or almost a decade later, when investors started to develop an appetite for investing in the Philippines.

As a result of the foreign exchange crisis experienced in the Philippines in 1983, the authorities tried to introduce structural and institutional reforms. Policies aimed at attracting foreign capital were adopted, keeping in mind the factors that had contributed to the foreign exchange crisis. Moreover, its debt monitoring system, which had been modified to take into account data requirements for debt rescheduling, was strengthened.

This paper attempts to present the basic features of the Philippine debt management system that were introduced or strengthened after the debt rescheduling experience of the 1980s, and which contributed towards maintaining a relatively strong foreign exchange position during the Asian crisis.

2. Comprehensive debt monitoring system

When the Philippines rescheduled its debts in 1983, it developed its own debt monitoring system which covered only the non-monetary sector (i.e. public and private corporate sector, excluding banks). Although computerized, the system had several limitations. The accounts were all denominated in US dollars, hence could not be marked to market based on current foreign exchange rates. Debt service had to be recorded manually, and individual exposures of banks could not be derived. Data also suffered from poor reporting by private companies. However, the biggest weakness was the failure to include the foreign borrowings incurred by banks, thus grossly understating the foreign exchange requirements for debt servicing. Total liabilities of banks were monitored separately on a consolidated basis and reported under the monetary survey. The structure and profile of these borrowings, which were predominantly short-term, were not closely tracked.

Learning from this experience, the debt monitoring system was redesigned to cover all foreign exchange liabilities of the private and public sectors – bank and non-bank. Separate modules were prepared for short- and medium-term debts, taking into account the rollover feature of short-term debts. The system captures the basic characteristics of all debts, such as repayment, availability period, interest rate and other costs, project and purpose, and counterparties. It also automatically computes the debt service schedule for each account, based on the specified terms of the loan.

The new system is maintained in the original currency of the loan, but has the facility to convert accounts denominated in third currencies automatically to US dollars at a specified exchange rate. This allows marking to market of Philippine debts denominated in currencies other than the US dollar which, including multi-currency loans, account for 47 per cent of total debt. It also facilitates analysis of the impact of exchange rate volatility on the country's foreign exchange position.

Recently, the Central Bank has also started to keep track of contingent foreign exchange liabilities, such as those arising from guarantees issued by local banks in favour of foreign entities and those arising from Build Operate Transfer and other similar financing arrangements, in a separate system. This financing arrangement has been encouraged to allow private companies to undertake and fund infrastructure projects on their own. Upon completion of the project, the Government pays capacity and service fees to the private contractor. In most cases, the Government issues some form of guarantee for the foreign obligations incurred by the contractors.

What is important to emphasize here is that coverage of debt systems should be subject to continuous review. Considering the various financing arrangements and financial products and instruments that continue to evolve, debt managers should have a clear understanding of how these transactions affect on foreign exchange liabilities, and they should be prepared to monitor these transactions.

3. Compulsory reporting by private companies of their foreign debt

Private companies have been more diligent in reporting the status of their foreign borrowings since the 1983 foreign exchange crisis. In 1984, they were required to report the extent of the arrearages they had incurred. Only those companies that reported were subsequently given foreign exchange allocation. Since then, borrowers have realized the importance of regularly reporting the status of their loans and have complied with requirements of the Central Bank. It also helped that the Central Bank had earned the trust of private companies because of the confidential manner in which it treats data submitted. There has never been an instance where borrowers have complained of information leakage.

Companies are required to submit their annual borrowing plans, which are then considered in the preparation of the country's overall borrowing programme. Reports for both short- and medium-term debts are required to be submitted monthly, although there is a move to require more frequent reporting of short-term debts to allow a closer monitoring of movement and status of accounts.

Diligent reporting by private companies has certainly helped to improve the quality of debt data. To ensure the quality of reports submitted, the Central Bank provides borrowers with an orientation on the concepts used and procedures for reporting their debts. Having developed this reporting discipline among private companies, compliance with reporting rules has not been a problem even after the rules on foreign borrowings were eased. Since 1993, companies that do not source their foreign exchange requirements for debt servicing from the banking system need not submit their borrowings for Central Bank approval. Nevertheless, they are required to report all their foreign borrowings, whether or not these were submitted for approval. There has never been an instance when companies refused to comply with the reporting requirement or sought to clarify the terms and conditions of their loans. Of course, there is no certainty that all private sector loans are captured. Companies having debts involving small amounts that can be easily serviced out of their own foreign exchange resources or by foreign exchange dealers may not be complying with the reporting requirements. However, loans involving big amounts, which are normally widely publicized, are captured by the system. The Central Bank reminds each company to submit reports whenever it learns of new loans being syndicated or negotiated. It also reconciles its data against other published sources.

4. Regular reporting and analysis of the debt situation at macro and micro levels

It is not enough to just summarize and generate debt statistics; it is equally important to analyse debt data and establish debt indicators that can serve as early warning signals for triggering certain courses of action to prevent crisis situations. Findings on debt structure, profile of debt service and debt service ratio provide basic inputs to guide a debt office in its day-to-day and long-term foreign borrowing operations. For instance, the debt service implications of loans payable on bullet terms are closely monitored to support the policy that requires borrowers (whether public or private) to lengthen the tenure and extend the maturity of loans, if necessary, to avoid bunching. The impact of foreign currency volatility, including the effect of multi-currency loans, is regularly reviewed.

Chief executive officers of major borrowers, whether in the public or private sector, are formally advised of the concerns of the Monetary Board with regard to the levels of their outstanding debts and debt service profile. Occasionally, they are requested to present their borrowing plans and strategy to the Monetary Board. They are also alerted if they deviate significantly from their borrowing programmes. These measures are intended to instill awareness on the part of major borrowers that the Monetary Board reviews their foreign borrowing activities, and that they should, therefore, be cautious in planning such borrowings.

5. Framework for approval of foreign-funded public sector projects

The public sector accounts for a sizeable proportion (65 per cent) of Philippine external debt. To ensure that public sector debts are used for priority projects, several government agencies are responsible for approval of foreign-funded public sector projects. Acting under the umbrella of the National Economic and Development Authority Investment Coordination Committee (NEDA-ICC), key government agencies review projects taking into account their economic and financial viability. Only projects that meet the Committee's criteria are approved and considered eligible for foreign financing and endorsed by the Central Bank's Monetary Board. The NEDA-ICC is composed of representatives from the key Ministries including Finance, Budget, Economic Planning, Trade and Industry, Central Bank, Environment, Agriculture, and Energy. There are two levels of approval required: that of the Technical Board consisting of department heads, assistant secretaries and undersecretaries, and the Cabinet Committee consisting of the heads of the different ministries and the Central Bank governor. The committee is very active and undertakes an exhaustive analysis of projects. Moreover, its decision is respected and implemented by the agencies concerned. Approval of public sector projects by NEDA-ICC is a precondition for approval of foreign financing proposals by the Central Bank. Since foreign loans are required by law to be approved by the Central Bank, agencies have no choice but to go through NEDA-ICC for approval of their projects.

The Central Bank's role is to evaluate the financing terms and conditions, ensure that these are market-oriented and the best possible in the prevailing market environment, and that they can be serviced taking into account the country's debt servicing capability.

6. Restrictions on foreign borrowings

Prior to 1993, the Philippines had a highly regulated foreign exchange environment. Residents were required to surrender their foreign exchange holdings to the banking system. Their foreign exchange requirements had to be bought from the banks, but only if they had properly documented eligible transactions, and the amounts they could borrow were limited. Central Bank approval and registration of all foreign borrowings, whether incurred by non-bank public or private entities, were mandatory. In the case of banks, loans, other than those considered normal inter-bank transactions, likewise required approval. The use and purpose of foreign borrowings were limited to priority projects, and only for financing of foreign costs. Longer-term borrowings were encouraged, and borrowers were required to renegotiate the maturity and pricing of their loans if these were outside the acceptable parameters and did not match the gestation period of the project to be financed. Failure to comply with the rules rendered the loan ineligible for debt servicing. Considering that the banking system was the sole source of foreign exchange, borrowers had no choice but to comply with the rules.

When the foreign exchange rules were liberalized in 1993, the policies on foreign borrowings were basically maintained. However, for consistency, since the mandatory surrender of foreign exchange has been lifted, residents with foreign exchange earnings are allowed to borrow without Central Bank approval, provided they do not source the foreign exchange needed to service the loan from the banking system. Notwithstanding this change in rules, private companies continue to submit their foreign loans for Central Bank approval. Creditors generally require Central Bank approval to ensure that their loan qualifies for servicing with foreign exchange purchased from the banking system, in the event that their borrowers' source of foreign exchange dries up. The new foreign exchange rules do not apply to public sector borrowings, which are required by law to have the prior approval of the Central Bank, without exception.

There was a temptation to revert back to foreign exchange controls during the height of the 1997 currency crisis. However, the authorities realized the negative implications of moving in this direction and the inadequacy of the domestic capital market in responding to the funding requirements of the private sector. Until conditions in the domestic capital market improved, stable foreign exchange policies were deemed critical for preserving confidence not only among foreign investors, but also among those residents who had substantial foreign exchange assets deposited in local banks.

7. Restrictions on maturity and interest rates on foreign borrowings

The liberalization of foreign exchange rules in 1994 contributed to domestic liquidity, and consequently, eased the availability and access to foreign currency loans. To reduce costs, borrowers sought to tap the short-term debt market. However, the Central Bank refused to approve short-term loans and required maturity of loans to be renegotiated, a requirement for which several private companies were thankful, when the Asian crisis erupted in 1997. Lengthening of the maturity of loans meant higher costs, but they were at least spared the problems and uncertainty of raising funds during those difficult times. The maturity profile of borrowings is closely monitored together with the debt service profile so as to ensure that there is no bunching of scheduled debt payments, particularly considering the sizeable portion of existing debts payable on bullet terms.

8. Observance of debt ceilings

The Central Bank sets an annual ceiling on the amount of foreign loans it approves, based on demand for such loans and the country's capacity to service its debt. The amount of foreign loans that may be approved are set for each maturity category (e.g. from more than 1 year up to 5 years, from more than 5 to 12 years, and more than 12 years). Foreign borrowing ceilings were observed even during periods when the country was not under any IMF arrangement. In addition, the Central Bank ensures that the debt service ratio does not exceed 20 per cent of foreign exchange receipts as required by law.

9. Strong and independent debt office

Responsibility for management during the debt rescheduling years lay with several departments, but was subsequently centralized in one department (Management of External Debt Department) when the Philippines exited from rescheduling in 1992. This department played a major role in ensuring the implementation of foreign borrowing rules, monitoring these debts, negotiating the terms and conditions of public sector borrowings with creditors, and advising public and private companies on market developments, sources of financing and acceptable terms and conditions. It is ideal to have a dedicated department or unit exclusively focusing on debt management. Debt management, being a highly specialized field, requires experienced staff who have the expertise to assess debt situations, foresee problems, review loan documents, negotiate loans, package loan proposals and handle the operational side of debt management. Even more importantly, the debt office should maintain its independence and not be subject to political pressures. The functions and responsibilities of the Central Bank's debt office were respected by both public and private entities and the office had considerable independence to tackle (what would have been) political issues on a technical basis.

10. Conclusion

A good debt management framework does not guarantee against future debt crises. Considering the highly globalized financial environment, it is evident that structural and institutional reforms need to be put in place, if the Philippines is to cope with the contagion effect of financial and economic instabilities brought about by developments in other countries. In this context, consistency and commitment in performing debt management tasks and objectives are a necessity.

Discipline plays a key role in management of debt – in borrowing, in complying with the rules, in reporting and in analysing the implications of debt data. Yet the need for debt discipline during good times is sometimes overlooked. When conditions are stable, there is a tendency to be lax in performing functions and implementing rules. An accommodating policy, particularly in the face of political pressures, might be pursued that could have a destabilizing effect. For instance, offers of banks and financial institutions to syndicate loans or underwrite bonds may be accepted even if there is no need for funds. This could lead to heavy borrowings, maturity limits could be breached, and debt servicing could become a burden due to high cost and unplanned borrowing. The resulting vulnerabilities in the debt structure and repayment schedule, if not addressed early enough, could compound debt servicing problems and lead to a crisis situation.

The debt office should be strong and independent in pursuing its tasks and should guard against such pressures. It should focus on its debt management task and be constantly attuned and responsive to developments in the international financial markets. It should be prepared to recommend policy and structural and institutional reforms as necessary. Moreover, it should continue to enhance its computerized system, so as to expand its coverage to include both real and contingent liabilities, to improve data consolidation and reporting capability and to update the system in line with changes in technology.

A good debt management framework, complemented by structural and institutional reforms in the economy and continued vigilance in identifying sensitive and vulnerable spots, would help arrest and mitigate possible crisis situations.

The Philippines' preparations for the euro:

1. Orientation seminar for Central Bank officials, the banking system and the general public.

2. News releases for the benefit of the public.

3. Issuance of a circular letter regarding the mechanics of the euro and the rules to follow with concerning reports submitted by banks regarding their assets and liabilities denominated in euro.

4. Letter to borrowers advising them of the shift to euro and requesting them to report the timing of the shift to the euro by their creditors, and balances of their accounts as converted.

5. Changes in currency library of the computerized system and reporting forms to include the euro.

6. Maintenance of account balances in legacy and euro-currencies during the transition period.

7. Setting up of euro accounts.

BRADY BONDS: ARE THEY STILL USEFUL?

Luis Foncerrada

This paper is divided in to three sections based on three questions: (i)What is the real nature of the Brady bonds?; (ii) How useful are these bonds? and (iii) What are the future challenges?

1. What is the real nature of the Brady bonds?

For a thorough understanding of the Brady bonds, it is important to bear in mind a few conceptual elements. The history of these Bonds, which were issued for the first time in the context of the Mexican crisis, starts in August 1982. Their design and characteristics were determined by the Mexican debt problem. It took eight years to find a solution to the debt problem, following different attempts by the many participants involved in the process to develop their ideas and to be able to accept new options. They also needed to be willing to change some usual practices and finally get a good understanding of the real dimension of the debt problem before implementing a sound solution to it.

This process can be best understood with the aid of a brief explanation of a strategy that I shall call "four conceptual stages". Each one of these "stages" is characterized by the goals pursued and the corresponding attempts to solve the problem, and the reactions generated by specific negotiations and their results. Actually, the results were a sort of mirror with of several kinds of reflections: the legal and financial capacity of creditors to undertake more definite steps and/or their understanding of the problem; the willingness of authorities in creditor countries to assume a flexible attitude; and, a most important factor, the capacity and political support of the negotiating debtor teams.

1.1. First stage

Taking time to understand and organize

The first stage took place from 1982 to 1985. Since 1981, as oil prices were falling, interest rates were growing. Both tendencies were thought to be "temporary", but they lasted several years, and these were the two most important variables for the Mexican economy at that time. After contracting over US$ 20 billion in 1981 – a move that raised the Mexican public foreign debt to a total of over US$ 80 billion in 1982 – and suffering serious capital flight in those two years, Mexico found itself without both foreign resources and further access to the markets. Additionally, the Mexican monetary policy did not help: the Government did not react in a timely manner nor appropriately to the urgent situation at hand.

During this period two different efforts to restructure the Mexican foreign debt took place. In 1983, the first concern was to reschedule the past due payments and to create at least some minimum breathing space to recover from the "temporary situation", and afterwards, it was argued, Mexico would recover its pace. In 1984, the Mexican Government presented a longer-term solution as well as a proposal to compensate the costly results of 1983.

The following, were the main results of the 1982-1983 negotiations:

a) Rescheduling of 17 months of principal payments due between August 1982 and December 1983;
b) US$ 5 billion of additional funds to be made available to support the economic programme;
c) An increase in interest rates (almost double that of the prevailing market rates and a very high fee for the restructuring!).

In 1984, there was multi-year restructuring of capital payments (MYRA) as follows:

a) Rescheduling of payments (including those of the previous negotiations) due between 1985 and 1990;
b) Rescheduling of the US$ 5 billion of new money lent in 1983;
c) Additional funds of US$ 3.8 billion.

Some advance was made in reducing interest rates, but the main achievement was an extension of the period of the payments by14 years.

This first stage can be characterized as a response to the urgent need to extend the time limit for repayments, as much possible. Time was needed in order to design a solution and to avoid the difficult and disrupting situation of a unilateral decision and a moratorium. There was certainly concern about reducing transfers, but the utmost priority was considered to be the need to gain time and some urgently needed breathing space. It is clear that this strategy did not represent a solution, since net transfers abroad were still required to be made.

1.2.   Second stage

The second stage can be characterized as the pursuit of the most important goal: the elimination of net transfers abroad, and achievement of the minimum conditions of stability for growth recovery.

In 1986, the Mexican Government made a proposal, the main feature of which was what it sought to achieve: a long period of a stable balance of payments that would protect the country from external shocks. Unquestionably, the reduction or elimination of net transfers abroad was fundamental and involved the two main variables of the Mexican external sector: interest rates and oil prices.The proposal included a link between these two variables, and it established a limit for the yearly payments abroad.

- The total debt to the banks was to be paid over the longest possible period, with normal interest payments, the first proposal stated a period of 30 years;
- However, if, in a given period of time, oil prices came to exceed the London Inter-Bank Offered Rate (LIBOR) by 2.5 times, then the principal payments should be increased to an amount equal to the total of the new surplus; and
- In the opposite case, if oil prices were less than 2.5 times the LIBOR, then the equivalent of that reduction should be deducted from the payments of principal; if that were not enough to compensate the reduction, then even the interest payments should be reduced. In that case, the amount of payments reduced would be added to the original principal.

It is clear that such a scheme would be able to offer protection to the economy from the brutal disruption generated by both soaring interest rates and plunging oil prices. In any case, the combination of both measures would guarantee stability in the balance of payments as well as in the monetary variables, and eventually, savings and investment would be generated. It is obvious that responsible monetary and fiscal policies represent another necessary condition for the possible success of this strategy.

Thus in brief, the main features of the Mexican proposal were:

- Interest rate protection;
- Oil price protection;
- Additional funds; and
- Debt relief over time: through a restructuring of principal payments.

Unfortunately, the final result at the end of the 1986 negotiations was not much more than a new copy of the two previous rescheduling exercises.

The 1986 agreement involved: A reduction on the spread to 13/16th; some oil protection in the form of emergency loans to compensate, to some extent, for the price reduction; rescheduling; and a longer amortization period.

It is clear that some improvements were made, but not enough. In the following two years, 1987 and 1988 transfers abroad continued to be made, and at very high levels. It is enough to look at the Mexican balance of payments during those years to realize that the situation remained unsustainable.

1.3. The third stage comprised a series of several different schemes and transactions designed to reduce the principal and transfers abroad

The debt-equity swaps programme was started in 1996, but negotiations were interrupted and reopened twice. It reduced debt by about US$ 10 billion and supposedly increased investments by US$ 15 billion. The programme, which was also implemented in Argentina and other countries, was difficult to monitor and did not offer sufficient evidence of the actual increase in investment. Another important concern was obviously related to the origin of the domestic resources. But some debt was reduced and a certain amount of investment took place.

The 1988 debt exchange offer with collateral floating rate bond. This is a strategy that was aimed at achieving real debt reduction and eliminating principal payments using zero coupon United States Treasury bonds as collateral. The underlying concept was that to take advantage of the current prices at which banks were selling and buying the Mexican debt, and exchanging it for a new Mexican bond which had, as collateral, a United States zero coupon bond. Under this scenario, the principal payment would cease to be a Mexican risk. The only remaining risk would be represented by the interest payments, which would have a fund to cover them for a predetermined period of time. These new bonds were indeed the predecessors, or one could say, "the grandfather" of the Brady bonds.

The exchange offer was for US$ 10 billion and a wide and very intensive "road show" took place all around the world in order to explain the mechanics of this strategy. The final result was a little over US$ 2.5 billion worth of new bonds issued. There were people, both in Mexico and abroad, that considered this outcome a failure but many others considered this new issue of bonds not necessarily a disaster.

In 1989, Mexico again made an offer to exchange old debt at discount for new debt, this time guaranteed with oil receivables. The offer was not very widely accepted at the time, with the exception of Spain, where it was very successful. This scheme turned out to generate enormous interest and proved highly successful a few years later.

1.4.   Forth stage

The final strategy can be summed up as grow to pay. It recognized the vital importance of limiting transfers abroad and achieving stability.

The following list enumerates the proposals of the Mexican Government at the time, which closely resemble the principles of 1986:

- Interest rate protection;
- Oil prices protection;
- Debt reduction; and
- Longer tenures.

In addition a very important element, derived from the 1988 experience, was a collateral with zero coupon bonds plus the experience gained through the swap programmes. Then there was also Nicholas Brady, a person who understood perfectly well the possibilities of the scheme, who was able to give the necessary political support when it was needed, and who pushed all those involved in order to find a solution. He was a man who did not allow anyone to leave the meeting room until an agreement had been reached.

The question now arises, what were the consequences of the negotiations? Interestingly enough, they were a combination of every single scheme and of lessons learned over the past 10 years. It constitutes a menu well known these days:

- Exchange of bonds at par and at discount values;
- Zero coupon bonds issued by the American Treasury as collateral;
- Additional funds;
- Debt- to-equity swaps;
- Interest rate protection;
- Oil price protection; and
- A fund to guarantee a minimum period of interest payments.

After eight years of practically zero growth and several attempts to limit transfers abroad, the Brady plan enabled the Mexican economy to achieve during the decade of the 1990s, a constant average level of growth of 3.0 per cent. In addition, its oil exports came to represent only 10 per cent of total exports, instead of the 85 per cent reached in 1982, domestic savings started to recover, and, last but not least, investment and employment started to recover.

The main achievement was, above all, the creation of a stable environment:

- Reduction of net transfers abroad;
- A foreseeable period of stability;
- Certainty for the future;
- Political and economic commitments; and
- An increase in domestic savings.

This is the story of the Mexican process, which ended with the issue of the Brady bonds. What was the real nature of these bonds? They were, strictly speaking, just another instrument of debt exchange: a collateralized bond exchanged at par or at discount. This shows that, rather than talking about the Brady bonds per se, we should really concentrate on the fundamental components of the Brady plan, which can be summed up us: Grow to pay. It was the understanding and consequent support of this concept that made an enormous and critical difference. The Bonds represented a practical solution with a menu approach to meet the different institutional and individual preferences, in a quasi-market-oriented scheme.

I believe that the real nature of the Brady bonds was that they represented a politically different concept. They recognized the critical importance, both economic and political, of growth.

2. What feature of the Brady bonds can be carried into the third millennium?

It is not necessarily the Bonds themselves, but the lessons learned from the approach used that is useful:

- The importance of growth and of the necessary conditions for growth;
- The use of all available financial instruments;
- The attempt to use, whenever possible, market-oriented solutions and designs;
- To try all kinds of debt relief, through market-oriented solutions;
- Additional funding and imaginative schemes were critical elements.

These are the attitude, the concepts, and the elements of the Brady plan worth retaining. As evident as they may seem, it took several years before they gained active political support. We can no longer accept the risk of having countries verge on political upheaval as a result of a pursuit of short-sighted goals.

3. What challenges does the new century present?

The same old ones: growth and stability.

Growth is the only solution, and stability the absolute condition, to solve poverty and inequality. A plan to achieve this should contain the following three elements:

1)   Continuous training, since human capital is the real key element. Would it be possible for us to constitute complementary training programmes with all the resources of our multilateral institutions?
2)   Sound economic programmes. The exercise of good internal and external monitoring in order to assure of sound administration.
3)   A global debt approach based on experiences, market transactions and multinational coordination. And at this point, training and constant updating would be helpful.

Let us work for the prevention of crises, and not just for trying to solve them once they present themselves.

THE BUREAU OF THE TREASURY AND THE DEVELOPMENT OF THE RETAIL MARKET IN THE PHILIPPINES

Leonor Magtolis Briones

This presentation offers a brief description of the experience of the Philippines in the development of the retail market for Treasury bills and bonds. Many countries have experienced both problems and successes in developing a retail market, and perhaps the experience of the Philippines will be useful for others when considering the development of their retail markets.

It has been mentioned that it would be a good idea to develop domestic savings in our respective countries to assure a steady source of financing for government programmes. The Philippines has the lowest rate of savings in all of Asia – just a little over 10 per cent. Whether our economy is growing or whether it is at a standstill, the rate of savings remains the same.

Also in the Philippines the issuance of government securities, whether Treasury bills or bonds, are through accredited government securities dealers comprising 47 investment houses and banks. The lowest denomination of our securities is 10 million pesos or US\$ 250,000. These are bought by securities dealers and then distributed, either through wholesale or retail institutions, to their investors. In the Philippines, as in many other countries, where there is wide disparity in income levels, where we have a large number of people living in poverty (more then 31 per cent), and very low levels of income, only a limited number of people can participate in the purchase of Treasury bills and bonds, and they are mostly institutional buyers.

The new administration's policy is to empower and democratize the economic system. One of the ways developed for giving citizens a sense of participation, a sense of ownership, a sense of contribution to financing of development, was to make these Treasury bills and bonds available to them. At the height of the financial crisis, the Government was paying as high as 21 per cent for 91-day Treasury bills, and of course, the clear beneficiaries were those who could afford the various denominations of these instruments. The instruction to us was to lower the denomination of the bills and the bonds from 10 million pesos (or US\$ 250,000) to at least 5,000 pesos (or US\$ 125) which is a tremendous drop. When that deal was first floated, we were advised that it would be an administrative nightmare, because issuing securities from US\$ 250,000 to US\$ 125 would result in their widespread purchase perhaps all over the Philippines. We, in the Bureau of Treasury, were fortunate that we already have an electronic system, called ADAPS (Automated Debt Auction Processing System), and a register for our securities, which did not require the use of a lot of paper. Part of the Bureau's preparatory work was, first to upgrade our electronic option system, because the prices of these bills and bonds were based on the weekly option of the large bonds and bills issued to the regular securities of dealers. Secondly, we upgraded, with Government support our Register of Securities, so that it would have the capacity to handle the large number of transactions expected (50,000 transactions a minute), since the intention was to make the Treasury bills available nationwide.

In an island country like the Philippines, with 7,100 islands and 70 million people speaking 86 languages, it is hardly democratic to have only 47 institutions benefiting from high earnings from security bills and bonds. Thus, the first thing we did was to upgrade our facilities to enable us to issue the Treasury bills on retail and at lower prices. Secondly, we developed an infrastructure which is connected to the Internet. This would make it possible for any buyer –

from the southernmost island or the northernmost city in the Philippines – to be able to buy electronically or to transfer his or her investments at real time gross settlement.

At the same time we engaged in a massive information campaign to make people familiar with these instruments, as they do not know about Treasury bills and bonds. Most of those small savers would just deposit their money at 2 per cent in savings accounts. The first stage of the campaign for Treasury bills was launched in metro Manila by no less than the President of the Philippines. Since then, the Treasury bill programme is now available in seven cities in the Philippines, and the response has been very enthusiastic. We observed that more than 50 per cent of the investors bought the lowest denominated Treasury bills (i.e. at US$ 125).

The second phase after the Treasury bill campaign was to launch the small-denominated Treasury bond, again for US$ 125 (down from the original US$ 250,000). This time we engaged the services of five underwriters and they were issued in two tranches, by the Philippines Government. In the first tranche, 5 billion pesos worth of small-denominated bonds were offered, which raised 11 billion pesos, and many people were angry because they did not have the opportunity to buy these small-denominated bonds. In the second tranche another 5 billion pesos-worth of these bonds were offered, which raised 18 billion pesos. Thus for 10 billion pesos offering we actually generated more than 30 billion pesos, and the demand is still very high.

What I am sharing with you, is the experience of information technology, which is responsive to particular requirements: at the Bureau of the Treasury, for example, it proved helpful in overcoming perceived administrative difficulties. What we have achieved is that more and more citizens belonging to the lowest income groups feel and believe that they own part of the economy, that they are participating in the development of the country, and at the same time, they are also earning very good returns. At present the Treasury bill for 91 days fetches 8.9 per cent. For Treasury bonds this would be about 13.5 per cent for 5 years, which the various investment houses and banks had been earning. But this time, whether one is a small depositor with only US$ 125 or a big investor, with billions of pesos available for purchase of government securities, the level of earning is the same.

During the launching in Manila by the President, the second person who made a deposit was a plumber from the Bureau of the Treasury; in the second city where we had the launching, it was a retired school teacher bringing a paperbag full of her retirement money; in a city in the south, a policeman was the first depositor, in another city it was an association of cooperative drivers of motorized vehicles, which are very popular in Asian cities. What I am trying to say is that it is possible to mobilize the rest of the population and encourage them to participate in the economy, and not give them a sense that only 47 institutions are providing the financing. It is possible to give them the sense that, if we want the country to develop, they also have to contribute towards the financing of such development.

Of course, there are still problems such as how such bills and bonds can be made available to the other islands – make it available in the sense of savers being able to buy these instruments at banks. And so it is still in the process of refinement; but as mentioned earlier, the public response has been tremendous. In the process of promoting the programme and of bringing it to the people, we did not employ a single additional person to help us out. We made do with the current staff of the Bureau thanks to the the information technology that was set up and which greatly reduced the administrative costs and procedures.

This is the experience I would like to share, since a good number of developing countries also want to mobilize domestic savings and encourage the average, small investor, not the billion-dollar type of saver, to participate, whether in a small way or in a big way, in the development and stability of the financial system of their country.

Part 2

Financial tools and risk management

STRATEGIC RISK MANAGEMENT FOR DEVELOPING COUNTRIES: COLOMBIA CASE STUDY[1]

Stijn Claessens, Jerome Kreuser & Roger J. B. Wets

1. Introduction

Uncertainty makes economic and project management more difficult for any entity. This is especially true for sovereigns that have experienced substantial financial volatility and shocks throughout the 1990s, particularly those with substantial debt and commodity price exposures. Furthermore, the development of a strategic approach at the country level for analysis of that uncertainty has lagged behind, as most approaches exclude, for example, trade flows and fiscal dimensions. A World Bank (WB) research project undertook to rectify that situation. In this paper, we present a case study for Colombia of the tools developed in that research project. We look at only one small aspect of the issues in order to illustrate how these tools could be applied and what might be examined.

2. Importance of a strategic approach to asset/liability management

Global financial markets have been very volatile in recent decades with extensive changes in commodity, foreign exchange, interest rates and capital flows. Many developing countries have considerable exposures to these risks. They often have large external debts and considerable foreign exchange reserves, exposing them to interest and exchange rate risks. Many developing countries depend on (primary) commodity exports for generating foreign exchange, or need to rely on imports for energy and for supplementing basic food supplies. Adverse movements in international commodity prices can affect them greatly. All these risks have played a role in raising the debt burdens and negatively affecting the economic performance of many developing countries.

Uncertainty makes economic and project management more difficult for any entity. This is even more so in developing countries: they experience greater difficulty in dealing with the booms resulting from increases in commodity prices, and external shocks, which appear small, have often created havoc in these countries. A variety of factors will continue to contribute to the greater impact of shocks in developing countries: companies in these countries have limited access to financing and hedging tools, and access may be cut off completely during periods of financial turbulence. In the mid-1990s, for example, private capital flowed into East Asia at the rate of about US$ 40 billion per annum, with a peak of about US$ 70 billion in 1996. In the second half of 1997, more than US$ 100 billion in bank loans pulled out of these same countries. As financial integration advances while international capital markets remain volatile, emerging-market economies will be exposed to many risks.

---

[1] Presented at the second Interregional Debt Management Conference in Geneva, 3-5 April 2000. We would like to thank the staff of the Central Bank of Colombia, in particular, Roberto De Beaufort Camargo and Laura Vila Londoño, for many discussions and help with the data. The views expressed do not necessarily represent those of the World Bank or the Central Bank of Colombia.

Improving asset/liability management (ALM) will thus be more important than ever before. During the last two decades, a broader range of financial tools such as credit swaps and derivatives has become available. The breadth of tactical risk management tools has expanded greatly and now includes many types of borrowings and assets, forwards, swaps, plain vanilla and other exotic options. Asset/liability management strategies have become more sophisticated, and concepts such as value-at-risk are now commonly used. Meanwhile, developing countries have, in recent years, gained some access to risk management tools.

Yet the development of a strategic approach for ALM at the country level has lagged behind. Typical approaches to country ALM, copied from approaches for firms and financial institutions, do not, however, incorporate country - specific factors, and strategic interactions are missing. They often exclude, for example, trade flows and fiscal dimensions. Modelling flexibility is very limited, with country adaptation often made using a piecemeal approach through basic analysis rather than optimization. More generally, their perspective is often the development of benchmarks. However, by requiring a benchmark, which is constant over time, they fail to incorporate the dynamic realignment of portfolios. The treatment of uncertainty is generally also very limited and constraints are typically not included in the optimization process itself, but rather through iterating around the solution.

Asset and Liability Management for developing country governments often has to consider risks on a much broader scale than for well-established corporations in developed countries. It is also essential that a truly dynamic approach be adopted. Risks should include not only the Government's own direct exposures, such as those arising from debt and reserves, but also those arising from contingent risks from the banking systems or State-owned enterprises. Approaches need to be related to measures of the Government's earning potential, such as the sensitivity of fiscal revenues to global factors. Without these factors, approaches to risk ignore the existence of natural hedges in the external and fiscal sectors, limit the analysis to "on-balance" liabilities only, and ignore many important constraints. At the same time approaches need to be dynamic: for example, developing countries face, many constraints in rapidly adjusting their assets and liabilities, as transaction costs can be high. ALM strategies pursued for corporations in developing countries can, thus, clearly be less than optimal, and may even add to risk for developing countries' sovereigns.

The events in East Asia have highlighted the complexities of ALM in a financially integrated world. East Asian countries had few of the traditional weaknesses in fiscal management: balances were generally in surplus and public debts were low. Yet, East Asian countries did witness a build-up of financial vulnerabilities in their private sectors. These were mainly the result of the macro-policies being pursued, particularly foreign exchange management, the sequencing of liberalization, and the poor process of domestic financial intermediation. But, a neglect of external asset and liability management was also an important factor in triggering the crisis in several countries. Affected East Asian countries are now trying to improve their ALM. The lesson may be that proactive ALM can reduce the risks of currency and balance-of-payment crises.

The changing nature of reserve management risk (see De Beaufort, 2000) also highlights the need for more sophisticated risk management tools. There has been impressive growth in the level of total foreign exchange reserves of central banks, of which Asia and Latin America account for almost all the increase. This growth implies an opportunity cost, so that central banks are considering more active investment strategies for a portion of their portfolio that has a low probability of being used for intervention purposes. The challenge then becomes how to apportion the portfolio between a liquid portfolio that could be used for intervention purposes, and another for investment purposes, while managing asset class risk, credit risk, currency risk and interest rate risk. The objective becomes one of enhancing returns, with sound ALM and a solid public mandate, while limiting risk to a suitable level.

3. The risk management issues facing the Central Bank of Colombia

Building on recent advances in technology and optimization techniques, it is feasible to address some of the weaknesses of existing ALM techniques.[2] To illustrate the techniques developed and their ease of application, we present the case of the foreign exchange reserve management of the Central Bank of Colombia. We first describe the ALM problem as faced by the reserve managers and the Government of Colombia, and then the approach currently taken by the Central Bank of Colombia for managing its reserves.

In deciding on the way it wants to manage its reserves, the Central Bank of Colombia faces a number of strategic objectives for holding reserves, as well as legal and other constraints. It also has to consider its relationship with the country's overall debt management and the budget. Moreover, it has its own institutional structure for management, including reporting on reserve management, which need to be taken into account in the modelling.

Strategic objectives: The management of Colombia's foreign exchange reserves is regulated by Law 31 of 1992, in which the responsibility of the Central Bank regarding the management of foreign reserves is defined in Article 14 as follows: "The Central Bank will administer the foreign exchange reserves in accordance to public interest, in support of the domestic economy and with the objective of facilitating the external payments of the country. The administration of the reserves involves its management, investment, custody and disposition of the assets. Its investment will follow criteria of safety, liquidity and return in assets denominated in freely convertible reserve currencies or in gold." From this general objective, follows a narrower objective on the desired size.

Size: The objective of the Central Bank of Colombia is to hold sufficient foreign exchange reserves to be able to intervene in the domestic currency markets, in order to ensure normal volatility in the exchange rate of the Colombian peso, to deter speculative attacks, and to provide an adequate guarantee for foreign investment in the country. There is no clear policy regarding the optimal size of the reserves. Although, in light of the risks arising from rapid movements of capital and currency substitution, the ratio of reserves to months of imports and the ratio of reserves to financial liabilities in Colombia (M3, including bonds) is watched, there is no expressly desired objective for a minimum or maximum level. No factors regarding private sector behaviour are taken into account.

Constraints: The Central Bank of Colombia faces a number of constraints, some arising from legal factors, some for financial planning reasons, and yet others for historical reasons.

- *Asset classes*:   As administrator of the foreign exchange reserves, the Central Bank of Colombia faces certain legal constraints. No borrowing is allowed, for example, except in the case of securities lending. All liquidity needs of the Bank are to be met by the liquidity portfolio, and the investment portfolio can only invest in highly liquid

---

[2] These results build on the earlier work reported in Claessens, Kreuser, Seigel and Wets, 1997 and 1995.

assets such as government bonds or very short-term time deposits. It can execute derivative transactions, but only in order to hedge. In such cases, it is allowed to deposit part of its reserve assets to cover margin calls or guarantees, or to purchase instruments to hedge. And by law, the Central Bank of Colombia cannot incur losses of principal, but currency gains and losses are not considered part of this constraint.

- *Policy, legal and other constraints*: Except for the limits on loss of principal, there are no policy constraints on realizing financial losses (or gains). Reserves are marked to market every day, thus directly affecting the profit and loss of the Central Bank. The legal limits of no principal losses, means that there is a policy constraint of avoiding negative returns within each currency over a given year.

Relationship with external debt management: Since there can be important synergies between the management of assets and liabilities, the Bank manages its reserves in coordination with the liability of the Republic of Colombia. There is a Risk Committee designed to coordinate reserve management policies with public debt policies. This leads to certain policy restrictions, which, to date, apply mainly to the currency composition of its reserves. In particular, the currency composition of foreign exchange reserves must match the composition of the outflows of the balance of payments in order to eliminate, as much as possible, cross-currency risks.

Institutional arrangements: According to the charter of the Central Bank of Colombia, the body responsible for defining the strategic objectives of reserves is the Bank's Board of Directors. The Reserves Committee makes strategy decisions on portfolio allocations monthly as a sub-committee of the Board. Most tactical and many strategic issues are addressed directly by the reserves department on a daily (tactical) and monthly (strategic) basis. However, if deemed necessary, a meeting of the reserve management committee can be arranged. The process for the review of strategic and tactical choices can also be revisited when needed.

Current Foreign Exchange Reserves Management Arrangements: Reflecting its objectives and these various constraints, the Central Bank of Colombia has the following policies currently in place for the management of foreign exchange reserves.

Size: The reserves are divided into two portfolios – the liquidity portfolio, which is equivalent to around 10 per cent of total reserves and is invested solely in US dollar-denominated overnight investments, and the investment portfolio. The liquidity needs of the Bank are met by the liquidity portfolio (as the investment portfolio can only invest in highly liquid assets, such as government bonds or very short-term time deposits, it can accommodate liquidity needs as well). The level of the liquidity portfolio is determined by an analysis of the historic behaviour of outflows, with a current range of US$ 500 million to US$ 900 million. The remaining reserves are invested in the investment portfolio. After deducting a reserve provision for future foreign exchange losses and the administrative expenses of the Bank, excess returns are transferred to the Ministry of Finance at the end of each year.

Currency and duration: As already noted, the currency composition of the investment portfolio is based on the balance-of-payments outflows by country of origin, and mirrors the average composition over a rolling two-year period, currently 80 per cent US dollars, 15 per cent in Euro and 5 per cent in Japanese yen. The interest rate exposure within each currency is set on an average two-year duration, achieved through a combination of 1 to 3 months money market instruments generally tied to the London Inter-Bank Offered Rate (LIBOR), and government bonds. Within each currency, the portfolio composition is set to ensure that the probability of negative returns over a given year is low. For the last three years, the asset allocation has been in the following broad ranges: US dollar portfolio: 20 per cent 1-3 month money market instruments and 60 per cent 1-5 year United States Government bonds; euro: 3.75 per cent 1-3 month money market and 11.25 per cent German Government bonds; and Japanese yen: 3 per cent 1-3 month money market instruments and 2 per cent 1-10 year bonds.

Currently, all money market instruments no longer than one year have to be issued by Governments having a minimum long-term rating of AA, banks having a minimum long-term rating of A+, or corporate bonds with a minimum long-term rating of AA. For bonds, the benchmark only includes government issues by the United States, Germany and Japan, although reserves can be invested in United States agencies, Eurobonds and supranationals with a minimum rating of AA. Derivatives are only considered for hedging purpose, and, so far, the Central Bank has only used foreign exchange forward contracts and futures on authorized instruments via recognized exchanges. The use of options has not been considered for reserve management.

Management: Almost 50 per cent of the investment portfolio is invested passively, in accordance with a benchmark portfolio and evaluated at the end of each month. The other 50 per cent are invested with active external managers, of which 5 per cent is invested directly by the Central Bank of Colombia. Aggressive active strategies are rare, however, and strategies tend to concentrate on deviations from the index.

Risk measurement: Market risk is measured by the modified duration of the portfolio and each of its components, currency risk by the difference between the benchmark and actual weights in each currency, and credit risk by the rating of every issuer. Managers are evaluated against the benchmark on a monthly basis, separating deviations due to currency risk, duration risk and credit risk. On a yearly basis the performance of each administrator is reviewed by the Board of the Central Bank of Colombia over a rolling three-year period compared to the tracking benchmark portfolio.

4. Strategic analysis using integrated advanced tools for ALM[3]

The problem faced by the Central Bank of Colombia in managing its reserves, while matching the currency composition of the outflows of the balance of payments and observing other constraints, is an optimization problem under uncertainty. A general model for this type of ALM-problem has been formulated and solved as a dynamic stochastic programming problem by Claessens et al. (1997). Further discussion of the technology is beyond the scope of this paper (readers are referred to Claessens et al. (1995 and 1997 papers); Ziemba & Mulvey (1998) provide a more general overview on asset and liability modelling). It is worth noting here, however, that the methodology is very flexible and allows for many different specifications of objective functions, stochastic behaviour and constraints. Specifically, the model has the following characteristics: it is based on cash flows for all currencies and at all future dates, not just the next period; it incorporates stochastic volatility constraints on the liquid portfolio; it allows for choices among all asset classes at all future dates; it incorporates transaction costs; and

---

[3] These were originally developed at the World Bank. They are now available from The RisKontrol Group GmbH, which continues to develop them in a package called RisKontroller. More detailed information on these tools and their use can be found at www.riskontroller.com.

its decisions are based upon maximizing a specific objective function (e.g. the expected value of the portfolio at the horizon in terms of a basket currency). Next, we show how these tools can be used by the Central Bank of Colombia.

(i) The base case

For the asset choices, we include short maturity and long maturity assets in each of US dollar, euro, and Japanese yen. We also include a liquidity portfolio of short dollars. The model allows for the sale of long maturity assets and any currency transactions, and includes transaction costs.

We make the following behavioural assumptions on interest and exchange rates:

- Expected values of interest rates are computed so that they satisfy statistically the interest rates implied in the term structure. In other words, in an expected value sense, the rates of return on long maturity assets are indifferent to investments in short assets at any time.[4] We apply this principle to the current rates as well as to any future rates by calibrating the expected interest rates in the future to the forward rates implied today.

- We compute the volatility of, and correlation among and between, the interest and exchange rates from historical information. The variability of the short-term rates is taken as the historical volatility over the last year and that of the long-term rates over most of the 1990s (we use a longer period to base the estimate on a statistically constant regime).[5]

- Going forward, we allow time-varying volatility to reflect the possibility of regimes over which the uncertainty is more or less stable and to incorporate the mean-reversion present in many asset prices. Consequently, the variance does not change exactly by time (and the standard deviation not by the $\sqrt{t}$) because the stochastic processes change over time.

- In terms of exchange rates, expected values are computed such that the Uncovered Interest Parity hypothesis holds (i.e. exchange rates are expected to appreciate or depreciate by the differential in interest rates).

These assumptions essentially mean that all assets have identical expected rates of return and the only difference is the variability of the various assets. Tables 1 and 2 provide respectively the expected values of the rates and the standard deviations of the various assets.

Table 1: Expected values of rates

Assets	1999	2000	2001	2002
Euro short rate	3.40	5.45	6.43	6.36
Euro long rate	4.99	8.57	9.88	9.04
US dollar short rate	5.23	6.41	6.73	6.20
US dollar long rate	6.28	7.99	8.52	8.07
Japanese yen short rate	0.12	0.08	0.14	0.35
Japanese yen long rate	1.11	1.48	1.74	2.22
Euro exchange rate	0.99	0.97	0.97	0.98
Japanese yen exchange rate	102.20	97.24	92.10	87.03

---

[4] As we have a finite horizon model, we make investments in long and short assets equivalent at the horizon.

[5] This estimate has been quite accurate to date. For more on regime matching, see RiskMetrics, *LongRun Technical Document*. In the next section, we will make some assumptions that reflect a change in the regime.

Table 2: Standard deviation of rates

Asset Class	2000	2001	2002
Euro short rate	0.68	1.29	1.45
Euro long rate	0.99	1.64	1.63
US dollar short rate	0.35	1.15	1.61
US dollar long rate	0.44	0.89	1.05
Japanese yen short rate	0.07	0.13	0.25
Japanese yen long rate	0.37	0.54	0.77
Euro exchange rate	0.08	0.19	0.30
Japanese yen exchange rate	6.83	8.99	12.39

We can represent the stochastic processes graphically. An example for the US dollar short rate is given in figure 1. The degree of correlation between the US dollar short and long rates can be assessed from figure 2. Both these figures are useful in understanding how interest rates might progress over time and in relation to each other.

Figure 1: US dollar short-rate scenarios   Figure 2: Short vs. long rates

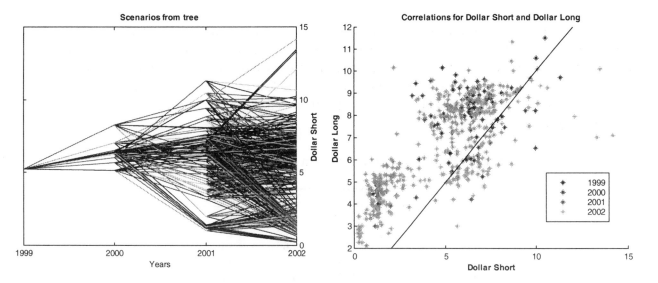

One must be careful in interpreting figure 1, as the scenarios do not have equal probability of occurrence (i.e. the density of the tree is not depicted, but rather, each scenario appears with equal likelihood, which is not what the stochastic process implies).[6] To better understand how rates are distributed, we depict the density functions[7] over time in figure 3 for the US dollar short rate. From this, it is easy to see that the interest rates are distributed over a smaller range in the first year, and, as time progresses, spread out.

---

[6] A single path along the graph from 1999 to 2002 is called a scenario.

[7] We obtain explicit expressions for these (See Wets, 1998). This allows us to integrate them to obtain the cumulative distributions and to obtain inverse values to create tables, like table 3, for any probability values.

Figure 3: Density functions of US dollar short rate

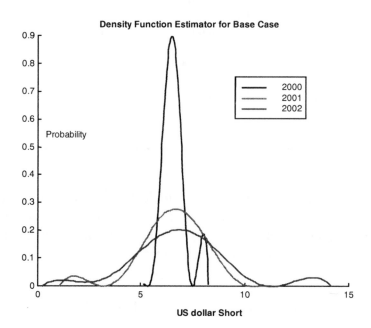

We can also use the densities to provide us with the cumulative distribution for certain cut-off levels(e.g. the probability of worst or best case interest rate outcomes (table 3)). The value, "2.16" in the first row of the column 2001 means that in "2001" there is a 3 per cent chance that the short-term US dollar interest rate will be less than 2.16.   Or, from the bottom of the column, the chance that it will be greater than 9.06 is 3 per cent. This can be used to identify "values at risk" measures.

Table 3: Probability distribution of US dollar short rate

Probability	2000	2001	2002
3	5.79	2.16	2.02
16	6.10	5.25	4.96
50	6.54	6.69	6.91
84	7.01	8.03	8.87
97	8.04	9.06	13.06

Note: The probability (per cent) that the rate will be less than the amount specified in the column (e.g. in the column, "2000", and row, "50", half of the interest rates will be below 6.54 and half above).

With the distribution of rates, we can derive the optimal asset allocation for a given objective function.   One of the considerations in the Central Bank of Colombia's reserve management is that the currency composition of foreign exchange reserves must match the composition of the outflows of the balance of payments to reduce as much as possible cross-currency risks. The resulting desired currency composition for reserves is currently 80 per cent US dollars, 15 per cent Euro, and 5 per cent Japanese yen. This combination can be thought of as a basket currency, implying that we can redefine the objective function to be the maximization of returns defined in the basket currency. This insures that any asset choices are evaluated relative to what is considered the most risk-reducing currency composition of assets. Table 4 provides a summary overview of the solution, on which we expand.

Table 4: Solution summary information
(All expected values, except for 1999)

Item	1999	2000	2001	2002
% US dollar	80.00	80.00	80.00	80.00
% Euro	15.00	15.00	15.00	15.00
% Yen	5.00	5.00	5.00	5.00
Expected yearly return in US dollar		5.23	5.69	6.14
Standard deviation of return		0.53	0.82	1.09
Weighted average maturity	5.09	5.00	5.00	4.33
Probability of returns 2.75%		0.00	0.00	0.02
Probability of returns 5.5%		100.00	48.20	30.34
Probability of returns 7.5%		100.00	100.00	100.00

When we solve the model by optimizing our objective, we derive the percentage asset allocation in each year (table 5). In terms of currency choices, this is, for the year 1999, exactly the same asset allocation[8] as currently suggested by the Central Bank of Colombia: 80 per cent US dollars, 15 per cent euro, and 5 per cent Japanese yen. This is to be expected since, by construction, the expected rates of return on each asset (after currency movements) are identical, and there are no bounds specified on any asset classes nor any other constraints imposed. We emphasize the point here to show the consistency of the model with the prior assumptions.

Table 5: Percentage of expected asset allocation

Asset Classes	1999	2000	2001	2002
Euro short	3.74	4.29	4.81	5.31
Euro long	11.26	10.71	10.20	9.71
Euro total	15.00	15.00	15.01	15.02
US dollar liquid portfolio	7.13	6.90	6.47	5.18
US dollar short	10.00	13.95	17.87	22.51
US dollar long	62.87	59.15	55.64	52.29
US dollar total	80.00	80.00	79.98	79.98
Japanese yen short	3.00	3.02	3.05	3.07
Japanese yen long	2.00	1.98	1.96	1.93
Japanese yen total	5.00	5.00	5.01	5.00

Table 5 suggests that the asset class proportions are (almost) constant over time. This is not necessarily the case, as the asset allocation in table 5 for the years beyond the first year are the percentage of allocations expected. As exchange and interest rate movements will occur, depending on the particular scenario which materializes, the portfolio manager may find that a composition is realized that deviates from the 80/15/5 split. In order to achieve the desirable mix at each future date, the portfolio will be rebalanced in a certain way, depending on the specific outcome in the year. As the outcomes themselves are stochastic, the allocation in the second year and beyond become stochastic as well. This element of dynamic rebalancing of the portfolio at every future event is a key element of the optimization technique. Different from most other ALM-models, the model explicitly allows, at date zero (today), for the possibility of rebalancing at future dates (i.e. the possibility of rebalancing in the future plays a role in current

---

[8] With some latitude as to the assumption of the percentage in the U.S. dollar liquid portfolio.

allocation of assets). This way we obtain the correct estimates for the density functions of activities that depend on future decisions, such as total wealth.

To illustrate, we plot the density functions of the proportions of dollars in the portfolio in figure 5. We see that, in the year 2000, there is little variability around the 80 per cent proportion, but that the variability expands somewhat in 2001, and even more in 2002. In none of the years, however, is the variation very substantial. In 94 per cent of the cases in the years 2000 and 2001, the proportion of US dollars is between 78 and 83 per cent. Put differently, the optimal portfolio is quite stable over time and requires only modest rebalancing.

Figure 5: Density functions of the percentage of US dollars in the portfolio

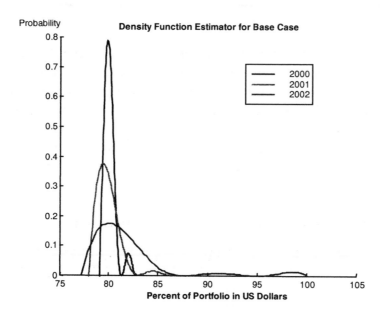

The modelling technique allows us to get the density functions of any decision and outcome variables at every date in the future. Following the portfolio allocation, figure 6 gives the density functions of wealth at different points in time. The figure shows that the densities for total wealth widen as time progresses, a reflection of the increase in uncertainty.

Figure 6: Density functions of total external wealth in millions of US dollars

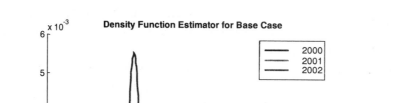

Using the densities, just as we did for the interest rates, we can generate a table of the distribution of wealth derived, which is given in table 6. The distribution of wealth is quite narrow: 94 per cent of the density mass is between US$ 11,401 and US$ 13,796 at the end of 2002, and 68 per cent between US$ 12,662 and US$ 13,544. This is partly due to the relatively low volatility measures used, and the fact that there were no other constraints imposed on the problem.

Table 6: Probability distribution of wealth in millions of US dollars

Probability	2000	2001	2002
3	11282	11658	11401
16	11488	12182	12662
50	11571	12371	13134
84	11638	12519	13544
97	11679	12599	13796

Note: In analysing the wealth in dollars at the horizon (year 2002), we must be careful to keep in mind that we are actually maximizing wealth measured in the basket currency. This is almost dollars, but not exactly. The expected wealth at 2002, for example, in millions of US dollars is US$ 13,134 and the maximum expected wealth in millions of the basket currency is 14,735.

(ii) An alternative scenario

The assumptions of the last section were based on an investment-neutral assumption, that is, we assumed that all assets were expected to yield the same rates of return. This is only one of the many possibilities. Specifically, typically three possible choices for predicting future rates are being used. First, the assumption we used above, that current market data embedded in the yield curve and in forwards and options contain the most accurate information on how future rates will move. Second, the assumption that rates behave as they have in the (recent) past and base the future stochastic processes on the basis of estimation using historical data. Lastly, one may use expert judgement. Our techniques allow for the use and integration of all three approaches.[9]

To explore the sensitivities of the outcome of the ALM model to the assumptions on rate movements, we conduct a test and alter the model by increasing the euro appreciation. Specifically, we assume that the euro appreciates at twice the rate indicated by the Uncovered Interest Parity assumption over the year 2000, and that the volatility of all the processes almost doubles. The new volatilities are given in table 7. Everything else is assumed to remain the same. We call this case the stronger euro.

Just as before, we present the summary solution information in table 8 first. Comparing this with table 4, we notice the wider dispersion in returns. On the downside, there is a 20 per cent probability that the compounded return will be less than 3.75 per cent in 2002. However, on the upside there is a 2.7 per cent probability that returns will be greater than 13.5 per cent. Looking at the standard deviation of returns, we see that they are much higher than before, with the possibility of substantial negative returns. However, the expected value of total wealth is higher, as the rate of return on the euro is higher.

---

[9] The latter integration is an extension of the technique proposed by Fischer Black and Robert Litterman, Global Portfolio Optimization, *Financial Analysts Journal*, September-October, 1992.

Table 7: Standard deviation of rates for a stronger euro

Asset Class	2000	2001	2002
Euro short rate	0.89	1.88	2.23
Euro long rate	1.39	2.91	3.27
US dollar short rate	1.10	1.65	1.93
US dollar long rate	1.31	2.41	2.79
Japanese yen short rate	0.16	0.30	0.39
Japanese yen long rate	1.48	1.79	1.63
Euro exchange rate	0.38	0.49	0.62
Japanese yen exchange rate	19.80	22.53	27.07

Table 8: Optimal solution with a stronger euro

Item	1999	2000	2001	2002
% Euro	92.83	92.71	92.74	92.76
% US dollar	7.17	7.29	7.26	7.23
% Japanese yen	0.00	0.00	0.00	0.01
Expected yearly return in US dollar		6.87	6.36	6.72
Standard deviation of return		11.10	11.63	11.92
Weighted average maturity	5.80	5.48	5.25	4.99
Probability of returns 3.75%		52.00	18.95	20.85
Probability of returns 7.5%		54.00	56.98	42.28
Probability of returns 9%		54.00	71.22	65.69
Probability of returns 13.5%		6.00	2.23	2.70

Table 9 provides more detail of the effects of this stronger euro assumption on the optimal asset allocation. It is no surprise that the modified solution produces a large position in euro (89 per cent in euro long assets).

Table 9: Percentage expected asset allocation for a stronger euro

Asset Classes	1999	2000	2001	2002
Euro short	3.77	7.82	11.89	15.88
Euro long	89.06	84.89	80.85	76.89
US dollar liquid portfolio	7.17	5.30	4.85	3.75
US dollar short	0	1.99	2.41	3.48
US dollar long	0	0	0	0
Japanese yen short	0	0	0	0
Japanese yen long	0	0	0	0

As noted, volatility was assumed to almost double, thus raising the riskiness of the rates of return, including the possibility of negative rates of return. In order to examine solutions with less volatility in returns, we use the techniques for restricting the density function of returns. We adopt an objective function[10] that weighs not only the expected value of the wealth, but also the uncertainty surrounding the distribution. We will also include, as required by the Central Bank, a constraint on negative returns. As noted, the Central Bank faced the legal restriction that there

---

[10] The objective is a piecewise linear-quadratic preference function of total final expected wealth. It tends to push the probability mass into a region defined by function parameters, determined exogenously.

should be no loss of principal. We will apply a no-negative-returns constraint to the total returns on the basket currency. This is most natural in our setting, since it captures all currencies at once. The solution, which we call the constrained solution, is given in table 10.

Table 10: Optimal solution of a stronger euro with constrained density

Item	1999	2000	2001	2002
% Euro	19.31	19.14	18.87	18.89
% US dollar	75.69	75.88	76.24	76.22
% Japanese yen	5.00	4.97	4.88	4.89
Expected yearly return in US dollar		5.54	6.41	6.74
Standard deviation of return		2.18	2.69	3.05
Weighted average maturity	5.18	4.86	4.58	4.34
Probability of returns 3.75%		4.00	5.66	5.03
Probability of returns 7.5%		98.00	100.00	99.74
Probability of returns 9%		100.00	100.00	100.00

Now the asset allocation proportions are closer to the 80/15/5 split for US dollar/euro/Japanese yen, as given in the Base Case. Moreover, on the downside, the probability of returns being less than 3.75 per cent is now only 5 per cent as compared to 20 per cent before. However, on the upside, there is now only a 0.3 per cent probability that returns will be greater than 7.5 per cent, whereas before, the probability was 58 per cent. All in all, the standard deviation of returns has dropped considerably, at a cost of lower rates of return.

In order to get a better understanding of what is happening, we examine various density functions. The first graph of figure 7 is the wealth in basket terms. The second graph in figure 7 shows the dramatic "squishing" of the density function of returns, leading also to a lower variability of wealth. Whereas wealth varied from 4 to 20 billion in the basket[11] currency, it now varies between 13 and 16 billion. However, this comes at a cost, as noticed in the expected value of wealth of about 56 million.

Figure 7: Density functions of wealth in 2002 – stronger euro versus constrained

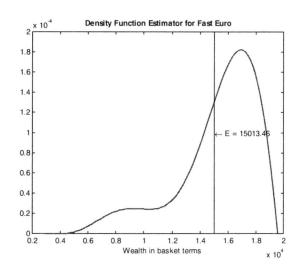 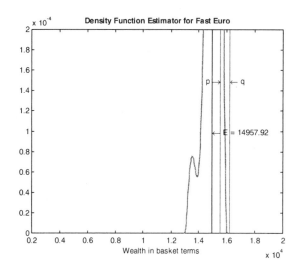

---

[11] We could have also graphed the returns in $US but these are not much different.

Figure 8 presents the densities of the returns on the assets. The base case basket returns vary from – 50 per cent to 20 per cent in all years, whereas under the constrained solution the densities of the rates of return vary from 0 per cent to around 10 per cent. This then maintains the no-negative-return requirement.

Figure 8: Densities of percentage returns - stronger euro versus constrained

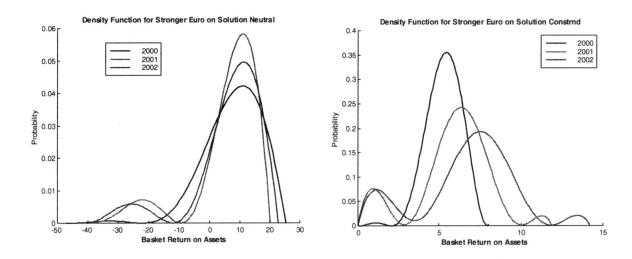

We also examine the maturity structure of the portfolio. Comparing tables 8 and 10, we see that the average maturity of the constrained solution is less in every year than the base case. This is consistent with a portfolio with less volatility. Moreover, the average maturity decreases in each future year within each solution under the constrained solution. To examine these phenomena, we plot the graphs of the densities of the average maturity of the portfolio in figure 9.

Figure 9: Densities of average maturity – stronger Euro versus constrained

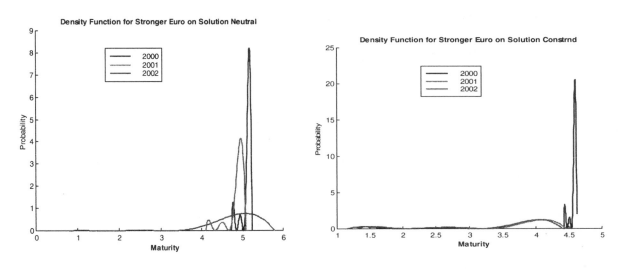

We notice that the densities are very narrow in both cases in the year 2000. However, in 2001 and 2002, the densities are much wider. Also, the average maturity decreases over time. One way to examine these issues is to look at the expected cash flows over time, given in table

11. We see that, to obtain a lower maturity, the model suggests selling some long assets and purchasing short. We see in table 11 that the main sale of assets (US$ 135 million) takes place in the year 2001. A further breakdown[12] of the line items of the cash flow statements for the sale of assets and for new assets acquired shows that the main sale of assets takes place in long dollars and the main purchase is in short dollars.

Table 11: Expected cash flows for the constrained case
(Expected sources of funds in millions of US dollars)

Category	1999	2000	2001	2002
Liquid assets matured	1 100.00	821.19	655.31	640.17
Other matured assets		1 714.35	2 522.15	3 373.37
Return on assets		569.55	638.60	701.80
Sales of assets	159.50	10.29	134.90	0.11
Total sources	1 259.50	3 115.38	3 950.96	4 715.45

The question is, why does this happen? If we look at figure 9, we notice that the density of the maturity in year 2001 has a long tail. What we would like to know is what the scenarios look like corresponding to that long tail (i.e. under which interest rate scenarios did the model suggest to sell long and purchase short?) For this, we examine all scenarios with an average maturity of less than 3, as shown in figure 10.[13] The chance that these scenarios will occur is only 1.8 per cent. From the figure, it is clear that these scenarios correspond to States of the world where there is a yield curve inversion. In this case, it makes perfect sense to sell long dollars and purchase short.

Figure 10: Scenarios for maturity < 3 for constrained case

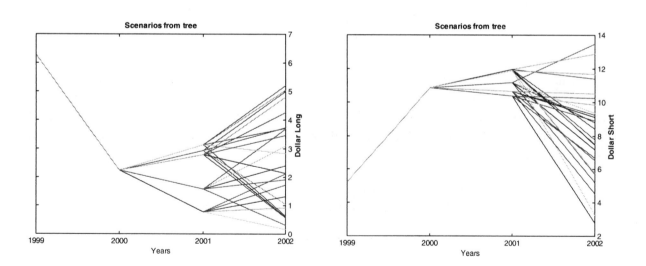

---

[12] We omit the details of that table and we omit the table of applications of funds.
[13] Within RisKontroller, we have the facility to specify a slice of any density function. That slice can then be used to generate scenarios, cash flow statements, new densities, or any other functions for those scenarios.

iii) A combined scenario

One other scenario of interest is the one where we constrain the densities, yet still wish to allocate currency in the ratios 80/15/5. Moreover, suppose we always rebalance the portfolio to maintain the same ratios? How do the solutions compare? There is much less left to optimize, but there is still freedom to choose the maturity. Figure 11 graphs the densities of wealth lost due to the policy decision to adopt an 80/15/5 currency composition instead of that suggested by the constrained case. In looking at these densities, we note that the distribution is almost centred on 0, with a potential for losses of up to 800 million, compared to the constrained solution. However, the probability of such losses is small. Nevertheless, there are opportunity costs to having additional constraints imposed.

**Figure 11: Densities of wealth lost due to policy decision
to enforce 80/15/5 ratios (in millions of US dollars)**

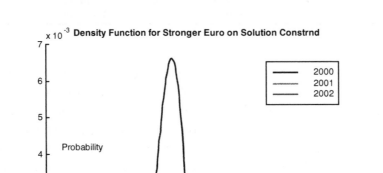

Table 12 provides a more precise answer for the distribution of costs. The expected loss varies from 16 to 24 million. In 2002, there is a 3 per cent probability that the loss due to the difference is more than 399 million. On the other hand, there is a 3 per cent probability that the 80/15/5 currency composition will give a $ 290 million gain over the solution suggested by the constrained solution.

**Table 12: Probability distribution for losses
due to policy decision to enforce 80/15/5**

Probability	2000	2001	2002
3	94	-206	-290
16	39	-103	-157
50	16	20	24
84	67	137	193
97	95	219	399

5. Conclusions

(i) ALM-modelling

The analysis demonstrates how to make informed decisions under uncertainty for debt and asset management. It shows that a rigorous process of analysis and the structured framework provide significant gains in modelling and insight. It also shows that one needs to investigate the whole spectrum of distributions of asset returns, exchange rate returns, and their effects on uncertainty of wealth currency composition, maturity, and asset composition to understand the reasons for their volatility, or lack thereof. While many have used simpler measures, such as value-at-risk, standard deviations, partitions of the densities, or probabilities on achieving specified intervals, these are most often only partial measures and less informative than the full density measures.

Applying the model to the problem of risk management for a reserve manager, we can analyse in more depth the currency composition and maturity choices. Using various "cuts" of the solution and different sensitivity analyses, we found robust support for the preferred choices. We also showed the trade-offs from making other policy choices, and provided statistical measures for different choices. On investigating the sensitivity of the solution to the stochastic processes used, we found that the results were very stable. More generally, the dynamic stochastic optimization approach leads to solutions that are quite robust to assumptions on underlying stochastic processes. The theoretical foundations for this model actually guarantee the stability of the proposed solutions under (not excessive) perturbations of the underlying stochastic processes.

The model can be extended to address more complex issues with active reserve management. One extension is the problem of liquidity portfolio size and the allocation of a part of reserves to active management. In this case, the model can be used to determine levels of reserves to go to active management, either in-house or through external managers with pre-specified risk profiles, with a desired overall risk profile of the portfolio. The model can also be extended to analyse disaster scenarios (with low probability and high impact).

(ii) More complex ALM models

The application to the management of a central bank's foreign exchange reserves shows both the ease of usage and some of the gains to be obtained from using this approach compared to approaches that are more traditional. It is easy to extend the model to more general problems, which reveals all the features and advantages of using a dynamic stochastic programming approach. One such more complex problem is that of a sovereign debt manager, for which the approach can be expected to be even more useful. Debt managers are likely to have to consider a much broader range of objectives and constraints than reserve managers. They will, for example, have to incorporate the evolution of fiscal revenues and the relationship between these revenues and external risk factors. They will also have to consider the risks coming from contingent liabilities, including government guarantees to State and/or private enterprises, and other contingent liabilities (most often these are not even budgeted or evaluated). In addition, the range of legal and policy constraints is likely to be greater. Furthermore, liabilities, be they loans from banks or bonds, are generally less easily altered than reserves, where short-term assets are generally liquid and can be easily marked to market and sold. The market for altering long-term liabilities is much less liquid, and, while they can be swapped in principle, this can often only be done at high costs.

(iii) Implementation

As with all models, their values depend on their application and on the context of usage. It is clear from many experiences with debt and reserves management that a proper institutional framework is key, including the availability of good personnel, data, reporting and accounting procedures, and accountability. Second, proper ALM requires a very careful analysis of the real underlying objectives and constraints. Often such an analysis will indicate underlying problems, which need to be fixed first before any ALM can be undertaken. And the analysis, as well as institutional weaknesses, might well suggest that the best way forward is to use very simple models to analyse specific areas of concern.

This does not necessarily mean that most countries should not pursue an ALM approach as laid out here. There are undoubtedly some countries which have addressed most of the pre-requisites. For those, a strategic ALM approach may be a useful tool. And even for those countries that do not yet have all the prerequisites in place, a strategic ALM approach allows them to evaluate the opportunity costs of the existing approaches. Regardless of the level of institutional development, the elements of a strategic approach provide a conceptual framework against which managers may wish to compare their existing approaches and assess whether they can be expected to address the underlying objectives and constraints. All too often, managers will "buy" very expensive technology or advice that only addresses a sub-set of their problems. It can then well be that the proposed solutions are far from optimal or even suggest a totally inappropriate position! It will often be more important to go through a rigorous process, in the government agencies and debt and asset management agencies, of identifying risks, constraints and objectives, than to adopt a technology for a sub-set of the overall problems.

References

Cassard M, Folkerts-Landau D (1997). Sovereign debt: Managing the risks. *Finance & Development, December.*

Claessens S, Kreuser J, Seigel L, Wets R (1995). Research proposal – A strategic approach to external asset/liability management in developing countries. The World Bank, Washington DC.

Claessens S, Kreuser J, Seigel L, and Wets R (1997). A Tool for Strategic Asset and Liability Management. Proceedings of the Interregional Debt Management Conference, UNCTAD, Geneva, December 10-19.

De Beaufort (2000). The changing nature of reserve management risks. Working Paper, Central Bank of Colombia, July.

IMF (2000). Debt- and reserve-related indicators of external vulnerability. Public Information Notice No. 00/37, May 19. International Monetary Fund, Washington DC.

Kim T, Maltz A, and Mina T(1999). *Long Run: Long-Term Forecasting for Financial Markets.* Technical document, RiskMetrics Group, The World Bank, Washington DC.

Wets R J-B (1998). Statistical estimation from an optimization viewpoint. *Annals of Operation Research, 84: 79-102.*

Ziemba WT and Mulvey JM (1998). *Worldwide Asset and Liability Modeling*: Cambridge, Cambridge University Press.

RISK MANAGEMENT AT THE SWEDISH NATIONAL DEBT OFFICE

Lars Kalderen

1. Introduction

Assessment and management of risk has always been an essential element of banking. Modern portfolio theory has made it possible for investors to develop, together with their bankers, instruments for the management of their assets. During the past 10-15 years, these techniques have also been adopted by liability managers. In some countries, such as Denmark, the risk control is effected simultaneously for the Government's external assets (i.e. the exchange reserves) and its liabilities in the form of currency loans. The central bank is in charge of the administration of both. In other countries, such as Sweden, risk management is undertaken separately by the bank and the Ministry of Finance (MoF) or by a special debt office. Initially, sovereign borrowers considered only their liabilities in foreign currency, but, increasingly, risk management techniques are spreading to the domestic loan portfolio, to State guarantees for loans raised by other borrowers, and to the Government's on-lending activities.

2. Sweden

Risk management is an essential part of the activities of the Swedish National Debt Office (SNDO) in the fields of:

- Borrowing and debt management;
- Raising funds in the domestic retail market;
- Deposit taking and lending to State corporations; and
- Issuing and administering State guarantees.

Thus, all departments of the SNDO are giving high priority to risk management, for which the Government has established the following goal: to observe best market practice, in accordance with legislation and the regulations issued by the Swedish Financial Supervisory Authority.

The SNDO gives special attention to three kinds of risk:

(i)   *Market risk*: To measure this risk, the SNDO has adopted the Value at Risk method, and has developed analytical tools to apply it to the currency debt. Moreover, the new back office system now being implemented will facilitate the application of this method. The currency portfolio is marked to market daily and limits are applied for the exposure to currency and interest rate risk. As of 1 January 2000, the portfolio has been split into an active and a passive part with regard to management. The former is to be vigorously managed with the aid of derivatives to obtain cost minimization, while the latter will be adjusted so as to correspond to the "benchmark portfolio" as regards currencies and interest rate types.

(ii)   *Operational risk*: This is defined as the risk that weaknesses in organization, systems and routines could lead to less than complete achievement of the goals set by the Government and the Board of the SNDO. The organization of the Debt Office is now judged to be satisfactory from the standpoint of good risk control, with a strict separation between front and back office. As for systems, a major overhaul has recently been concluded, with the aim of improving back office work in particular. Moreover, a series of comprehensive product programmes are being undertaken in order to analyse each step in the handling of various debt instruments, to make sure that all risks are identified and covered. To reach standard market practice of risk minimization, these organizational measures must be supplemented by process thinking as well as quality and competence in management; to achieve this, internal training programmes are applied.

(iii)   *Credit risk*: The SNDO is mostly exposed to such risks through the choice of counterparties to derivative contracts. Longer-term transactions are done with borrowers who have at least an AA rating, while A is sufficient for short-term deals. The risk incurred is calculated as the risk-exposed amount multiplied by the probability that payment under the contract will be suspended. The SNDO applies certain limits to the risk which is acceptable on the basis of such calculations. In general, the Debt Office uses best market practice to assess and determine credit risk.

The broad guidelines for debt and risk management are set annually by Parliament on the basis of proposals from the MoF, which receives background material and requests for authorization from the SNDO. Parliamentary decisions are then handed down to the Debt Office by the MoF as part of the budget process. The broad guidelines concern the duration for the total nominal debt during the following fiscal year, with limits for permitted deviation from the target, either way. The Government also establishes guidelines for the proportion of foreign currency debt in the total debt and for the share of index-linked debt.

After receipt of the Government's decision, the detailed framework and guidelines for risk management are set by the Board of the SNDO, whose Director-General is responsible for their implementation. There is a credit committee and a committee for operational risk, to take the lead and push progress in these two areas, including reminding department heads of their responsibility to enforce the directives. A central unit for risk control, comprising a director and four officers, has been set up with the task of monitoring financial and operational risks, as well as for initiating limits to financial risk. The unit reports to the Board on a monthly basis. The SNDO reports every six months to the Ministry of Finance and annually to Parliament.

HELPING COUNTRIES DEVELOP THEIR DOMESTIC DEBT MARKETS

Thomas P. Briggs

This summary, which represents my personal experience in helping a number of countries to develop their domestic debt markets, will focus on operational issues. My views do not necessarily reflect the experiences of the United States Treasury debt managers, nor do they represent Treasury or United States policy on any of the subjects addressed. These remarks were made at a panel comprising a number of other experts, each of whom took a separate part. This contribution should therefore be viewed in connection with the remarks made by my colleagues on the Risk Management Panel. Finally, this summary was created after the fact and may contain additional material, although I attempted to limit the written summary to the oral original.

The great management consultant, W.P. Deming, who rose to fame in Japan following the Second World War, noted that managers should "watch what you measure, because what you measure you will manage." Lawrence Summers, Secretary of the Treasury, said the same thing, just more economically, "What you count, counts." The point is, that the selection of a risk measure or benchmark is serious business. The selection of the measure itself may direct the course of policy implementation in ways that were not contemplated or planned. Paul Sullivan, a senior debt manager in Australia, noted at a recent World Bank conference that "All benchmarks should carry a government health warning. Wrongly used, benchmarks can be dangerous. With care, benchmarks can be very useful. Benchmarks are nontrivial."

The problem is that without formal benchmarks, human nature seeks informal benchmarks. People naturally try to find a reason for their decisions. These reasons can be selected, on the one hand, in a process characterized by great analytical rigour or, on the other hand, on the spur of the moment as a thought strikes us. One example is a country that sold five securities with different maturities on the same day at auction. It had no formal benchmarks for decision-making. The yield curve was positive. The Minister of Finance, rationally seeking some basis for decision-making, selected the lowest-yielding securities, often resulting in rejection of all bids for longer maturity securities. Over time, this practice could have led to an assumption of significant refunding and interest rate risk, as portfolio duration diminished. Another example of inappropriate outcomes from the lack of a policy-making framework is that decisions are made at the wrong level in the organization. Ministers are burdened with operational-level decisions, or policy is made through practice initiated by operational-level staff. Either of these can be disastrous to public accountability and to debt management.

One additional principle to be considered is that debt management is risk management. Debt management is not accounting. A sound accounting system that delivers accurate information on time to the appropriate user is part of the institutional framework necessary for debt management. It is not an end in itself.

Many sovereign debt management observers state that the critical risk to be managed is volatility in cost. Obviously, volatility is important. State budgets suffer from the tendency of expenditures to remain fixed when revenues decline in an economic downturn. That can put pressure on debt service capacity. At a minimum, debt managers should deliver a steady and predictable stream of cost to the budget authority. But debt managers have another important role: providing liquidity to the State so that the spending plan in the budget can be fulfilled.

There are both short - and long-term aspects to this issue. Over the long term, we must be able to redeem, either through repayment or refunding, prior debt obligations. In the short term, we need to be able to fill cash flow gaps. Accordingly, I would like to suggest a second critical risk to be managed, that of illiquidity in the State treasury.

Risk Analysis

A Sovereign faces two fundamental risks:

- volatility in cost
- illiquidity in the state treasury

There are three main categories of the decomposition of these risks:

1. Market Risks – risks that arise from normal operations in the market.

2. Operational Risks – risks that arise from administrative operations in the debt issuance, trading and redemption processes.

3. Country Risk – risks arising from the overall financial, economic and political status of the country.

Issue:
Reconciliation of Conflicting Objectives

Conflicting objectives
- It is impossible to minimize both cost and risk simultaneously.

Trade-offs among objectives
- minimization of funding risk increases interest rate risk
- minimization of currency risk (hedging) introduces counterparty risk
- refunding risk minimization increases cost
- support to the market may increase cost
- focus on cost raises macroeconomic stability risk
- an embedded option increases the price in the IPO but increases the all-in cost of a financing instrument
- . . . and so on

Risk cannot be eliminated.
- Risks can be measured, monitored and mitigated but never eliminated.

These two fundamental risks of volatility and illiquidity can be disaggregated. One disaggregated list includes interest rate, currency, funding and refunding instrument, counterparty, and internal control. All are subject to measurement and benchmarking. Focus on risk is a useful organizing principle for sovereign debt management operations. Debt managers and their political superiors must comprehend that not only must they understand each individual risk, but they must also understand and analyse the trade-offs between risks and between risk and cost. For example, currency risk usually is mitigated through transfer via a hedging operation. The transfer is to another party that may have to perform on the contract at a point in time in the future. This process creates counterparty risk. In a positive-yield curve environment, reduction of refunding risk through extension of duration will increase cost. Decreased cost through shortened duration will expose the issuer to refunding and interest rate risk. Funding risk may be increased in the effort to reduce interest risk if long-term investor capacity is approached or exceeded. An embedded option may increase the price of a security when it is issued, but exposes the issuer to increased all-in cost if the option comes into the money at a later time.

Typical reference points focus on the stock of debt. If one is to consider illiquidity as a risk, additional focus should be placed on flows. My experience is that the most useful market feedback will occur from observing the reactions of market participants to funding and refunding operations. Such feedback is crucial to validating benchmarks derived from models or other sources. Thus, our experience is that construction of benchmarks should focus on two areas: the classic one of a set of reference points for the portfolio, and a second set of measures of efficiency and durability of debt issuance operations.

Benchmarks provide a number of important benefits, as follows:

- Benchmarks quantify the sovereign's debt management strategy. This provides guidance to government debt management officials for their operations, and transparency to the government's financing operations for market participants. The reduction of uncertainty provided by the transparency usually produces lower costs over time than opportunistic debt management methods.
- Benchmarks provide a means of holding government officials accountable for their actions.
- Benchmarks do not change with staff. Many debt management offices suffer from high staff turnover. Benchmarks may bridge this turnover and provide consistency to operations.
- Benchmarks should reinforce a culture of risk management.
- Written benchmarks tend to force debate, hopefully informed by analysis, when changes are proposed. This is a more deliberative means of policy-making that should produce superior results and more predictable debt management practices.
- Benchmarks can help focus officials at various levels in the Government on the issues that are appropriate to their level. Benchmarks should allow policy formulation, programme development and transaction management to occur at different levels of government in an appropriate and orderly manner.

The latest trend in debt management is to focus on asset/liability management (ALM) techniques. This trend mirrors and imitates the revolution in bank management that has occurred over the past 30 years. The problem is that State balance sheets and bank balance sheets are significantly dissimilar. Bank balance sheets are dominated by financial assets and financial liabilities. Sovereign liabilities, on the other hand, tend to be financial, but sovereign assets are both financial and non-financial, and the non-financial assets are substantial. State non-financial assets are much greater in proportion to total assets than those for banks, and the non-financial assets can be both physical and non-physical. A look at the State budget for education and health shows that these often dominate expenditures. They create human capital – extraordinarily difficult to measure but crucial to success in technologically-advanced economies. I was told by a former United States debt manager that the Treasury effort to implement ALM foundered on the issue of including human capital on the balance sheet. Countries with which I am familiar that have implemented ALM have not included human capital.

The creation of a balance sheet for ALM is difficult; it presents enormous challenges of measurement and definition. The Republic of South Africa is committed to adopting an ALM framework, but overtly recognizes that construction of the balance sheet cannot be completed before 2005. This raises the issue of what is to be done in the meantime. My answer is that we can find significant useful information from the debt portfolio itself, without reference to the asset side of the balance sheet, and we should not, therefore, abandon sound debt management practice simply because creation of the ALM framework may take several years. We should not let the perfect be the enemy of the good.

Another issue is that ALM does not provide information about funding and refunding instruments or counterparty risk. As I travel around the world and visit debt managers, I have observed that these managers spend far more of their working day solving funding and refunding problems. In most cases, interest rate and currency risk are reviewed infrequently, such as quarterly or annually, while debt managers make decisions almost daily about their funding and refunding operations in the weekly or monthly auction. Obviously, interest rate and currency risk is important. But, judging from the behaviour of real debt managers, so are refunding, funding and the other risks. (There was a misunderstanding on the part of at least one member of the original audience who got the impression that I said that refunding and funding risk cannot be modelled. Obviously, they can be modelled, just not in an ALM framework.) ALM offers important insights into currency and interest rate risk and should be exploited. Other risks should not be ignored simply because they do not fit the ALM model.

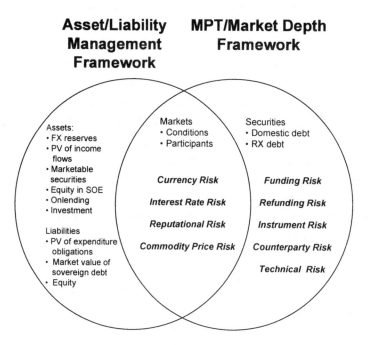

In conclusion, I go back to Deming and Summers – watch what you measure because it will drive your results. Sole reliance on ALM could be dangerous, because it does not measure risks that are faced every day in debt management operations. ALM is a great tool that offers enormous promise for debt managers. However, until ALM can be fully implemented, modern portfolio theory and analysis, based on first principles, offer useful information that can be used immediately. Together, analysis based on modern portfolio theory and first principles can be combined with insights gained from ALM to develop a comprehensive source of information for debt management policy-making and implementation.

DEBT MANAGEMENT IN THE AFRICAN CONTEXT

Trevor de Kock

1. Introduction

My aim is to provide a perspective of debt management from the African context. The extent of the debt management problem in Africa is quantifiable through the following figures:

- Of the approximately 36 countries qualifying for debt relief under the enhanced Heavily Indebted Poor Countries (HIPC) Initiative, 30 are from Africa;
- At the end of the 1970s Africa's external debt was some US$ 31 billion, accounting for 79 per cent of exports and 21 per cent of gross domestic product (GDP), and debt service was taking up 7 per cent of export earnings;
- During the 1990s the external debt was at some US$ 312 billion accounting for 220 per cent and 57 per cent of exports and GDP respectively compared to the average of 175 per cent and 36 per cent for all developing countries.

Since 80 per cent of African external debt is owed to bilateral and multilateral creditors, the debt problem relates basically to official debt. In some cases, the concessional resources from the multilateral development banks, rather than providing the solution, became part of the problem. Much of the increase in debt from the late 1980s related to concessional lending by multilateral institutions for policy reform programmes, which provided quick-disbursing balance of payments support. The extent of the debt problem has been well analysed; the question is, therefore, how it is to be tackled.

2. Risk management

As with many things in life, debt management is easier said than done. Many aspects of debt management may appear obvious, but when we come to implementing them in the real world we often run into difficulties. The same can be said about risk management. This is even more so in the developing than in the dustrialized than in the economies.

Debt management requires the balancing of a number of conflicting objectives relating to the reduction of the cost of debt over time, but subject to a number of risks and constraints. Indeed, the best debt managers are not those who achieve the lowest cost of borrowing. Very often a low cost hides a high level of risk which may not be glaringly obvious. A puttable bond, for example, gives the bondholder the right to sell the bonds back to the issuer, a right for which the issuer obtains a lower cost. Such a structure, however, puts the power in the hands of the lender, which he may exercise when the borrower can least afford it. Callable bonds, on the other hand, give the borrower the right to call bonds issued and such a right is paid for through a higher borrowing cost. This higher cost may, however, be worth more to a borrower than the exposure created by the puttable bond. It is often worth paying more for a structure that is robust under a range of scenarios rather than one that is optimal under one particular scenario.

So how can risk management help us to manage debt more effectively? Risk management conjures up ideas of complex derivatives structures leading to the problems experienced by the likes of Metallgesellschaft, Barings and others. However, details of various derivative instruments that may be used is beyond the scope of this presentation.

3. Special challenges of emerging markets

The design and implementation of a risk management system for use in an emerging region poses significant additional challenges beyond those normally associated with the process of measuring and managing risk. These challenges include:

- The absence of developed markets from which it would be possible to construct meaningful yield curves;
- The absence of reliable forward markets;
- The absence of deep and liquid derivatives markets with low transaction costs;
- The increased potential for foreign-exchange-rate disruptions due to changes in currency regimes or currency devaluation;
- The existence of political risk; and
- The existence of foreign exchange controls.

It has even been said that emerging-market debt managers need to be better than their counterparts in industrialized countries because of the ease with which industrialized economies are able to access sophisticated instruments and markets. In fact, only five African countries – Egypt, Mauritius, Morocco, South Africa and Tunisia – are currently rated by any of the major international ratings agencies. These countries can generally, to a greater or lesser extent, borrow from the international capital markets. In addition, these five countries have domestic financial markets, albeit at varying degrees of development, which would enable them to enter into hedging agreements with suitable counterparties in order to manage market risks.

But good risk management does not only mean the use of derivative instruments. In many developing countries operational risk may be the most important risk factor inhibiting effective debt management. Institutional capacity in debt management and risk management has been determined as being the main constraints faced by Governments in surveys conducted both by the World Bank and the African Development Bank. A lack of capacity leads to deficiencies in such areas as policy formulation, data recording, monitoring and analysis, all of which increase the risk of something going wrong when one can least afford it. It is safe to say that the more sophisticated the risk management instruments to be used, the more complex the organizational set-up would need to be. In addition, more complex instruments would also probably require tighter administrative procedures.

4. Developing domestic markets

In my view, one of the areas of importance for developing economies to better manage their debt is the development of their domestic capital markets. Once again, this is easier said than done and is a long-term process. In many developing economies, there is the illusion that because the local interest rate is higher than the foreign interest rate, the local debt is more expensive than the foreign debt. Sharp currency depreciation can make foreign currency debt much more expensive than local currency debt. Being able to borrow locally means developing local markets, and, over time, pushing out the yield curve by issuing longer-term debt. Without a developed domestic market, countries will always be reliant on foreign sources of finance and be exposed to the risks of foreign currency fluctuations. Well developed domestic markets would, over time, make the use of derivative instruments more possible. Currency risk between the local and foreign currency can only be managed through the ability to price into the future, which requires a well developed interest rate market and a longer-term yield curve. Needless to say, while these developments are important, they can only be achieved in a framework of sound monetary and fiscal policies.

5. Managing liguidity risk

One of the most important lessons to be learned from the debt crisis of 1997-1998 was the importance of managing liquidity risk. Liquidity risk relates to the ability to roll over maturing debt and the cost at which it can be rolled over. This is one area where derivative instruments are not necessary. General strategies for managing liquidity risks are:

- Extending portfolio maturity;
- Avoiding bunching of maturities;
- Pre-funding and the generation of large cash balances;
- Diversification of funding sources; and
- The development of liquid bond benchmarks.

Many developing countries also have to contend with the risks associated with fluctuating commodity prices, which are often the major source of foreign exchange. While many commodities have deep and liquid derivatives markets, not all producers are able to access them for the reasons stated above. An international task force under the leadership of the World Bank is currently investigating ways in which commodity price risk for developing countries can be managed.

6. Conclusion

In conclusion, I believe that the use of sophisticated risk management tools and instruments are undoubtedly beneficial to debt managers but their accessibility is limited to the more developed economies. As with any powerful tools, however, they need to be correctly used and they require adequate controls.

PUBLIC DEBT MANAGEMENT: THE BELGIAN EXPERIENCE

Louis de Montpellier

1. Introduction

In 1995, the Belgian Treasury, started working on a framework and methodology for establishing the public debt portfolio structure that minimizes the financial cost of the public debt at an acceptable level of risk, while taking into account the constraints imposed by budgetary and monetary policies. This was two years before the Government formally established the Debt Agency within the Treasury as the centre of public debt management expertise. The Belgian Debt Agency has now refined this method in several technical respects and is continuously attempting to improve it. This paper seeks to explain the reasoning which supports what has become, for several years, a real management tool for the public debt.

2. Trends in Belgian public indebtedness

This undertaking is the last step of several fundamental reforms in public debt management implemented since the beginning of the 1990s. These reforms were especially crucial given Belgium's high public indebtedness, the causes of which are briefly mentioned below.

The Belgian public sector has traditionally experienced rather high indebtedness, in contrast to the private sector. In this respect, Belgium differs from other European countries, such as Denmark or the United Kingdom, where the reverse is true. At the end of the 1960s, Belgian public debt as a percentage of gross domestic product (GDP) was already twice the European average. The accumulation of budget deficits during the 1970, following the energy shocks, exacerbated this trend. In 1981, the Belgian public deficit stood at 13.5 per cent of GDP, debt service cost was close to 8 per cent, and total debt stood at 82 per cent.

The cost of debt service had by then reached a level that generated a snowball effect, that is to say, an automatic increase of the debt due to the financing of the cost of the existing debt. This effect, combined with lower economic growth and inflation and higher interest rates in the 1980s brought the public debt to a level of 130 per cent of GDP at the end of 1987, where it stabilized following a first period of public sector austerity from 1982 to 1987. By 1987, the deficit was restored to a level of 6.8 per cent of GDP. The economic recession at the beginning of the 1990s, which threatened to inflate deficits and debt once again, prompted the Government to take a drastic new set of austerity measures. In 1993, the debt to GDP ratio peaked at 135 per cent, while the deficit stood at 7.2 per cent. Thereafter, the debt to GDP ratio declined by 21.5 per cent to 114.5 per cent of GDP at the end of 1999, and the deficit was 0.9 per cent that year. The fall in debt ratio was achieved by building up a large primary budget surplus (over 6 per cent of GDP in 1999). This policy of high primary surpluses is set to continue in the coming years, as prescribed by the Stability and Growth Pact.

Foreign debt increased in the late 1970s and the early 1980s due to continuing balance of payment and budget deficits. The National Bank needed to replenish the stock of its reserves during several periods of weakness of the Belgian franc, and the Treasury met these needs by issuing foreign currency debt. As a proportion of total debt, foreign debt grew from 1 per cent in 1978 to 24 per cent in 1984. As a result of the efforts to stem the budget deficits at the beginning of the 1980s, the return to a balance-of-payment surplus and the formal peg of the Belgian franc to the strongest currencies of the European Monetary System (EMS), particularly to the deutsche mark, the proportion of foreign debt decreased regularly between 1985 and 1992 to reach 12 per cent of the total debt. During the EMS crisis of 1993, intervention in the foreign exchange market by the Belgian National Bank was partially financed by borrowing abroad. The foreign debt proportion hedged back up to 17 per cent in 1993. Since then it has been brought back regularly, to represent, at present, less than 4 per cent of the total debt.

For the last 15 years, Belgium has been pursuing a tight budgetary policy and a stable anti-inflationary monetary policy, reversing the trend of the two previous decades. These policies have been mainly motivated to prevent an unsustainable public debt accumulation, which would have prevented the country from meeting three fundamental challenges: in the long term, the ageing population and the resulting growing pension liabilities; in the medium term, the recovery of budgetary freedom to meet new or recurring public sector or society needs; and in the short term, accession to the European Monetary Union (EMU). The establishment of economic policies necessary to meet these challenges has completely redefined the macroeconomic context in which public debt management is being operated.

3. Market reforms at the beginning of the 1990s

At the beginning of the 1990s a fundamental reform of the Belgian capital markets was undertaken. New fully computerized instruments were introduced in the money market (short-term Treasury Certificates at 3, 6 and 12 months) and in the capital market (linear bonds with maturities ranging from 1 to 20 years). The banking consortium system was abolished and competitive auction systems were introduced.

From the point of view of debt management, the main effect of these reforms was to significantly reduce the financial cost of the debt, while allowing for a diversification and a lengthening of the maturities of the debt portfolio. From a broader macroeconomic perspective, these reforms improved the efficiency of the monetary policy (by enabling open market operations), established a clear dividing line between monetary and budgetary policies, and allowed for more controlled budgetary management. The reforms also substantially improved the general context of savings and investment in Belgium, which benefited economic activity as a whole.

At the same time, the authorities embarked upon a structural adjustment of the public debt portfolio to reduce budget vulnerability to financial changes; they started to lengthen the debt maturity spectrum and reduced, whenever possible, the proportion of the foreign debt. In order to refine this broad debt portfolio strategy, the Treasury decided to develop a benchmark debt portfolio.

4. Defining a public debt management strategy

In embarking upon such a thorough strategic exercise, it is crucial, first, to define clearly the objective pursued by, and the risks involved in, the exercise of public debt management. Second, the question arises as to whether public debt management should be approached as an asset/liability management problem or a portfolio management problem. Third, the public debt manager should have a clear understanding of the macroeconomic context and the constraints imposed by that context. All these elements have institutional implications, and clear knowledge of these objectives and constraints should assist the establishment of an efficient institutional framework. However, historical developments specific to a country should never be underestimated when an institutional framework is discussed.

5. Objective and risks

Since 1997, the objective of public debt management has been defined in the law establishing the annual budget as being "...to minimise the financial cost of the public debt, while maintaining market and operational risks at an acceptable level, taking into account the general objectives of the budgetary and monetary policies".

Several concepts of this definition should be emphasized. First, the objective of the Belgian administration is to minimize the financial, long-term cost of the debt, and not only the current budgetary cost. A financial long-term cost measure of the public debt should adequately capture the cost of debt servicing on all future budgets.

Second, it is crucial to define the precise nature of the risks run by the sovereign debt manager. It is useful to distinguish two types of risk. As any market participant, the manager of the public debt is subject to financial risks (i.e. market risks, credit risks and operational risks). However, the manager of the public debt is also subject to risks, specific to funding a sovereign State, which could be qualified as "macroeconomic" risks. This is the risk that public debt management runs contrary to, or endangers some, economic policy objectives of the Government.

As an example, take the case of an extremely steep yield curve, as was the case in Europe in 1995-1996 (the difference between the six-month and 10-year rates was about 300 basis point). In such an environment the sovereign debt manager could be tempted, even in a conservative financial risk management framework, to maintain a sizeable proportion of floating rate debt in order to save costs to the taxpayers. However, when the sovereign is running a high debt to GDP ratio and is following a stable exchange rate policy, the proportion of floating rate debt should be limited to leave full freedom to the central bank to raise short-term rates rapidly in order to defend the parity of the currency in case of speculative attack, without endangering the current budgetary objective of the Government. If the interaction between sovereign debt management, and monetary and budgetary policies are not fully understood, quantified and integrated into the public management framework, public management may run into conflicting objectives, possibly with disastrous consequences.

6. Financial approaches

Two financial approaches spring to mind when it comes to managing public debt. The first one starts by defining the State's respective financial assets and liabilities, and tries to establish a risk-neutral position by matching the two. Albeit simplified, this is what any financial intermediary does, and there is no reason why a public debt manager should not try the same ploy. After all, tax receipts can well be considered as cash flow returns from assets. The Treasury could then manage both tax receipts and public debt. The snag is that tax receipts do not show the same sensitivity to financial variables, such as interest rates and currency exchange rates.

While impractical, the approach of managing both assets and liabilities offers a few valuable hints:

- Tax receipts are, for the greater part, in the national currency. Logically, debt ought to be denominated also mainly in the national currency;
- Tax receipts occur year after year and have regular patterns and levels. They are, in a sense, long-term cash flows. Logically, debt ought to be long-term fixed-rate debt;
- In the case of a diversified, market-based economy, external revenues are commercial surpluses, which, when accumulating into currency reserves, provide foreign currency cash flows. The public debt manager should then consider a match between foreign debt (if any) and foreign exchange reserves.

But these considerations are clearly insufficient to build a thorough public debt management strategy. The public debt manager should, therefore, resort to a second approach: that of managing public debt pretty much as a portfolio fund manager would do in reverse. Fund managers try to maximize their return by taking a certain risk. The risk they take will depend on the risk aversion or appetite of their clients. A public debt manager, as opposed to a fund manager, does not strive to maximize return but to minimize cost, and this under the constraint of maintaining risk at an acceptable level.

But what level of risk? A public debt manager should try to assess the risk aversion of the Government and the public in general to financial risks, and to "macroeconomic" risks, in particular. By definition, the risk profile will be very conservative; not necessarily towards financial risks of which the Government and taxpayer do not have a clear idea, but towards "macro-economic" risks. It is the latter which will impose the greater constraint on public debt management.

7. Policy constraints

Two policies impose constraints of a macroeconomic nature on public debt management: monetary policy and budgetary policy. The constraints are best explained by taking a specific example – that of Belgium before EMU[1].

---

[1] The example is out of date, and given the current context, not always relevant. Nevertheless, it is more appropriate than, for example, taking Belgium after EMU.

We first look at monetary policy. Before EMU the Belgian National Bank's monetary policy consisted of closely pegging the exchange rate of the Belgian franc to the strongest currencies of the EMS, and, in particular, to the deutsche mark. The effect on debt management was twofold:

- It affected the proportion and composition of the foreign debt; and
- It affected the proportion of floating rate debt in the domestic debt.

First, a monetary policy aiming at stable exchange rates influences the proportion and the composition of foreign debt, as such a policy necessitates a sufficient level of foreign exchange reserves and a smooth access to the international money and capital markets. The surest way to meet these constraints was to maintain a certain level of debt in the markets for reserve currencies. On the other hand, the proportion of foreign debt could not be too high. If the central bank needed to intervene, the foreign debt would increase. If the proportion of foreign debt were already high, central bank interventions could have destabilized the debt portfolio.

Two additional economic factors have led the Treasury to gradually reduce the proportion of foreign debt in Belgium's total debt. On the one hand, the country had been accumulating reserves for several years in the form of sizeable balance-of-payments surpluses. Borrowing in a foreign currency had lost much of its sense. On the other hand, once Belgium had joined EMU, the management of international reserves for intervention purposes was to disappear as a priority at the national level. Taking these considerations into account, it was unlikely that the actual proportion of foreign debt would be increased in the run up to EMU, and so it turned out.

Second, a monetary policy aiming at stable exchange rates limited the proportion of domestic floating rate debt to assure the central bank the greatest possible flexibility to influence short-term rates through open market operations. This objective is difficult to quantify. It is to meet this constraint, as well as to improve budgetary control, that the Treasury progressively reduced the proportion of domestic floating rate debt from 35 per cent at the end of 1990 to 20 per cent at the end of 1999.

8. Budgetary policy, a second constraint[2]

Two specific objectives of the Belgium's current budgetary policy are major determinants of its debt management: the annual budgetary objective limiting the public deficit as a set percentage of GDP, and the annual reduction of government debt as a percentage of GDP. The first objective imposes constraints on the average duration of the debt portfolio, on the fix/floating ratio and on the amount of annual refunding. The second objective imposes a constraint on the volatility of the euro-value of the total debt.

First, the Government's budgetary objective dictates a maximum amount per year in euro devoted to servicing the debt. It is intuitively clear that the shorter the average duration of the debt portfolio, the larger the refunding amounts due within the year, and, consequently, the greater the volatility of the annual budgetary cost of the debt. Therefore, the budgetary objective imposes a minimum average duration on debt management. Furthermore, the budgetary objective is more likely to be met if the proportion of floating rate debt is not too large. Finally, the budgetary constraint will apply in any future year. It is therefore crucial to ensure a "smooth profile" to the debt repayment schedule till maturity.

---

[2] Of the two constraints mentioned this one has lost none of its relevance.

Second, the objective to gradually decrease debt/GDP ratio will be assured over the years by a combination of a continuous primary budget surplus (targeted at about 6 per cent over the next several years), normal economic growth, resulting diminishing interest charges on the debt, and shrinking public deficit.

Though this objective is not quantified in terms of GDP percentage points, it is clear that it imposes a constraint on the volatility of the total value of the stock of debt expressed in euro. Therefore, this constraint aims at limiting the proportion of foreign debt in the total debt and at favouring foreign debt in currencies which have historically experienced low volatility vis-à-vis the euro.

9. Institutional implications

A clear conceptual framework defining the objective of public debt management and the cost and risks inherent to it, and organizing the interaction between sovereign debt management, monetary and budgetary policies, is crucial to the efficient conduct of public policies and debt management. A proper conceptual framework should clarify respective tasks and responsibilities. The actual institutional arrangements then become secondary, though some are clearly more conducive to an optimal public management than others. The most obvious example, now largely adopted as a model across the industrialized world, is an independent central bank to conduct monetary policy.

In Belgium public debt management is run by the Debt Agency within the Treasury. It operates independently from the other functions of economic policies (mainly the budgetary and fiscal) within the public administration. Annually, a strategic review takes place to determine a benchmark debt portfolio as a reference for the management of the public debt in the coming year. The benchmark portfolio quantifies the main portfolio parameters used by the Debt Agency in managing the portfolio during the coming year: currency exposure, average duration of different currency components and the level of future refinancing for each maturity.

This exercise has also enabled a clarification of some aspects of the institutional framework of public debt management. A relatively straightforward definition of the objective and risks of public debt management has been integrated into the annual budget law, together with an explicit reference to the context of monetary and budgetary policies in which this management has to take place. The law makes reference to General Guidelines relative to the management of the public debt during the budget period. The Minister of Finance adopts these Guidelines based upon the benchmark debt portfolio at the beginning of the budgetary year on the basis of a proposal put forward by the Debt Agency.

The Debt Agency is expected to optimize the financial management of the public debt, with reference to the benchmark debt portfolio, as prescribed by the General Guidelines. This transparent framework has strengthened risk management and performance assessment. It should also present decisions and operations pertaining to public debt management, convey signals about the government's macroeconomic policies, and thereby improve the transparency and efficiency of the domestic financial market.

THE IMPACT OF THE INTRODUCTION OF THE EURO ON DEBT MANAGEMENT IN HUNGARY

Mr. László Buzas

1. Introduction

Before trying to assess the impacts of the introduction of euro, I would like to draw attention to one specific aspect of Hungarian debt management. For the past 30 years, Hungary has been an active participant in the international capital markets, having issued more than 100 public bonds in 13 different markets, including those of the so-called legacy currencies (deutsche mark, Austrian schilling, Netherlands guilder, French franc, Luxembourg franc and Spanish peseta). Due to this active fund-raising from the international capital markets, Hungary has a relatively high share of foreign currency debt, which constitutes 36 per cent of the public debt portfolio.

In line with the debt management strategy of the Government debt management agency the budget deficit, including interest payments on external debt and the maturing domestic debt, is exclusively financed by the domestic market. As only the maturing principal of the foreign currency debt is being rolled over in the international capital markets, the share of the foreign currency debt will gradually decrease. A more radical decrease of this part of our debt portfolio is not contemplated.

2. Role of the euro

So what role does the euro play in our debt management? First of all, the euro is the major component of our benchmark. When the Government's debt management agency started to manage external debt, having taken over this function from the central bank in 1997, the major objective was to limit the foreign exchange risk. In search of the least risky solution, we had come to the conclusion that swapping the foreign debt into the structure of the currency basket of our domestic currency – the Hungarian forint – would limit the foreign exchange risk to the extent of the crawling peg devaluation of the HUF. At that time, as the currency basket contained 30 per cent US dollars and 70 per cent deutsche mark, (the latter was replaced by the euro in 1999), cross-currency swaps were used to replicate that currency structure. As from 1 January 2000, the HUF basket contains 100 per cent euro, all existing non-euro debt has been swapped into euro, and all future issues in US dollars or Japanese yen have to be swapped into euro as well. This also gives us the possibility to compare different financing alternatives on a euribor basis.

As frequent issuers, we had expected that the creation of the euro and the consequent elimination of the foreign exchange risk for European investors would enable us to widen the existing investor base by issuing large liquid euro-denominated issues. So far that has not happened. The European investor base is still very fragmented, and since the pricing of our issues is driven by our traditional (predominantly German and Austrian) investor base, it makes it very difficult to reach other European (e.g. French, Spanish or Scandinavian) investors. The participation of United States and Asian investors in our euro-denominated issues is also below expectations (to a large extent due to the weak euro).

Hungary, being a convergence country, certainly has a special position. Membership of the European Union (EU) is expected in early of 2003, and of the EMU two years thereafter. Thus according to this, admittedly, very optimistic forecast, by 2005 the euro will be our domestic currency, and that has some additional implications also for the domestic market.

With the creation of the euro many European investors found that the room for manoeuver within the euro zone was rather limited, and that they would have to look elsewhere for diversification of their investments. As a consequence, the convergence countries experienced a huge inflow of foreign capital into their domestic bond and equity markets. The typical maturity preference of these investors is 2-3 years, which makes it clear that they are the so-called convergence players, who will move to the next group of EU-candidates as soon as the first wave are admitted to the EU.

In this context it is important to realize, that domestic bonds owned by foreign investors are by no means domestic debt. In fact these types of liabilities may be very volatile and do not bear the low-risk profile of the domestic debt. This leads us to an issue that will become extremely important for debt managers in convergence countries. Is domestic debt free of foreign exchange risk? To take an example, in January 1999, Hungary issued a 10-year fixed-rate HUF-denominated bond and almost simultaneously, a 10-year fixed-rate euro-denominated bond. If both are repaid in 2009, by which time Hungary will have become a member of the EMU, which bond carries a higher foreign exchange risk?

3. Implications of EMU membership

It may seem premature to try to assess the implications of the euro as the domestic currency of Hungary, but preparation for EMU membership might be very time-consuming. We can consider the experience of smaller EMU members (Austria and Portugal) or the next EMU candidate (Greece) and make the following conclusions.

With the redenomination of our domestic debt at the time of joining the EMU, our financing needs in euro will suddenly increase from the current 1.0-1.5 billion to 13-15 billion euro per year. There are arguments that this will not be a problem, as domestic investments will also be made in euro instead of HUF, and Hungary's membership in the euro zone itself will attract additional euro-based investments. While that might be true, it is obvious that, at the same time, we shall loose a very significant part of our investor base.

On the one hand, domestic investors, who currently buy Hungarian government securities because of the benchmark status, will have to move their investments into bonds that serve as the euro benchmarks. They might buy Republic of Hungary issues as credit products. On the other hand, the so-called convergence players, as mentioned above, will also move to the next group of potential EU members. Even investors who are comfortable with the risk of the HUF-denominated assets today will look for further asset diversification as soon as the HUF ceases to exist. This may lead to a situation where the loss of certain groups of our current investor base will not be compensated by the increase in the investments attracted by Hungary's EMU membership.

4. Preparing for EMU membership

Whether these projections will prove to be correct or not is difficult to predict. Certain preparatory measures, however, can be taken. First, in order to maintain, and, to the extent possible, widen the existing investor base, we have to continue to issue euro-denominated bonds. These bonds should be of relatively long duration that will help us to avoid bunching of redemptions around the date of Hungary's EMU-entry. This seems to be important, as the duration of our domestic portfolio is still very short, and about 60 per cent of the domestic debt will mature within one year.

Second, further development of the institutional framework for the distribution of our bonds may also help, and the primary dealer system should also include investment banks that are currently not incorporated in Hungary, but that have significant capacities in distributing Hungarian papers.

Third, as investor diversification is key to any successful financing strategy, we shall put more emphasis on investor education outside Europe. Wide access to the United States and Japanese capital markets might offer an alternative source of funding in case of turbulence in the European market

Finally, a gradual decline in financing needs as a consequence of appropriate fiscal policies and a decrease in the debt in real terms will certainly make the task of the public debt managers a lot easier independently of the currency of fund-raising.

ASIAN DEVELOPMENT BANK'S EURO STRATEGY

Julia Holz

1. Introduction

On 1 January 1999, the euro became the official currency for 11 European countries. How did this affect the borrowers of the Asian Development Bank (ADB)? I will present a brief picture of the ADB's euro strategy and the impact on ADB borrowers. The presentation is divided into four parts: the first part describes the ADB, who we are and what we do; the second discusses the euro and its impact; the third describes ADB's euro strategy; and finally, the results of that strategy.

2. Asian Development Bank

The ADB was established in 1966 and is now owned by 58 member countries, with all but 16 from the Asian and Pacific region. These 16 members are: Canada, the United States of America and 14 countries in Europe. The ADB has its headquarters in Manila, and it has 20 resident missions in the region, plus offices in Germany and the United States. The mission of the Bank is to foster social and economic development in the region through financial assistance in the form of direct equity investments, technical assistance grants and loans. The largest assistance is in the form of public sector loans and these come from two sources.

The main source of funds is from ordinary capital resources (OCR). The Bank borrows funds for its ordinary operations from the capital markets of the world. The interest rate on these loans is typically between 6 and 7 per cent. The major currencies borrowed and lent for OCR loans are the yen, US dollar and Swiss franc. Thus, there is no euro impact on OCR lending. The other source of loans is from the Asian Development Fund (ADF), which carries a service charge/interest of 1 to 1.5 per cent and a repayment of 32-40 years. ADF lending is intended for the poorest member countries. The source of these funds is voluntary contributions from members who contribute funds in their own convertible currencies. It is these currencies, in turn, which are lent to the poorest countries on concessional terms. The ADB lends out these currencies on a pro-rata basis. As a result, any loan may consist of disbursements in up to 16 different currencies. Now let us relate this back to the euro.

LOANS
as of 31 Dec. 1999

- **Ordinary Capital Resources (OCR)**
  - $27.8 billion outstanding
  - 495 loans
  - Borrowings

- **Asian Development Fund (ADF)**
  - $15.5 billion outstanding
  - 736 loans
  - Contributions

3. The euro

The European Union (EU) is made up of 15 countries, of which 11 are currently members of the new European Monetary Union (EMU), or euro bloc. Of these 11 countries that have agreed to make the euro their official currency starting in 1999, eight have contributed their own currencies to the ADF. Thus, eight of the 16 currencies disbursed as loans under ADF, belong to the euro bloc.

We have seen that the euro mainly affects the ADF loans of the ADB because ADF donors (including eight of the euro bloc countries) contribute their own currencies for on- lending. These same currencies must then be repaid. Let me now explain the particular aspects of the euro which formed the basis for the Bank's strategy.

EMU Composition

European Union (EU) Members	Economic and Monetary Union (EMU) Members	ADB Members of the EMU
Austria	Austria	Austria
Belgium	Belgium	Belgium
Denmark		
Finland	Finland	Finland
France	France	France
Germany	Germany	Germany
Greece		
Ireland	Ireland	
Italy	Italy	Italy
Luxembourg	Luxembourg	
Netherlands	Netherlands	Netherlands
Portugal	Portugal	
Spain	Spain	Spain
Sweden		
United Kingdom		

There are three important features of the impact of the euro: a three-year transition period, fixed exchange rates and no compulsion/no prohibition. Regarding the transition period first, during the three-year transition, period, payers may use the national currencies or the euro for settlement of accounts. By June 2002, the legacy, or national currency units (NCU), will be withdrawn from circulation and will no longer be accepted as legal tender. The adoption of the euro is, therefore, predictable and inevitable.

The second impact is a result of the fixed exchange rates. There is no financial gain or loss from converting NCU to euro at the beginning or the of the transition period. Why? Because the exchange rates for each NCU to euro were fixed as of 1 January 1999.

Fixed Conversion Rates

Austrian Schilling	13.7603	Irish Punt	.787564
Belgium/Lux. Franc	40.3399	Italian Lira	1,936.27
Finnish Markka	5.94573	Neth. Guilder	2.20371
French Franc	6.55957	Portug. Escudo	200.482
German Mark	1.95583	Spanish Peseta	166.386

The third impact, which determines whether the euro or the NCU will be used to settle accounts, is called "no compulsion/no prohibition". This means that the payer can neither be forced to pay in euro nor prohibited from paying in euro. The choice lies with the payers. Now let us relate these three aspects to ADB strategy.

4. Euro Strategy

The ADB euro strategy offered borrowers the conversion option of eight NCU to one euro currency to achieve the following benefits:

- To consolidate and simplify ADF borrowers' outstanding loan balances by reducing the number of currencies on each loan;
- To minimize borrowers' transaction volume and related fees for repayment settlement through this consolidation; and
- To provide the technical services and expertise of ADB to implement the conversion on the borrowers' behalf at the earliest opportunity (i.e. 1 January 1999).

The strategy was implemented through an awareness campaign using letters, visits and technical presentations. As a result of this focused and consistent effort, there was a 99 per cent success rate of conversion. Of 26 borrowers, 25 indicated their acceptance of the ADB's offer to consolidate their legacy currencies outstanding into euro. The one borrower who did not respond was Afghanistan, with two loans outstanding. Since ADB only acted on the basis of positive acceptance, this country's outstanding loans will remain in the various legacy currencies until conversion is mandated in June 2002.

The strategy

- Offer borrowers a conversion option at the beginning of the transition period:
  - To consolidate their account;
  - To simplify their loan service payments; and
  - To minimize the transaction fees.

Implementation Process

- Prepared conversion programs
- Sent letters on 31 July 1998
- Visited borrowers
- Organized technical sessions

---

5. Results

I would like to close by noting some key success factors. It was not sufficient for ADB to just state a euro strategy. This had to be translated into action. What was the action plan to obtain acceptance of the conversion option from ADF borrowers? ADF borrowers are diverse countries, some quite remote and others newly established, with unsophisticated and highly bureaucratic institutions. ADB has to take a proactive lead and had three lessons to share as key success factors, which are applicable when introducing any new change:

- *Start early.* In the case of the euro strategy, the ADB started this planning in May 1998;
- *Involve stakeholders.* ADB did this through targeted visits, letters, follow-up communications, and explanations to ADF borrowers of the benefits of early conversion; and
- *Provide technical support.* The ADF borrowers were devoting their resources and strategy to Y2K preparedness and did not have the budget or the human capital to dedicate to the euro conversion. The ADB, therefore, used its own expertise and resources on the borrowers behalf.

The Bank believes its early and proactive response has facilitated debt settlement for its borrowers and facilitated better debt management.

PREPARING FOR THE EURO IN THE PHILIPPINES

Cristina Orbeta

The impact of the euro on the Philippines is not particularly significant considering only about 1.2 per cent of the country's liabilities are denominated in euro. However, it has required the same amount of preparation in terms of reporting as in terms of introducing awareness about the euro. And in this respect the Central Bank's debt office was at the forefront of all of the preparations for the euro. We were responsible for arranging orientation seminars on the euro for Central Bank officials, for banking system managers and for the public, and we issued several news releases for the benefit of the public. We also issued a circular letter, which outlines the mechanics of the euro and the rules to be followed with regard to the reports that would have to be submitted by banks. We also sought to orient the public on the new format of our foreign exchange bulletin.

Every day the Central Bank would issue a foreign exchange bulletin, which indicates the conversion rate of all the currencies. There were modifications to this bulletin, because previously, it would only indicate the conversion rate of the currency to US dollars and to our local currency, the peso. We therefore added another column – the conversion rate of each currency to euro.

From the debt-monitoring standpoint, nothing had to be amended in our system, because it is already original-currency-based, but we changed the currency library to include the euro. As for corporations, we notified them of the conversion and requested them to indicate to us whether they had received notifications from their creditors, or the official conversion of their liabilities to euro so that we could also effect the appropriate changes in our own database. Considerable effort was required for actually reporting banking system liabilities, because their reports were more balance-sheet-oriented and more structured, also, they were denominated in US dollars and converted from original currencies to US dollars. Thus, there were some modifications to the system that involved a change in the reporting format to incorporate the euro as a currency.

With regard to the accounting system, the Central Bank had to maintain, and is still maintaining, four records: one in original currency, one in US dollars, one in pesos and one in euro. Accounting and bookkeeping of our own obligations are somewhat complicated, butI think it is also important that the Philippines is one of the first, if not the first, country to have issued euro-denominated bonds in the market, in April 1999. Prior to that had been in the market for foreign currency bonds, mainly United States capital markets, but this was the first time that we were issuing in the Euro market. And since we were the first, it was difficult to analyse the structure of the market – whether the market was likely to accept the amounts and the maturity. We had problems in determining and assessing how the price would (take off) from the existing United States bond market in terms of our own issues for corresponding maturities. Thus there were some difficulties in determining and sizing up the market. Although we had a lot of experience in the United States market, we had some difficulties in the Euro market. While we welcomed the opportunity to extend our investor base, it was also more difficult; when promoting bonds in a new currency for the first time, a number of questions are going to be asked and there are concerns that are different from those that apply to United States investors.

But bond issuance was successful, and from that we learned an additional experience that we really need to tap the euro market as a source of funding on a continuing basis.

That was last year and there has not been any new issue denominated in euro since then. And, as far as I know, there is no intention to tap the euromarket at this time (not even for the purpose of realigning the Central Bank's international reserves for instance). They have not issued or adopted any policy concerning a more active and greater share for the euro as far as international reserve realignment of currencies is concerned.

In addition, since we had a lot of Paris Club obligations, we wrote to the different Paris Club creditors to advise us of the conversion in their own records so we could be consistent. I do not think that most of the Paris Club creditors have converted their own accounts to euro, probably because some of the accounts are maturing by 2001; they, have therefore, chosen to refine the obligations in legacy currency rather than to make an effort to convert to the euro.

INTERNATIONAL USE OF THE EURO AS A FINANCING CURRENCY

Ettore Dorrucci

This presentation on the implications of the advent of the euro for debt managers will focus on the track record of the euro as an *international financing currency*, that is, a currency used by private and official borrowers who reside outside the euro area.

First a few general remarks: by severing the traditional link between money and State sovereignty, the euro has become one currency issued by one central bank in an area of, for the time being, 11 States. In this respect, they have become one economy – the euro area. Although the single largest country in the euro area accounts for slightly more than 4 per cent of world GDP, the euro area as a whole accounts for 15.5 per cent. This is less than the share of the United States, at 20.8 per cent of world GDP, but about twice that of Japan, at 7.4 per cent. Moreover, the euro area has the highest share of world trade, with a ratio of area-wide exports to total world exports of 19.6 per cent, well ahead of the shares of both the United States and Japan, at 15 per cent and 8.5 per cent respectively.

Given the weight of the euro area in the world economy and the legacy of the former currencies of the euro area countries that have been replaced by the euro, it is no surprise that *the euro is the second most widely used currency at the international level*. In this regard, the stance of the Eurosystem, consisting of the European Central Bank and the national central banks of the euro area, is based on two basic principles. First, since the internationalization of the euro is mainly a market-driven process, the Eurosystem adopts a neutral stance, neither fostering nor hindering the international use of its currency. Second, the implications of the international role of the euro for domestic monetary policy will not prevent the Eurosystem from maintaining price stability as its primary objective. Price stability is also a key precondition for a currency to develop an international role. It is a necessary requirement for investors outside the euro area to be confident that their purchasing power will be preserved over time, since price instability constitutes one of the main factors which cause exchange-rate and asset-price volatility.

Although residents outside the euro area make use of the euro for several other reasons (e.g. payment, as a vehicle in currency exchange, investment, pegging, holding of foreign reserves), *trends in the international use of the Euro as a financing currency have been the most significant development so far*. This holds true for both international bank liabilities and international debt securities, but it is much more impressive for the latter.

In the field of international debt securities issuance, in 1999 the euro was more widely used than its legacy currencies up to 1998. This emerges from the database of the Bank for International Settlements (BIS), which allows singling out the truly international (i.e. non-domestic) component of issues denominated in euro (around 10 per cent of total euro issues). According to this statistical source (see table 1), in 1999 euro-denominated gross issues of money market instruments, bonds and notes by residents outside the euro area accounted for 28 per cent of total issues denominated in a currency other than that of the geographical area where the borrower resides. By comparison, in 1998, the combined share of the former national currencies of the euro area and the European Currency Unit (ECU) was only 18 per cent of total gross issuance. The euro's growth was mainly at the detriment of the US dollar, the share of

which declined from 58 per cent to 48 per cent between 1998 and 1999. The comparison is even more favourable to the euro if one focuses on:
- shares calculated at constant exchange rates, given the depreciation of the euro;
- the bond and notes segment of the market, where, in 1999, the share of the euro (33 per cent) was just slightly below the share of the US dollar (37 per cent).

Of course, one-off factors may partly explain the development of the euro in 1999: for instance, some international issuers may have deliberately postponed deals arranged in 1998 until after the "changeover weekend". However, international issues in euro have been growing continuously throughout the year. In the second half of 1999, in particular, euro-denominated bond issues have exceeded those in US dollars both at constant and current prices.

		TOTAL	of which: EUR		of which: USD	
		bn USD	bn USD	% of tot [1]	bnUSD	% of tot [1]
1998	**Total**	**1027.1**	**181.1**	**18%**	**590.6**	**58%**
	Bonds and notes	618.8	143.7	23%	290.6	47%
	Money market instruments	408.3	37.4	9%	300	73%
1999	**Total**	**1182.5**	**329.1**	**28%**	**570.1**	**48%**
	Bonds and notes	709.2	232.8	33%	264.9	37%
	Money market instruments	473.3	96.3	20%	305.2	64%

Table 1 - Debt securities' issues denominated in a currency other than that of the geographical area where the borrower resides

Source: Bank for International Settlements.
[1] Percentage share at current exchange rates.

Besides one-off factors, other factors are therefore likely to have played a role. One of these factors may *be market expectations concerning the future development of the domestic euro area financial markets.* The introduction of the euro, in fact, involves a process of integration of national financial markets of the euro area into an area-wide single market, the size and liquidity of which will exceed that of the constituent markets. This implies a reduction in transaction costs and greater choice of financial instruments, which make the euro attractive as both a financing currency and a vehicle for portfolio diversification. A virtuous circle may therefore develop – the increasing international use of the euro as an investment and financing currency may feed back into the depth and breadth of Europe's domestic financial markets, thus encouraging further restructuring of the euro area's financial system.

Evidence shows that the euro area money market is already highly integrated and liquid. Significantly higher trading volumes in this market have already led to lower bid-ask spreads for very short-term maturities. Efforts to integrate national securities markets and settlement systems are under way. The euro is also leading increased to competition in the banking sector, thus strengthening existing trends towards securitization. Securitized financial instruments are easier to trade internationally. Furthermore, the unprecedented size of mergers and acquisitions within the euro area is encouraging the development of a large domestic market for corporate bonds.

It should be acknowledged, however, that a number of obstacles to the full integration of the euro area's financial markets still remain: separate national fiscal policies lead to discrepancies in credit and liquidity risk premiums across the area; equity markets and securities settlement systems are still segmented; and differences in financial market conventions persist. Hence, the short-term liquidity and efficiency gains are smaller than a simple aggregation of national markets would suggest. Most of the potential gains will only materialize fully over time.

I would like to conclude with some remarks about the *geographical composition of euro-denominated issuance of bonds outside the euro area*. I will base my remarks on the data made available by the European Commission, which cover the period from January 1999 to February 2000 (see chart 1).

First, during this period, around 75 per cent of non-euro-area bond issuance originated from the industrialized countries, mainly other EU countries (Denmark, Greece, Sweden and the United Kingdom), which accounted for 44 per cent of total issuance, and the United States (26 per cent). EU accession countries (10 per cent) and Latin America (10 per cent) made up the bulk of the remaining issues by developing countries and economies in transition.

Second, issues from industrialized countries stem mainly from the corporate sector, whilst those from emerging-market countries are typically sovereign issues. Since the first months of 1999, countries, such as the EU accession countries, Brazil, Argentina, South Africa and the Philippines, have launched euro issues in significant amounts in order to reallocate towards the euro the currency composition of their foreign debt.

Third, the geographical composition of euro-denominated bond issuance indirectly mirrors the euro's capability of acting as an anchor for many currencies in the so-called "Euro-time zone", which comprises non-euro-area countries in Europe, as well as Mediterranean and African countries. Out of 87 countries belonging to the euro-time zone, currently 36 are somehow linking their currency to the euro (e.g. through currency boards, pegs, crawling fluctuation bands, and in the context of managed floating). In particular, Lithuania is the only EU accession country that currently does not involve the euro in its exchange regime. It is therefore no surprise that about 56 per cent of non-euro-area bond issuance originates from the Euro-time zone.

Chart 1.

Euro-denominated bond markets: gross issues by borrowers residing outside the euro area

(January 1999 - February 2000; % of total issues outside the euro area)

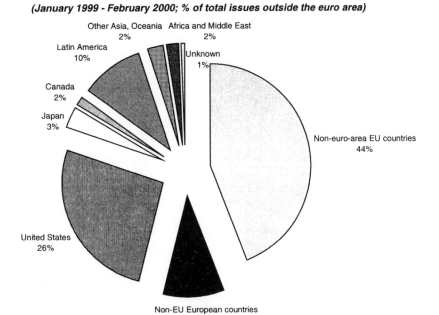

Source: European Commission

PANAMA – INVESTMENT GRADE POTENTIAL

Richard Fox

The aim of this presentation is to give a rating agency perspective on Panama and to discuss credit ratings in general, and Fitch IBCA's rating process in particular. Panama presents an interesting case study. Fitch IBCA takes a positive view of Panama, having signalled that we were thinking of upgrading the country to investment grade in February 2000. One of the reasons for that decision is Panama's very successful debt management strategy.

1. Introduction

Credit rating of emerging markets is a fairly recent development. For ourselves, even though Fitch and IBCA, which merged in 1997, have been around for decades, we published our first sovereign rating only six years ago, and our prospective partners, Duff and Phelps (with whom a merger is due to be finalized soon), have been rating sovereigns only since 1997. But we think there are advantages to that. Emerging markets are constantly changing and we think that by being new, we are a bit more open minded. Latin America in particular – with a range of very distinct economies and a spectrum of policy regimes – often challenges our way of thinking about ratings. We therefore attach great importance to having a dialogue with our clients. When we visited Panama in November 1999, there were some important policy debates going on, and discussing these with the authorities certainly helped focus our mind.

Secondly, although the final product of the rating process is the rating, this is just our opinion. Rating is as much an art as a science, and it is very difficult to summarize a whole range of complex judgements on different aspects of a country's political and economic make-up in the familiar letter score (BB+ for Panama). Thus, as important as the rating is, so is our explanation of why a country is rated where it is. Our reports are therefore very comprehensive.

This presentation looks at Panama against this investment grade yardstick, as a way of explaining the reasons behind our decision to consider an upgrade. Without going into what investment grade means, it is useful to review the implied default probabilities. Unfortunately, the only long run of data refers to United States corporations. Here the ex post incidence of default over 10 years at BB+, where Panama is now, is 15 per cent. At the lowest investment grade (BBB-) level, it falls to 10 per cent. Investment grade does not, therefore, mean that investors are certain to get their money back – not even AAA guarantees that – but the probability of default is 5 per cent less. That is the hurdle Panama has to jump to achieve investment grade status – it is significant, but not huge.

So what does an investment grade country look like?

2. Fitch IBCA rating distribution

Of the 63 countries we rate, 43 are investment grade and 20 are sub-investment grade. So that is 43/63 or just over two thirds of our ratings at investment grade.

Fitch IBCA Rating distribution

	Investment grade	Sub-investment grade
All countries	43	20
High income	29	nil
Low/middle income	14	20
Latin America	**2**	**6**
Asia	3	2
Europe	6	8
M. East/Africa	3	4

The table divides countries into high income (World Bank definition) – mainly the industrialized countries, but it also includes Hong Kong (China) and Singapore and a few Middle East countries – and the low-/middle-income countries, more commonly called emerging markets.

Two facts stand out: First, Latin America has the lowest proportion of investment grade countries of any region – only two out of eight, namely Chile and Uruguay. That is a quarter compared to about a half for the non-Latin American emerging markets. Secondly, over two thirds of the investment grade countries (29/43) are high-income countries. Indeed, of the 29 high income countries we rate, none are below investment grade. That does not mean a country has to be high income to be investment grade – there are 14 emerging markets which are investment grade – but being high income certainly helps. This is partly because richer countries can sustain a higher level of debt, and because high income levels tend to be associated with more developed social and business infrastructure – better education and health systems, better legal systems and basically better places to do business. So how does Latin America look in terms of income?

3. Per capita gross national product

In order of declining creditworthiness, we rate as first the two investment grade countries, Chile and Uruguay; then Panama, which we are reviewing for investment grade, followed by Colombia, which only recently lost its investment grade rating. Mexico, Argentina and Peru are all at BB; Venezuela at BB-; Brazil at B+, and finally, Ecuador is currently in rescheduling negotiations. (For comparison, dotted line shows the average for the 12 countries in the BBB range, which is the lowest investment grade range). A mixed bag of

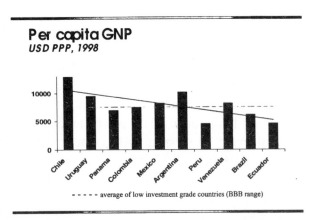

Czech Republic, Egypt, Estonia, Greece, Hungary, the Republic of Korea, Latvia, Malaysia, Poland, Thailand, Tunisia and Uruguay are in the BBB range, Chile is rated A, which is above this comparator group.

Thus in Latin America we find that two investment grade countries have per capita incomes higher than the BBB average, and at the other extreme, Ecuador is amongst the poorest. But although the trend is clear, there are exceptions. Peru is just as poor as Ecuador, but is rated higher. Mexico, Venezuela and especially Argentina all have per capita incomes higher than the BBB countries but are rated sub-investment grade. These exceptions remind us that the rating process looks at a whole range of variables and these other variables, which are discussed later, are what keeps Argentina, Venezuela and Mexico below what might be expected from just looking at their relatively high per capita incomes, and which, by contrast, support the ratings of Peru, despite its relatively low income. Panama comes out slightly poorer than the BBB average. That does not preclude investment grade because there are a number of poorer countries than Panama at investment grade, such as China and Egypt. But it does mean that we look for a stronger performance in other areas to compensate.

Probably the most important consideration in the rating process is the strength of the policy regime. Unfortunately, this is very difficult to measure. There are some specific indicators, discussed later, but an alternative approach is to measure policy outcomes.

4. Inflation

Consistently low inflation tends to reflect a strong policy regime, and investment grade countries generally have low inflation – 4 per cent on average for BBB countries. Thus the low inflation of Chile and Uruguay is consistent with investment grade, and at the other extreme, it is no coincidence that weaker credit-rated countries – Venezuela and Ecuador – have the highest – inflation. But again there are outliers, such as Argentina, with the lowest inflation in the region, and Mexico, which has the highest inflation among the stronger rated Latin American countries.

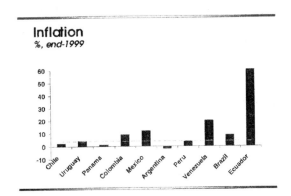

Inflation
%, end-1999

Panama does very well. As already mentioned, Latin America often challenges conventional rating wisdom, and Panama's US dollar-based system is a good example. Panama cannot print money as it has no central bank. It has no monetary discretion and faces the discipline of having to run a budget in line with available finance. This amounts to a very strong policy regime and certainly supports Panama's rating.

5. Per capita gross domestic product growth

Per capita GDP is the other major outcome variable we look at. In the past five years, only Chile comes anywhere near to matching the growth performance of the BBB countries. The Andean countries have performed very badly. That is partly because the past two to three years have been very difficult due to falling commodity prices. But Peru has faced just as harsh an external environment, as has Chile. And it should be remembered that these two also have very good inflation records. Their experience shows how important a strong policy regime is in overcoming other handicaps. This is not to say that Peru did not have a bad time during the Asian crisis, but without its strong policy regime it could have fared as badly as its Andean neighbours.

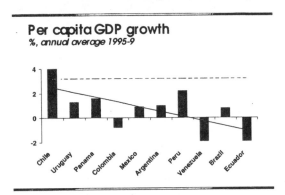

Per capita GDP growth
%, annual average 1995-9

Panama has been the third fastest growing country in the region over this period. We would like it to be stronger, because that would bring its per capita income closer to that of the investment grade peer group and help tackle some of its problems of poverty. Looking ahead, we expect that to happen, as the increased investment in the Canal zone, since its reversion to Panama, raises medium-term growth potential. However, that is not the main trigger for the rating review. For that we have to look at the debt position.

6. Net external debt/exports

A country's external debt burden, not surprisingly, gets a high weight in the rating process. We prefer to look at net debt, netting off official reserves and banks' foreign assets. We measure net debt in relation to current external receipts, which include merchandise exports, services and transfers. Because external receipts are, for the country as a whole, the main source of foreign currency for debt service, this ratio is a key measure of external debt sustainability. It increases along the rating spectrum, from Chile, with one of the lowest ratios (close to the

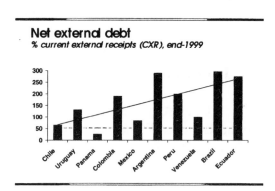

BBB average), to the weakest credit ratings, Brazil and Ecuador, with the highest ratios. This highlights the key constraint on Argentina's rating, and, to a lesser extent, Uruguay and Colombia. By contrast it reveals a key support for Panama, with the lowest net external debt burden in Latin America and one that compares well with BBB countries. Mexico and Venezuela also do well on this criterion.

There are two components to this ratio – debt and exports – discussed below.

7. Exports/GDP

Panama obviously stands out with regard to this criterion. No other country in the region can match the 50 per cent export/GDP ratio of the average BBB country; even Chile and Mexico only manage just over 30 per cent. A key reason why the debt/export ratios of Argentina and Brazil are so high is because their exports are barely 10 per cent of GDP. Panama is slightly unusual because of the size of its duty free zone, based on the Canal, which is similar to Mexico's *maquiladora* sector. And it is no coincidence that these are the only two countries to have significantly diversified into manufactured exports.

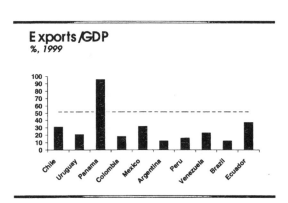

8. Commodity dependence

Manufactured exports constitute over 80 per cent of exports in both countries, which is even better than the average BBB country. By contrast, the rest of the region still gets about threequarters of its exports from commodities, compared to only a third for the BBB countries. Brazil is the only other country with reasonable diversification into manufactures. The problem with commodity exports is that , an average, they do not grow as fast as manufactures and they can be quite volatile from year to year. Thus manufactured exporters tend to be less vulnerable to external shocks.

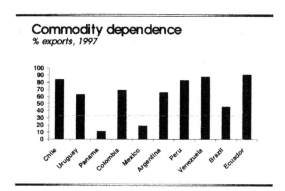

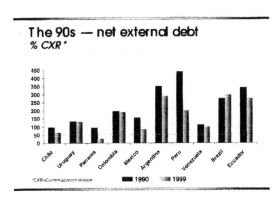

9. The 1990s: Net external debt

This figure shows how successful Mexico and Panama have been in reducing their debt burden over the past decade. Peru has done even better, which is a testament to its economic revival. Chile continues to make progress; Argentina and Ecuador have not done badly, but their debt burdens are still very high. Brazil's debt burden has increased, however, which shows that a strong manufactured export base does not automatically reduce the debt burden. Traditionally, sovereign risk analysis has looked at the external debt of a country as a whole – both public and private sector. That is because, in a crisis all debt claims compete for the same scarce foreign exchange. And this is often a source of misunderstanding between rating agencies and debt managers, since the latter are obviously focused on public debt. But the Korean crisis showed that even where a State has little debt of its own, private sector debt can bring the State to the brink of default if official reserves are used to support private sector claims. However, this does not mean that the specific position of the Government should be ignored. Sovereign risk is, after all, about the payment capacity of a Government. The further the country is in the investment grade spectrum, the less likely it is either to need or be willing to support corporates and banks in the event of external shocks. So in investment grade countries we tend to attach more weight to the position of the sovereign State.

10. External debt structure

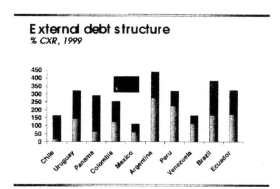

Comparing the gross external debt burden of a country as a whole with that of the Government, in some countries the distinction makes little difference – in Argentina, Peru and Venezuela for example, the sovereign is the biggest debtor. However, in Chile especially, but also in Uruguay and Panama, the private sector's external debt is bigger than the public sector's. In Chile, it is the foreign-owned corporations, and in Uruguay and Panama it is mainly non-resident deposits in offshore banks that we classify as external debt. But in these three countries, where private sector debt has been stable despite external shocks, the rating attaches more weight to the relatively lower debt burden of the Government.

Panama's public external debt is second lowest in the region after Chile, and Mexico's is almost as low. But a big difference between Mexico and Panama is that Mexico's banks are much weaker than Panama's. We can, therefore, be more relaxed about Panamanian banks' external debt than we can about the debt of Mexican banks. Thus for Mexico, we continue to attach more weight to the external debt of the country as a whole and less to the relatively low public external debt. All the recent emerging-market crises – in Mexico, the Republic of Korea, the Russian Federation and Brazil – have been triggered by short-term debt. Consequently, we pay particularly close attention to this.

11. Short-term debt by debtor

This confirms that Uruguay's and Panama's short-term debt is overwhelmingly non-resident bank deposits. Indeed, for most countries, short-term debt is mainly inter-bank deposits. We therefore spend a lot of time analysing banking systems, and include a section on the banking system in every sovereign report.

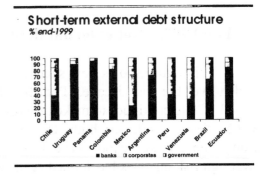

Short-term external debt structure
% end-1999

Argentina is a very useful case study, where the authorities have worked very hard, since 1995, to strengthen the banking system. And this paid off when, in contrast to the *tequila* crisis in Mexico, when bank deposits fell by a third, last year they continued to grow, despite the problems caused by Brazil's devaluation. By contrast, in Brazil, the authorities had to negotiate with international banks to keep inter-bank lines rolling over.

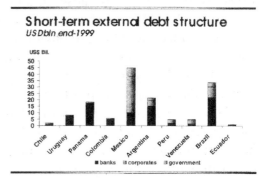

Short-term external debt structure
US Dbln end-1999

Bank short-term debt is a much lower proportion of the total in Chile, Mexico, Peru and Venezuela. However, the reasons are different. In Mexico, weak banks mean foreign banks are more comfortable lending direct to corporations – particularly the big exporters; in Venezuela, private sector external trade is very limited; in Chile, inter-corporate loans are more prevalent since the internationalization of the private sector; and in Peru, with the banking system 80 per cent dollarized, the need for external US dollar credit is limited.

Note that short-term government debt is generally very small. The *tequila* crisis saw to that.

12. Short-term external debt

In absolute terms, Mexico has the highest level of short-term debt, which we have been watching very closely recently. This is because while short-term debt gets rolled over in normal times, as soon as there is a crisis it causes problems, as we saw last year in Brazil. As mentioned earlier, we are comfortable with the relatively high level of bank debt in Argentina, Panama and

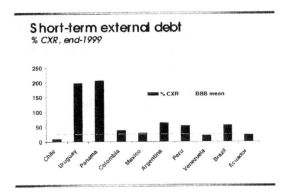

Short-term external debt
% CXR, end-1999

Uruguay. We are also getting more comfortable with Mexico's short-term debt. As we have seen, most of it is corporate debt, held by exporters, and the reason it is so high in absolute terms is because Mexico's trade is also high. We have a 25 per cent rule of thumb for a comfortable level of short-term debt in relation to trade and this also happens to be the average in BBB countries too. Mexico's short-term debt has gradually fallen closer to this ratio and is not that far off from Chile's ratios.

This chart brings home the size of Panama's and Uruguay's IBCAs in relation to their trade. And the high level of bank debt also swells the ratios in Argentina and Brazil.

13. Debt service ratio

With regard to debt service ratio (DSR), a traditional measure of sovereign risk, there is quite a strong correlation along the rating spectrum. Panama's DSR is as low as Chile's and equal to the BBB average. Mexico and Venezuela also have relatively low DSRs for their rating level, which supports their ratings. Splitting the ratio into interest and principal one sees that in the countries with higher DSRs, Colombia, Argentina, Ecuador, and especially Brazil – the problem tends to be

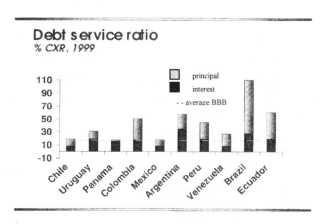

Debt service ratio
% CXR, 1999

high amortization rather than high interest. That is something an active debt management strategy can help alleviate. Thus, a successful debt management strategy can certainly raise a country's rating. However, a problem with the DSR is that it only includes amortization of debt.

14. External liquidity ratio

We have constructed a vulnerability measure that expresses international reserves, including banks' liquid foreign assets, as a ratio to all debt service, including short-term debt. A 100 per cent ratio means a country can pay all its interest, amortization, and pay off all its short-

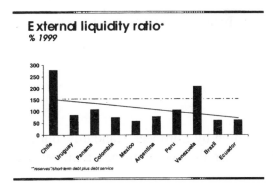

External liquidity ratio·
% 1999

term debt in a year. That puts Panama and Peru in a very comfortable position. But BBB countries have an even higher ratio, of 150 per cent. Chile and Venezuela do better still. On the other hand, Mexico, Brazil and Ecuador come out quite weak, at just over 50 per cent.

As with any summary measure, this is only a starting point. Just because a country has a weak liquidity ratio does not mean it cannot be investment grade. Most developed countries have appalling liquidity ratios. That is because external confidence is higher, so they do not need such high reserves as emerging markets. Ultimately, a detailed analysis of the debt structure of the banks, corporations and the Government is a key part of the rating process – and not a summary liquidity ratio or debt service ratio.

The next section takes a closer look at government debt, as it is sovereign debt that is being rated, after all.

15. General government debt/GDP

This measure is one of those used in the Maastricht Treaty to judge the appropriateness for entry into the euro area. General government includes local authorities but excludes public enterprises; thus, although one may not be familiar with our numbers, they are comparable across countries. Many Latin American Governments do better than the Maastricht criterion of 60 per cent. Many of them also match or come close to the 42 per cent average for BBB countries. The exceptions are the weaker credit-rated countries – Brazil, Ecuador, Panama and Venezuela. This is the first real weakness we have identified for Panama.

Note also the different proportions of domestic and external debt. Panama's external public debt/GDP is one of the highest in the region. By contrast, in Chile, public debt is overwhelmingly domestic, a result of its long standing pension reform which has created a big domestic investor base. Investment grade countries can usually finance themselves domestically. Elsewhere, only Brazil and Mexico have higher domestic than external debt. Their better access to domestic finance is important for their foreign currency rating, but not for

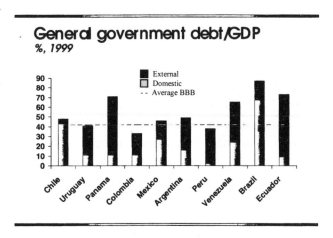

their overall rating because their domestic finance is fairly short term, especially in Brazil. This contrasts with the situation in Argentina, which has hardly any short-term public debt. This is because it makes more use of external finance, which is cheaper, with longer maturity and avoids rollover risk. The downside is that it puts Argentina at the mercy of volatile foreign sentiment.

The scope for domestic finance is becoming a key issue, especially for Latin American ratings. In Argentina and Mexico, for example, growing pension funds are gradually increasing the scope for domestic finance.

I wish to emphasize the fact that it is Panama's relatively high public debt burden that has been the main constraint on its rating.

16. Public debt/revenue

Panama's high public debt burden may not seem that high by European standards, but the higher debt levels we see in Europe are more sustainable because they go alongside a higher tax base. This chart measures debt in relation to the tax base, which is particularly relevant in developing countries because there are often weaknesses in collecting tax revenue.

There is a strong correlation along the rating scale. Only Uruguay comes anywhere near the BBB standard; Ecuador Mexico and Panama come out with particularly high public debt burdens.

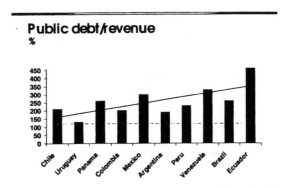

Public debt/revenue
%

17. Public debt interest/revenue

This comes out even stronger if you look at interest on the public debt in relation to revenue. So given this constraint on Panama's rating, obviously we are very interested when we hear that the Government is contemplating a major debt buyback.

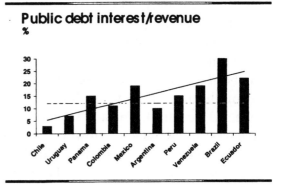

Public debt interest/revenue
%

18. Public debt/GDP

This chart shows the possible impact on the public debt ratio of Panama's proposed buyback; this could fall by around 20 per cent of GDP, bringing it below 50 per cent of GDP – to the sort of level seen in most of the rest of the region, and not far short of the BBB average.

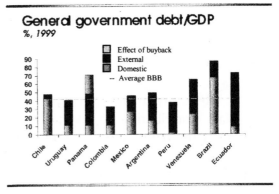

General government debt/GDP
%, 1999

- Effect of buyback
- External
- Domestic
- -- Average BBB

19. Public bonded debt

Since it is sovereign bonds we are rating, there is an impact here too – public bonded external debt would fall from 35 per cent of GDP to less than 15 per cent of GDP, which will be one of the lowest in the region. However, there is no magic level of debt that triggers an investment grade rating. Brazil, Colombia and Peru already have lower debt on this measure than Panama will have. But because, in Fitch IBCA's view, the debt level is the only major

constraint on Panama's rating, in combination with other factors, which might support an even higher rating, we feel comfortable proposing the upgrade, provided the buyback goes ahead.

But we would also expect Panama to pursue policies that stabilize the debt burden at the new lower level. The buyback proposal has stimulated an important debate about the appropriate use of the proceeds from privatization. We treat privatization receipts as a financing item

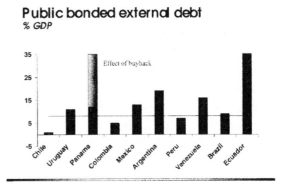

Public bonded external debt
% GDP

Effect of buyback

rather than as a revenue item; therefore, we would be concerned if privatization proceeds were used to finance current spending, simply because privatization receipts are non-recurring. If we thought current spending was rising to unsustainable levels, then, obviously, that would be negative for the rating. The beauty of debt reduction, of course, is that it brings a permanent reduction in interest payments.

20. Budget deficit

We have been impressed by the progress made by the new Government of Panama in reducing the budget deficit. These figures again are for the general government, and so are on a comparable basis, but not necessarily those most familiar to you. Brazil's high budget deficit has long been its Achilles heel; Colombia's deficit is one of the reasons it is no longer investment grade. By contrast, Panama's deficit is one of the lowest in the region. However, it should be borne in mind that the deficits of Chile and Peru

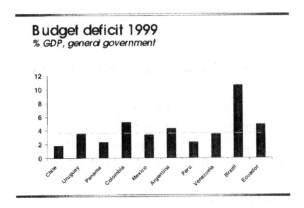

have been swelled by recession. Panama has been less hard hit by the regional crisis and so has not been under so much fiscal pressure. Its deficit has been more prone to political cycles, and we would hope that, in future, fiscal policy will be set in a more medium-term framework.

21. Savings ratio

Obviously public savings can make an important contribution to overall savings in a region where saving ratios have traditionally been weak. Again, Panama scores well; only Chile and Panama beat the 24 per cent average for BBB countries. Higher domestic savings reduce the reliance on foreign savings.

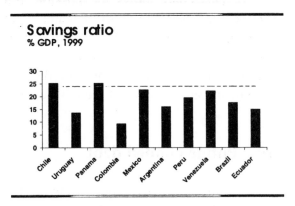

22. External market finance

Finally, looking at dependence on private external market finance is a way of judging countries' vulnerability to loss of market access. This indicator is the current account deficit, plus amortization payments by all sectors, less foreign direct investment (FDI) and credit from official sources (fairly stable). What remains is borrowing from banks, bond markets and suppliers (i.e. external market finance). The figures are for 1998, which is deliberate, to measure vulnerability going into the Russian and Brazilian crises.

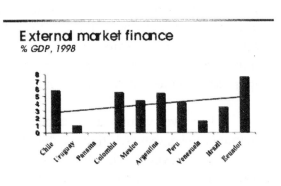

Excluding Chile, where the current account deficit was swelled by an unusual combination of overheating and low copper prices, the stronger credit ratings, as for Panama and Uruguay, are less vulnerable to disrupted access to external credit. Other things being equal, that would be reflected in a higher rating, whilst the higher vulnerability of, say, Argentina would be reflected in a lower rating. But it is important to distinguish between a "lower rating", reflecting vulnerability to loss of market access, and a rating which moves around with market mood swings. Our ratings are not cyclical, and have changed very little despite waves of pessimism and optimism in the markets.

23. Conclusion

I have outlined the reasons for our decision to review Panama for investment grade and in so doing, I have identified some of the key variables we look at. There are others, more subjective ones, which are difficult to measure. These include the strength of the policy regime; the strength of institutions, administrative capacity, business climate, and last, but not least, debt management policy. All of these variables can change and can change in opposite directions. A rating change is usually the result of a critical mass of changes in several indicators in a particular direction. It is unusual for a specific event to trigger a rating change as it may do in Panama. But this is because, as I hope is clear from my presentation, the debt burden is the main constraint and is something that may change significantly, assuming the proposed buy-back goes ahead. Thereafter, the key to maintaining the rating will be maintaining a sound policy regime. In the case of Panama, because of its unique monetary arrangement, that boils down to fiscal policy – maintaining a sensible budget, over the medium term, that stabilizes the prospective lower debt burden. If we were not confident of that, we would not be contemplating an upgrade.

SECURITIES ISSUANCE ON THE EUROPEAN UNION MARKET: OPPORTUNITIES AND CHALLENGES

Erkki Vehkamäki

1. Introduction

The introduction of the euro – which meant the controlled transfer of monetary power from the member States of the European Union (EU) to the European level – was a significant event in the recent history of Europe. European integration was founded on the strong desire of post-war Europe to sweep away nationalist tensions. The continuing problems in the Balkans remind us that peace cannot be taken for granted.

Today, goods and capital can move as freely between EU member countries as they can anywhere in the United States of America. European Monetary Union (EMU) is the natural result of this economic integration process, which otherwise would not be sustainable.

In this context, the integration of the securities systems' infrastructure will be one of the most important elements in supporting a single of the European financial market, and is, as a result, a necessary contribution to the European project. The project will not be an easy one, but it will substantially increase competition between the players on the financial market, which only a few decades ago was tightly controlled by the authorities.

Figure 1

2. Changes in the market

In Helsinki, Finland, the most notable changes in the securities market have taken place on the equities side, as shown in Figure 1. The chart clearly shows that, at least from Finland's point of view, the market has become extremely international. Non-residents hold almost 70 per cent of the total shares of Finnish enterprises. During the period from early 1996 to end 1999, not only has the market capitalization jumped, but trading volumes have also increased in the same proportion.

However, this development can only partly be explained by the creation of a single currency. The Finnish economy has boomed following a deep recession in the early 1990s. Annual average GDP growth (Figure 2) has, for many years, been over 4 per cent, and in some years, it has been close to 6 per cent. The GDP per capita has increased from US$ 19, 000 to well over US$ 22, 000.

The success of Nokia Corporation has probably been one of the key factors in attracting new investors to the Finnish equities market. Other factors, such as privatization of some State- owned companies and mergers between Finnish and Swedish corporations, have also contributed to this growth. Finland's membership of the EU and EM has also played an important role, as it has given Finland the necessary creditworthiness and increased outsider's general knowledge about the Finnish economy.

If we look at how the public debt has developed, the picture is not as rosy, yet, amazingly, the stock has begun to melt down in recent years. This has led to rather good liquidity on the market, and because State finances are in good shape, the bond market has not grown any further.

Although the new euromarket is still evolving rapidly, some observations can already be made. The euro has multiplied investors' opportunities to diversify their portfolios, as investments throughout the euro area are free from exchange rate risks. Investors can now buy government bonds or other securities denominated in the same currency in all 11 EMU countries. In 1999, the European market witnessed a significant growth in corporate bond issues, a phenomenon which is expected to continue. The average size of bond issues since the launch of the euro has considerably increased. The same phenomenon has been observed for trades in the money market in general, although not in Finland.

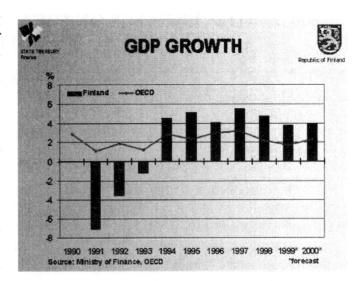

Figure 2

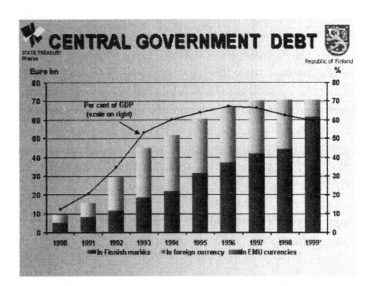

Figure 3

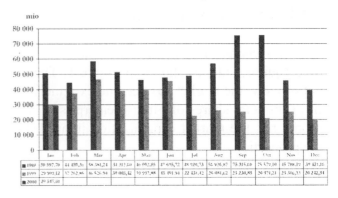

Figure 4

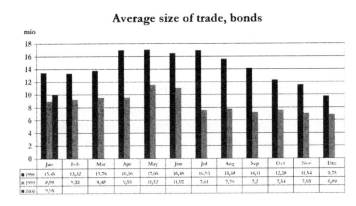

Figure 5

The total amount of issues of euro-denominated bonds in Europe accounted for about 50 per cent of the total issues in the first quarter of 1999. This was more than the total amount of dollar-denominated bonds. For the former European currencies, the share of bonds accounted for only 24 per cent of the total. In many European countries the re-denomination of existing bonds into euro has probably been the primary reason behind the development of this market.

Because of these developments, the issuers are now facing increased competition. Liquidity of instruments seems to play an important role and is also a major reason for a significant increase in the size of new issues. Almost 10 times as many issues with a total value of over two billion euros took place in 1999 compared to 1997. For a relatively small borrower, it might be necessary, in order to ensure liquidity, to offer to swap less liquid small bond issues with other larger and more interesting issues. As far as government bonds are concerned, the competition to obtain benchmark status, is keener than before, and depends on the duration of the issues. Liquidity has always been important, but the launch of the euro gave it added significance. Poor liquidity is also costly in terms of interest. Besides liquidity, it is also important to emphasize the need for marketing, unless the borrower is widely known, as on a large market small issuers are easily forgotten.

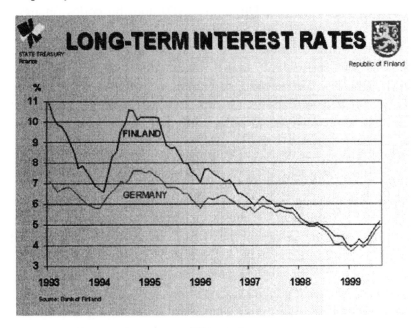

Figure 6

3. The supporting infrastructure

Though rapid development in the bond market has been evident, private bond and equities markets in Europe are still fairly fragmented. There are still 20 - 30 exchanges and "national" securities settlement systems left in Europe, including two international central securities depositories (CSDs), namely Euroclear and Cedel. The word "national" should be put in quotation marks because a number of them are private and profit seeking corporations and because there is often more than one CSD and one exchange in a country. In Spain, for example, there have been, at least until recently, six CSDs.

The solutions in different countries vary considerably. The systems operate under different conditions, laws, regulations and supervision. Market conditions also differ. Some CSD's have a monopoly in their country. However, typically they are very tightly controlled by local banks or brokerage companies, which sometimes see them as competitors or even a threat.

The euro is rapidly changing the European financial landscape. A common feature of the securities market infrastructure providers is that cross-border competition has become more obvious. Current trends include financial deregulation, alliance arrangements and technological developments that facilitate market access. These developments imply that location will gradually cease to be important. With continuing agglomeration development, some specialized centres might survive in competition against the major centres, which, in all probability, will anyhow attract the majority of trading volumes. Further centralization is, however, going to happen and networking effects can only postpone it. This trend is clearly suggested in a study by KPMG. According to the study, some 23 per cent of international banks have centralized their back offices, and an additional 50 per cent plan to do so.

From the regulatory standpoint, current market legislation has removed barriers between markets with implementation of the Investment Service Directive (ISD) and the codes on free movement of capital of the Organisation for Economic Co-operation and Development (OECD). The primary effect of the ISD on market infrastructure can be seen in equity and derivative markets, where the role of exchanges has been significant. In the bond markets, trades have been executed on an over-the-counter (OTC) basis. The secondary market now functions within a competitive regulatory structure. The requested services could, to a large extent, be provided via electronic networks. On the primary market, however, in order to be successful, contact with investors cannot be avoided.

The development of service providing infrastructure has so far been in the hands of the service providers themselves. Because of this, progress has been slow, and only some alliances have been formed: (i) between the nine exchanges in Germany; (ii) between the exchanges of Oslo, Copenhagen and Stockholm in the Scandinavian countries, (iii) between the exchanges in the Benelux countries and France; and (iv) the Eurex system, including exchanges from Austria, Germany and Finland. These arrangements are more or less operational. As mentioned earlier, the alliances are formed on the conditions accepted by the exchanges. However, it seems obvious that much closer cooperation is to be expected. If major banks are centralizing their own operations, they are unlikely to accept a situation in which they are forced to be in contact with several exchanges.

A similar development is obvious with regard to the Central Securities Depositories. The CSDs formed an association in 1978 which is expected to solve the technical problems created by cross border trading and securities settlement. The driving force behind this development was, however, the European Central Bank (ECB) and not "market forces". The ECB's predecessor, the European Monetary Institute (EMI), published nine standards for the use of securities settlement systems. The ECB's/EMI's goal was to facilitate the use of adequate collateral in the credit and monetary policy operations of the national central banks that form the Eurosystem, which is the European version of the Federal Reserve system. These standards give advice on settling legal, custodial, operational risk management and disclosure issues. They also cover issues such as regulation, and use of central bank money.

The Eurosystem has created a unique list of eligible assets, divided into two tiers. Tier one assets are the most liquid and marketable , while tier two assets are non-marketable and more domestically oriented. Given the principle of equal treatment between banks located in the different European countries, the ECB decided to both adhere to the principle of uniqueness of the list and to accept the cross-border use of collateral.

What is more, in response to ECB requirements, the European Central Securities Depositories Association (ECSDA) was established, with the purpose of strengthening co-operation between the European CSDs. In March 1998, the ECSDA published its first report on collateral management for the credit and monetary policy operations in the Eurosystem. The report presented a model for cross-border, free-of-payment transfers of securities that are to be used as collateral in credit operations between credit institutions and central banks outside the country of issuing. ECSDA members are currently implementing the recommendations offered in the report. For example, the Finnish Central Securities Depository has established links with Frankfurt, Paris and Amsterdam.

The next step in the ECSDA's development is to address and respond to the needs of the private sector participants in an environment where cross-border securities trades have increased remarkably in recent years. In particular, the ECSDA has to provide a safe and efficient solution for settling cross-border transactions, based on delivery versus payment (DVP). The solution must comprise transactions that are the result of over-the-counter trading (OTC transactions) and trading at an electronic exchange (exchange transactions).

The ultimate goal is to create a network of CSDs. This would provide domestic issuers access to the larger European market without the need to be in contact with markets in other countries. In fact, this has already become a reality among issuers in those countries that have established links according to the ECSDA's recommendations. The links developed from Finland have quite successfully been used to both transfer foreign bonds to Finland and to transfer Finnish bonds to other countries. The links also take care of redemptions, interest payments and transmission of some market information and market events.

Figure 7

Plans for competitive alternatives to the network also exist. Cedel and Deutsche Börse have agreed to create the European Clearing House, while Euroclear invited national CSDs to participate in its hub and spokes model. In the Scandinavian countries, the CSDs are seeking cooperation,and a plan to create a joint CSD already exists. From the issuer's point of view, these links or hubs do not take away the need to market the new, and the old, issues of bonds or other instruments. However, thanks to the links, the issuers and investors do not have to worry about legal differences, payments and other practical matters. Instruments issued in the home country can, with the help of these links or other future arrangements, be made available in other countries for trading and for use as collateral. The links also facilitate the diversification of the borrowing portfolio; and nothing; prevents issuers from outside the euro area from benefiting from these links and getting their debt instruments simultaneously on all major European markets after having issued them in one of the member States of the euro area.

FROM THE PARIS CLUB TO THE CAPITAL MARKETS: PANAMA'S SUCCESS STORY

Aracelly Mendez

1. How it all started.

In the early 1980s, many countries, including Panama, suffered from a shortage of funds, which led them to seek additional borrowings, thereby creating a problem. Furthermore, since much of the borrowing was done at floating interest rates, when rates began to rise, this further hindered the capacity of these countries to service their debt obligations. Eventually, commercial banks refused to continue lending, and in August 1982, Mexico declared a temporary moratorium on its debt payments. Soon afterwards, as other developing countries followed suit, an international debt crisis erupted. This resulted in many commercial banks being left with large amounts of defaulted syndicated loans which they were not able to write off even partially due to their large exposure and their limited capital base.

Starting in 1987, many banks began to set aside reserves against their exposure to least developed countries (LDC), and were then able to sell those loans at a discount. In order to find a solution to the debt crisis, many debt relief formulas were implemented:

- Debt buybacks;
- Swapping loans for exit bonds; and
- Converting of loans into local currency for equity investment, including in newly privatized enterprises.

Finally in 1989, the then Secretary of the Treasury, Nicholas Brady, announced a new coordinated restructuring plan. The so-called Brady Plan offered official credit in return for the implementation of IMF-sanctioned structural reforms. Debtor countries were required to make fundamental changes, which would foster investment and internal savings, and promote capital repatriation. At the same time, the official credit of the Brady Plan would be used to help reduce debt levels through Paris Club restructuring and the issuance of a new class of securities, thus enhancing the creditworthiness of the debtor countries. In other words, the Brady Plan required countries to establish an IMF-sanctioned stabilization plan and negotiate its Paris Club debt prior to renegotiating its commercial bank debt. Furthermore, the plan required banks and debtor countries to resolve or negotiate arrears in interest payments.

The Brady Plan recognized that the problem of developing country debt was one of creditworthiness and liquidity. Therefore, one of the fundamental tenets of the new plan was the provision of guarantees for new securities that would be exchanged for the existing commercial bank loans. In the process much of the credit risk was transferred from the commercial banks to the multilateral lending agencies. In contrast to the Baker Plan, the Brady Plan focused more on obtaining debt reductions than on providing new credits, and very flexible debt reduction mechanisms were negotiated on a case-by-case basis. They also were allowed to take the form of buybacks, swaps for new instruments and debt-equity swaps. The World Bank and IMF agreed to set aside 25 per cent of their funds for debt restructuring programmes. Finally, several creditor countries agreed to make changes to their domestic laws in order to facilitate the reduction of debt levels.

2. The story of Panama

In 1987, Panama ceased payments of its external debt, resulting in interest accruing and the debt stock climbing, from US$ 3.8 billion at the end of 1987 to US$ 5.8 in 1991; the country was declared ineligible for new financing by the international finance institutions, including the World Bank and the Inter-American Development Bank (IDB).

In 1990, Panama initiated the process to normalize its relations with its foreign creditors. In 1992, its defaulted bilateral debt of US$ 180 million was rescheduled under Paris Club agreements. At the same time, the country entered into a standby agreement with the IMF and contracted loans with the World Bank and the IDB to finance the economic development plan proposed by the Government.

In 1995, the country began negotiations with its commercial banks creditors. The debt stock owed to commercial banks was US$ 3.9 billion, including US$ 1.9 billion of arrears in interest payments. Creditor banks were provided with a menu of three options for the restructuring of commercial debt, under the Brady Plan. This set of options allowed banks to exchange loans for a series of new sovereign bonds. Banks could either exchange the original face value of the loans for new 30-year par bonds that paid fixed (but below market) interest rates. Otherwise, the banks could exchange the discounted amount of the loans, at 45 per cent discount, for new 30-year bonds that paid a floating interest rate based on the London Inter-Bank Offered Rate (LIBOR) plus 13/16th, or exchange the original face value of the loans for new 18-year bonds that paid fixed, below market interest rates for a 7-year period, and then a floating interest rate of LIBOR plus 13/16th.

Bank or creditor preferences were not only contingent upon institutional constraints, such as whether they would be penalized for accepting a sharp discount of the face value of the loan, but also on what the outlook was for future interest rates. For example, institutions expecting a decline in interest rates would tend choose the fixed-rate option because the value of their bonds would increase as global interest rates declined and prices of fixed-rate securities increased. Those institutions expecting an increase in global interest rates, however, would prefer to lock into floating-rate instruments in order to obtain rate protection.

Finally, on 17 in July 1996, the country issued US$ 3.2 billion worth of Brady bonds, with an estimated net debt reduction of US$ 1.2 billion. During that same year, under the San José Accord, the country also cancelled its arrears with Mexico and Venezuela, which totalled US$ 307 million.

The "Rise" of the Brady Market

Country	Issue Date	Billions of US Dollars
Mexico	March, 1990	29.60
Costa Rica	May, 1990	0.60
Venezuela	December, 1990	14.60
Uruguay	February, 1991	1.10
Nigeria	January, 1992	2.10
Philippines	December, 1992	3.40
Argentina	April, 1993	25.10
Jordan	December, 1993	0.70
Brasil	April, 1994	40.90
Bulgaria	July, 1994	5.10
Dominican Republic	August, 1994	0.50
Poland	October, 1994	8.00
Ecuador	February, 1995	5.70
Panama	July, 1996	3.20
Peru	March, 1997	4.90
Vietnam	March, 1997	0.90
Ivory Coast	June, 1997	4.90
	Total	151.30

After successfully closing its Brady deal, Panama considered increasing its presence in the capital markets and further reducing its debt and debt service levels. The Brady deal signalled Panama's re-entry into these markets. Since the country was in the process of implementing several structural market-oriented reforms, investors' risk perception of Panama improved significantly. In early 1997, Standard & Poor's and Moody's gave Panama a BB+/Ba1 credit rating.

It was clear for the economic team at the Ministry of Economy and Finance, that debt management has become increasingly complex with the globalization of the world economy, exacerbated by liberalization of the capital markets and large-scale capital flows. The team realized that there was a need to develop the country's capacity to manage risks associated with increased currency and interest rate volatilities, as well as liquidity risk. Without a formal public sector debt management scheme to identify, quantify and manage financial risk, a debt problem can easily turn into a major macroeconomic crisis. In Panama, the debt management objectives sought to:

- Maintain government solvency;
- Avoid seemingly cheap but high-risk debt;
- Issue debt that does not lead to sudden increases in debt costs or a need to refinance large volumes in short periods;
- Suggest long maturity, fixed rate, US dollar bonds (legal tender in Panama since 1904);
- Smooth debt servicing over time;
- Assist in developing domestic bond markets, which would reduce the vulnerability of private sector borrowers; and
- Manage the risks of contingent liabilities, which can lead to sudden increases in government debt.

These objectives were implemented when the country decided to take advantage of the complexity in valuation of the Brady bonds. This complexity derives from the fact that these bonds are hybrid instruments and their valuation is based on an analysis of the three basic components: the United States Treasury zero-coupon principal guarantee, the rolling interest guarantee (RIG) and the pure, unenhanced sovereign risk. Because of this, Brady bonds offer higher spreads when compared to non-Brady bonds of the same duration, giving an opportunity to:

- Capture the arbitrage between the Brady market yields and the international bond market funding levels;
- Eliminate artificially high-yielding, inefficient instruments from the yield curve;
- Reduce outstanding nominal amount of debt, which improves credit ratios;
- Reduce current debt service, and, therefore, reduce current financing needs;
- Replace floating rate Brady bonds with fixed-rate instruments, which eliminates exposure to rising interest rates;
- Extend the maturity profile; and
- Widen distribution and improve secondary market liquidity of benchmarks.

In trying to take advantage of this opportunity, Panama issued its inaugural five-year Eurobond on 13 February 1997. This issue was considered one of the most successful for a BB+/Ba1 country since the 1982 debt crisis. The issue was oversubscribed by more than three times and paid a lower spread than the United States Treasury benchmark. The main purpose of the issue was to fund a series of open market buy-back operations to retire and cancel collateralized Brady bonds due to their "cheapness" relative to the new issue. During a period of two months, US$ 505 million at face value in Brady bonds were retired using only 79 per cent of the new issue, with real cash flow savings of US$ 77 million.

To take further advantage of the arbitrage between Brady bonds and the international bond market, in September of the same year,

Outbreak of "Inaugural" Eurobond Issues

		Amount (US$ MM)	Spread (bp)	Maturity (years)
Jamaica	Jul-97	200	345	10
Ecuador	Apr-97	500	470	5
Oman	Mar-97	200	73	5
Croatia	Feb-97	300	80	5
Panama	Feb-97	500	175	5
Khazakstan	Dec-96	200	350	3
Russia	Nov-96	1,000	345	5
Slovenia	Aug-96	325	58	5
Indonesia	Jul-96	400	100	10

Panama offered to exchange Brady bonds for a new global bond maturing in the year 2027. Submitted offers amounted to US$ 600 million, for which US$ 713 at face value in Brady bonds were exchanged. An offering for cash was also made for the new bond, raising an additional US$ 100 million. This additional cash was used to cancel the debt of the commercial bank creditors that decided not to participate in the exchange of the Brady bonds. This operation resulted in real savings of US$ 30 million.

Market conditions deteriorated drastically in 1998 following the Asian and Russian crises, and the devaluation in Brazil. Consequently, there was a rapid reduction in the expected benefits of any open market operation. That called for a revaluation of tactics and so the country focused on optimizing its indebtedness by,

- Reducing vulnerability to swings in portfolio flows;
- Lengthening maturity;
- Maximizing secondary market liquidity and monetizing volatility.

In that sense, Panama entered a reverse repo operation to lock in the prices of the Brady bonds it intended to cancel and to adopt the policy of using a portion of every new issue to retire debt from the secondary markets, thereby minimizing the budgetary impact of the new issues. The refinancing risk has been minimized by extending the duration of the debt portfolio. Whenever the market conditions have prevented the issuance of long maturity bonds, the decision has been to maintain at least a two-year period between maturity dates, to further minimize refinancing risks. Following this principle, Panama issued a US$ 300 million 10-year Yankee bond in 1998 and a US$ 500 million 30-year Global bond in 1999 to fund the budget and to further retire Brady bonds from the markets.

Recently, the Government favours the use of the funds deposited in the Trust Fund for Development (established in 1995) to retire all of its outstanding Brady debt, in order to:

- Generate savings to finance high priority investment programmes;
- Maintain fiscal discipline consistent with economic and financial goals;
- Invest US$ 2.1 billion during 2001-2004;
- Generate an increase in the overall surpluses; and
- Obtain investment grade status from rating agencies.

Part 3

Financial management systems

THE ROLE OF INTEGRATED FINANCIAL MANAGEMENT SYSTEMS IN PREVENTING FRAUD

Jim Wesberry

1. Introduction

There are two major governance eruptions that are issuing in the twenty-first century: the "Corruption Eruption," so named by Moises Naim early in the last decade, and the "Anti-Corruption Eruption," the former's logical counter-reaction, as citizens across the planet repudiate and reject growing fraud and corruption in government. Historically, since the beginning of recorded civilization, fraud and corruption have erupted cyclically, to then be counteracted by citizens aroused to reform those defects in the prevailing governmental system that permitted the first eruption. At times the corruption-reform eruptions have involved revolutionary changes in the form of governance.

The present fight against global organized crime and corruption, the twin eruptions of our era, has already been described by United States Senator, John Kerry, as the Third World War. Professionally qualified financial managers strongly supported by top management are indispensable soldiers in the global fight against fraud and corruption in government.

One of the most powerful, yet least recognized, anti-corruption weapons at the command of those who govern is the establishment of sound financial management and internal control practices within an Integrated Financial Management System, made credible by punctual, professional review by internal and independent auditors.

Often, where plans are made to combat fraud and corruption, legislators, government commissions and officials place great emphasis upon legal and prosecutorial mechanisms together with punitive measures. Many persons do not realize that, in business, one of the major purposes of a sound financial management system is to combat and disclose internal white-collar crime, and so it should be in government. Others mistakenly think that the requirement of an annual audit is all that is needed, not realizing that auditors' hands are tied where inadequate accounting systems obscure the "audit trails", which permit auditors to find irregularities and determine who is responsible for them. Poor, disconnected and untimely accounting systems and disintegrated approaches to financial management provide opportunities for fraud, serve to cover it up, and, worse yet, if fraud is discovered or reported, make it impossible to determine and punish the person(s) responsible.

The tools of the trade of professional government financial managers, sound integrated financial management and internal control systems and practices – including timely and professional internal and external audit – counteract corruption in many ways. Perhaps even more importantly, in these days of wide media exposure of fraud and corruption, they *protect honest employees from unjust accusation by making it possible to quickly identify the guilty.*

2. The threat of "narcocybercryptocorruption"

Corruption in cyberspace will challenge corruption fighters of the twenty-first century on a scale greater than we can possibly imagine. The battle between "Transparency International" and "Opaqueness Intergalactic" – *World War III* – will be fought digitally with subatomic particles in a cyberjurisdiction never visited by humans, which has no laws and is not on any map.

Here is a flashforward to the possible future:

April 5, 2034 - The New York Times – Dateline, Cyberspace:

Cybercorruption has created a new class of electroelites, richer than all the kings, emperors and billionaires since time began. Thirteen supermagnates now control all economic transactions on earth. They are the creatures of cybercorruption, which, beginning early in the new millennium, began to bypass all jurisdictions and borders, move at the speed of light, be cryptologically impenetrable, and defy tax collectors, auditors, criminal investigators and prosecutors.

The originally illicit proceeds from narcocorruption, pornocorruption, gamingcorruption, eroscorruption, and armscorruption passed through multiple cyberlaundromats across the planet instantaneously, and within a few seconds, were available for reinvestment in legal enterprises, which remultiplied profits through cyberevasion, until ultimately, the group of individually sovereign cyberzillionaires came to economically dominate the earth and control all organized affairs.

The decline in strength and eventual division and disintegration of the nation State created the opportunity to maximize the economic power of the most lucrative transactions of the free economy democracy – those involving crime and corruption. Transparency has been opaqued by the "cybernarcocryptocorruptors". Bottom line: crime and corruption now pay...and pay better than ever.

Now fastscan back 39 years.

December, 1995: Dateline, Buenos Aires. Argentine officials today confiscated a computer from the home of a 21-year-old Argentine student. The United States Attorney General publicly charged him with illegally entering computer systems at the United States Defense Department and the National Aeronautics and Space Administration (NASA), including the Naval Command, Control and Ocean Surveillance Centre in San Diego, California, the Naval Research Laboratory in Washington, the NASA Jet propulsion Laboratory in Pasadena, California, the NASA Ames Research Centre at Moffet Field, California, and the Los Alamos National Laboratory in New Mexico. He obtained access to unclassified information about satellites, radiation and engineering but apparently did not access any classified information...(or at least, if so, it was not admitted publicly by the Government).

He first gained access through the Internet to a computer system at Harvard University's Faculty of Arts and Sciences, then moved into the United States government systems. He was also reported to have gained access to computers at the California Institute of Technology, the University of Massachusetts, and North-Eastern University as well as others in Brazil, Chile,

Mexico, the Republic of Korea and Taiwan, Province of China,...all without leaving his parents' home in Buenos Aires.

The United States Attorney General used cybersurveillance, through court-ordered wiretaps, to gather evidence on the Argentine hacker, but he is not extraditable under existing treaties.

Many of the world's countries are invaded daily through the invisible border of cyberspace, defying all possibility of the maintenance of controlled national territorial boundaries.

One of the major problems of the Information Age is that most people do not feel as if they are doing anything wrong when they are just "borrowing", perhaps not even printing out, electronic data from across the world that someone left unprotected.

Now forward to today, 2000:

- *An accountant alters accounting records in order to conceal inventory shortages or accounts receivable kiting or diversion.*
- *A Finance Ministry staffer obtains access to future project budget or tender records and communicates this information to a bidder.*
- *A clerk issues bogus cheques or cheques to phone suppliers.*
- *A purchasing manager buys from a colluding vendor at inflated prices.*
- *A payroll clerk sows disaffection amongst the staff by disclosing executive salaries.*
- *Vehicle use records are altered to conceal unofficial use.*
- *A hacker impersonates a legitimate client or organization and fraudulently obtains products, materials or confidential data.*
- *A debt manager wire transfers the proceeds of an international loan to an offshore account and flees to a safe jurisdiction where he cannot be extradited.*

There is not too much that has not been invented in the fraud department, but computers facilitate new and innovate ways to implement time-tried methods.

Today, here are some ways the computer can be used for protection:

- Force the selection of complex non-word passwords so that dictionary-based password-cracking algorithms cannot be used. And of course, require that passwords be changed on a regular basis. This can be done automatically.
- Activate a password-enabled screen saver that kicks in when you leave your computer unattended for 5 or 10 minutes.
- Encrypt all sensitive files and their backups.
- Use hierarchical permission structures to limit each staff member's access and even the content of their computer screens to the areas that they are authorized to work in.
- Incorporate into all applications comprehensive, historical audit trails that help identify users who make improper entries or manipulate data without proper authorization.

What will we do tomorrow, when all transactions and communications are digitalized and opportunities for cybercorruption multiply faster than techniques for protection?

What will we do tomorrow, when cyber-rich "supernarcocrooks" are able to buy whole Governments at a single purchase instead of the old way of bribing one official at a time?

What will we do tomorrow when proliferating new micro-States cater to the whims and needs of the cyberwealthy while larger Governments go bankrupt due to electronically diminishing tax revenues, which escape jumping from one tax-free jurisdiction to another?

What will we do when cybercorruption becomes a way of governance?

3. Some frightening lessons from current events

Here are a few statistics and the lessons they are teaching:

1. Electronic bank robberies average a quarter of a million dollars each. Only 2 per cent of the cyberrobbers get caught and only 1 per cent go to jail. Old fashioned pistol-toting bank robbers average about US$ 7,500 and 80 per cent are imprisoned, if not shot in the act.

Lesson: Cybercrime is more efficient and less risky than any other type.

2. Bank robbers are estimated to grab about US$ 60 million a year in the United States, of which about US$ 10 million is recovered. Cyberrobbery profits cannot be so readily measured, but could be about US$ 10 billion. They are almost never reported, nor is the money ever recovered.

Lesson: Cybercrime is almost unmeasureable, unspeakable and unstoppable, even today.

3. Of the Fortune 500 companies surveyed recently, 42 per cent reported unauthorized penetration of their security systems. Of major business and public entities polled recently, 75 per cent reported computer fraud losses in excess of US$ 100 million, but only 17 per cent reported the crimes to public prosecutors.

Lesson: Cybercrime is often quickly covered up and forgotten.

4. The United States Defense Science Board's Task Force on Information Warfare has warned of a potential national security disaster, predicting that, by the year 2005, attacks on United States information systems by terrorist groups, transnational organized crime syndicates and foreign espionage agencies are likely to be "widespread."

Lesson: Watch out! "The Sendero Electrónico" terrorists are coming.

The Third World War is being fought today against globally organized "narcocybercryptocorruptors" capable of paying enormous tax-free salaries to obtain the services of the best accountants, lawyers, economists and computer specialists available on the planet. Only one thing stands in their way to total victory – ethics and integrity in the public service in support of the peoples' anti-corruption eruption.

4. How financial managers counterattack fraud and corruption

Professional government financial managers are proficient in the techniques and practices of sound accounting, budgeting, cash and debt management, including the required internal controls which must be built into such systems. These techniques and practices inhibit, disclose and help confirm and identify fraudulent practices and their perpetrators in the following ways:

1. **Impose discipline.** Financial manager supported practices and procedures force a disciplined, on-time approach to public activity and financial reporting, as opposed to laxity permitting long delays in presenting information, thus impairing its usefulness and making its acceptance long after the fact practically automatic, since to question it would be to waste time on long-past transactions. Professional financial managers set up requirements that all transactions adhere to the same rules, eliminating the loopholes and alternative mechanisms that foster and cover up corrupt activities.

2. **Strengthen probability of detection.** Strong internal managerial controls put in place by professional financial managers, including appropriate audit trails (requisites of sound financial management), increase the probability that corrupt practices will be discovered and identified as such, permitting more prompt investigation.

3. **Create a disadvantage for the corrupt**. A professionally directed financial management system surrounds the potentially corrupt person with internal control mechanisms and vehicles which promote and require transparency and timeliness in reporting. They thereby place that person at a real disadvantage over those working in situations where lax controls and/or "false controls" provide cover. False controls are those controls, often legally imposed, which appear to impede criminal conduct, but actually foster and camouflage it. They are abundant in developing countries and often are designed intentionally to aid the corrupt, or are well intended, but facilitate corruption. They now seem to be growing in the developed countries, and are also often found in the international financial institutions themselves.

4. **Protect highly vulnerable areas.** Internal managerial controls are implanted by professional financial managers, especially as regards discretionary power over those resources and expenditures which are typically subject to a high degree of vulnerability. Typical areas of abuse are travel expenses, consulting contracts – often subdivided to come below thresholds of review – particularly valuable or attractive and portable assets, such as vehicles and portable computers, not to mention the inevitable temptation for kickbacks posed by very large capital expenditure projects or acquisitions in large amounts.

5. **Permit proper management and oversight.** Proper and timely managerial reporting on financial operations produces the feedback necessary to supervisory and oversight levels within the organization.

6. **Facilitate audit.** Professional and timely internal and independent audit, which focuses upon highest risk areas, is made possible where financial managers are present to insist upon adequate systems, especially accounting systems that comply with internationally accepted professional standards.

7. **Provide psychological control.** It has been well established that fear of discovery and punishment is a prime factor in discouraging corrupt practices. The knowledge that internal managerial controls are in place, constantly being emphasized and improved by financial managers and subject to selective audit review is a powerful disincentive to the potentially corrupt.

5. The anti-corruption advantage of integrated financial management

In the United States, the Office of Management and Budget reguires Integrated Financial Management Systems (IFMS), a term first coined and used to describe the new systems developed after the near financial collapse and impending bankruptcy of both the City and State of New York due to financial management inadequacy and fragmentation in the 1970s). Professionally directed IFMS provide powerful new high-technology tools, which can be applied in the fight against financial fraud and corruption as well as mismanagement. The following are some of the ways that IFMS counteract fraud and corruption:

1. **Multilevel budgetary control.** Budgetary review and control may be exercised at the operating, supervisory and central levels based upon varying thresholds of activity or other factors. Automatic flash points may be built in to call attention to deviations in areas of high vulnerability and to repetitive inappropriate budgetary manipulations.

2. **Avoidance of cash flow "surprises".** Actual cash flows can be monitored at appropriate levels through effective and timely cash management practices (as is done in business), cash flow forecasts can be prepared, and the typical cash unavailability "surprises", causing draconian austerity crises that destroy possibilities of achieving budgeted objectives, can be avoided.

3. **Spotlighting weaknesses.** Exception reports can be designed by professional financial managers to provide prompt feedback to operating managers in areas where weaknesses are arising.

4. **Internal validation of integrity.** The appropriate internal validation of the integrity of transaction data is provided for at each key step during the processing of transactions, and duly documented electronically, so that internal controls do not delay execution, and external controls may be limited to the post-audit function.

5. **Accounting control over resources.** The accounting system maintains general-ledger controls over all valuable resources which are independent of the operational level. Many Governments (both for internal purposes and project accountability) have, hitherto, been unable to control or account for important assets such as receivables, land, buildings, other fixed assets, vehicles, computer equipment, software, and all types of electronic equipment.

6. **Transparency in public reporting.** Complete and timely monthly, quarterly and annual financial reports are available for disclosure as is appropriate to legislative oversight committees and their staff and to the public at large, as provided for in most national constitutions, but rarely accomplished. Once transparency is achieved, it is hard for officials to cover up "bad news" when it is contained in financial reports. The tendency to

ensure that "bad news" is never published has been a major reason why disciplined and transparent financial reporting has long been avoided.

7. **Consistent enforcement of criteria.** The consistent policies and practices required by a professionally directed IFMS as regards resource control, such as a single Treasury bank account for all public funds and the prohibition of "off budget" expenditures, inhibit corrupt and collusive practices, and even where they persist, result in the entry into the accounting system of non-acceptable transactions which are labelled and reported as such (unless responsible officials are fired, which, in itself, results in disclosure of corrupt practice). In the United States we have been unable to prevent off-budget expenditures, and even manipulations, to move items "on and off" the budget in different years to suit non-professional needs, thus proliferating inconsistency. However, at least we do record all such items in our accounting systems and publicly report them. In many countries, "off budget" also means "off accounting."

8. **Decentralization of authority and accountability.** All unit or activity chiefs are in charge of financial planning and transaction authorization within their specific areas of responsibility; original transaction entry is at the operating level and managerial reports are immediately available. Thus, they may be held accountable for the planning and execution of their own financial transactions, yet are subject to either online, or very timely, supervision and oversight from higher levels.

9. **Reduced need for accountants.** Typical and repetitive transactions are precoded according to type and amount entered, and therefore, appropriate accounting entries are made automatically, thus reducing the need for accounting expertise, while at the same time reducing the possibility that transaction data can be manipulated.

10. **Immediate audit capability.** Timely entry of transaction data at point of origin permits immediate attention of the internal auditors to areas and kinds of activity identified as vulnerable to corrupt practice.

11. **Disclosure through comparability.** High-speed computer comparison of data available in comparable format (such as double salaried staff, retirees also drawing remuneration, or duplicate payments to suppliers) can disclose patterns of corrupt practices and their overall impact.

12. **Computer-assisted audit.** Computer audit software may be utilized in selecting transactions for audit sampling, vastly decreasing audit costs and increasing attention to areas which demand more frequent audit coverage. This is an anti-corruption measure which has traditionally been unavailable in developing countries due to the incompatibility and disintegration of any existing computerized systems.

6. Advantages to the honest

Finally, there is a tremendous need to protect honest employees from temptation as well as from any shadow of suspicion, which falls over them where corruption is suspected or discovered, involving either international projects or public sector activities in general. Every professional government financial manager has a double duty to do everything possible to protect other public servants, i) from temptation to perform dishonest acts; and ii) from damage to personal reputation due to unproven or unprovable allegations of wrongful acts, by ensuring that internal managerial controls are adequate. Here is how professional government financial managers provide an integrity safety net for the many dedicated and honest public servants:

(i)   **Limit the number placed under suspicion.** Professionally directed, sound financial management and internal control systems, especially IFMS, establish clear lines of responsibility and authority, provide for appropriate segregation of incompatible duties and provide for clear audit trails which limit the number of individuals placed under suspicion during investigations where irregularities are discovered.

(ii)   **Appropriate documentation.** Professionally designed, appropriate paper-based and electronic documentation of evidentiary matter which supports financial flows assures the eventual exoneration of the honest, even when they may temporarily be placed under suspicion.

(iii)   **Discouragement of pressure and executive override**. Pressure may be applied directly (by higher officials or peers) upon financial managers, staff or others to act in disobedience to established standards and policies that inhibit corrupt practices. Pressure may also be indirect, in that they are urged to (or rewarded for) do nothing, where duty demands action or reporting of irregularity. In this situation, professional financial managers can appeal for professional organizational support and resist such pressures. Tragically, honest staff soon leave public service if they have no means to resist undue pressures. A cadre of professional government financial managers, backed by a professional organization which supports them, can strengthen their resistance capabilities and give those under attack the courage to resist. Professionally directed IFMS provides a disciplined control environment and a series of specific control practices, which act to diminish the force of corrupt official and/or peer pressure upon financial staff. This, in turn, makes their professional career service more personally rewarding, as opposed to being an unbearable burden upon their conscience.

7. Conclusion

The Treadway Commission and the Committee of Sponsoring Organization in the United States, the Cadbury Commission in the United Kingdom and the Criteria of Control Board in Canada have focused private sector attention on the importance of internal controls for safeguarding resources and assets. But internal controls still need emphasis in the industrialized countries, and are basically in their infancy in most developing countries, the Governments of which have, so far, preferred to rely upon false and external controls, thus fomenting fraud and corruption.

The concept of internal control, which originated in the accountancy profession during the 1940s, has been expanded to now encompass the entire scope of managerial responsibility. It forms today's generally accepted framework for the safeguard and maximization of limited resources in the private sector, and should do the same for the public sector and for international development projects.

Fraud and corruption can never be eliminated, but they can be substantially counteracted, and, hopefully, diminished by professional government financial managers, duty – bound to insist upon sound, integrated financial management policies and practices. They can be accompanied by appropriate internal managerial controls, applied together with other disciplinary measures in the criminal prosecutorial and justice fields.

Finally it is imperative that the areas of government auditing, criminal investigation and justice administration be completely de-politicized so that they can be independent, effective and credible in our global society.

THE PUBLIC CREDIT SYSTEM IN GUATEMALA

Osvaldo Albano Landesa

1. The community and the public sector

A process of State reform has been launched in Guatemala, the first stage of which consists in strengthening the financial management capacity of the Government. This reform is based on a new approach to the role played in society by the public sector and by the civil service.

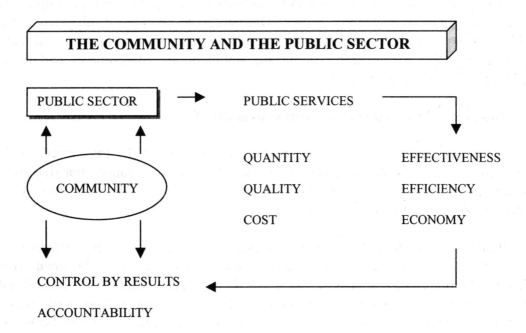

The goal is to bring the public sector closer to the community, which means interpreting what citizens want of the Government to improve their quality of life, while at the same time involving them in a joint endeavour to achieve it.

Citizens assess public management according to the services they receive, including, amongst others security, health, education and justice. They assess the quantity of services they receive, their quality and their cost and from the balance of this equation will emerge the community's degree of satisfaction. The systems developed for the reform of financial management are, therefore, based on a series of principles aimed at strengthening the above-mentioned objectives:

- The principle of effectiveness, in terms of the quantity of services which the public sector makes available to the population in fulfilment of targets established by the Government, linked to implementation of the peace accords and fiscal agreement;
- The principle of efficiency, based on an optimum combination of human, material and financial resources used for providing the services;
- The principle of economy, that is, seeking the minimum cost in the combination of resources; and

- The principle of normative centralization combined with operational decentralization, in order to take financial management to wherever services are provided and projects are implemented, in order to stimulate social control of public management.

If these principles are applied, we should achieve results-oriented public administration and enhanced performance by public managers, who, in addition to being assessed for the rectitude and honesty of their management according to the principle of accountability, will be under an obligation to account for their actions in the light of the results obtained.

2. Integrated public management system

The goal of the reform process in Guatemala is the organization and implementation of an integrated public management system, consisting of a series of subsystems, handled by different players, but all developed according to complementary conceptual and technological models, in an effort to generate synergy and optimum use of resources and technological, computing and communication tools.

2.1. Integrated financial management system (SIAF)

Operating under a unified computing system, the SIAF, introduced in 1998, has decentralized the financial management of the Ministry of Finance, transferring it to the ministries and departments of the President's Office. The SIAF is composed of budget, accounts, treasury and public credit modules.

The budget system: The budget is drawn up according to results, establishing physical and financial targets for the services offered to the community during the financial year; it is implemented through a dynamic system of quarterly reprogramming of budgetary allocations, the fixing of quotas for the execution of revenues and payments; and a process of monitoring and evaluation, including physical and financial performance indicators. The General Income and Expenditure Budget includes all the expenses and revenues of the central administration, while each ministry prepares its own budget on a decentralized basis, uploading it to the Ministry of Finance, where it is consolidated for submission to the Congress of the Republic.

Integrated Government accounts: Thirty-six entities execute their budgets in real time; data are transmitted to the Ministry of Finance by digital optical fibre channels; there they are validated and automatically converted to the State accounting system by double entry, and the liabilities generated are processed for payment by the Treasury within 72 hours through the banking system. The system in turn provides information to the lower levels of the public sector in the form of aggregated data; data originate from the executing units on the level where services are provided and projects implemented, and are forwarded up to higher levels, where they are aggregated for the preparation of national accounts and to supply information to international organizations.

The effect of the SIAF is to decentralize the financial management of the internal Financial Management Units (UDAFs) towards the implementing units (e.g. hospitals, health centres, educational departments). A Government communication network has been set up to operate the SIAF in Guatemala City.

INTEGRATED PUBLIC MANAGEMENT SYSTEM

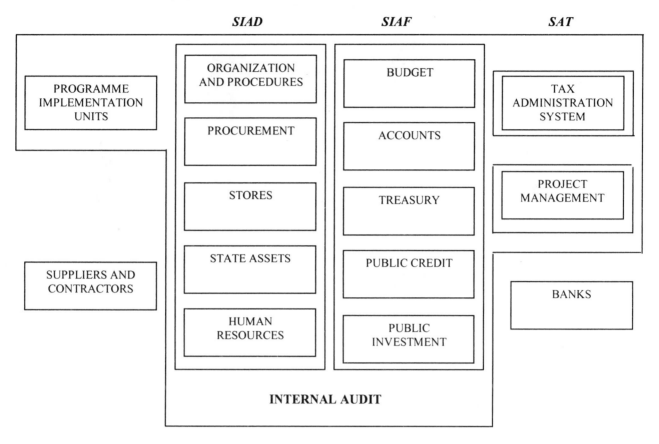

The treasury system, organized on the basis of a single Treasury account, each day programmes expenditure and income flows, coordinates the execution of the General State Income and Expenditure Budget according to tax revenues with the Technical Budget Directorate, and proceeds to pay moneys owed by the State to suppliers and civil servants by crediting cash accounts.

The system of public credit is being organized for efficient management of the internal and external public debt. Operations are being centralized, and procedures and relations with external and internal credit agencies improved. The system relies on an information system, which guarantees the timely payment of liabilities and registration of disbursements made by financial entities.

As of 2000, the SIAF is being applied in the judicial system and by decentralized, independent entities (including the Guatemalan Social Security Institute, Directorate of Tax Administration, National Technological Training Institute and port enterprises). SIAF III is currently at the design stage; it is intended to take the decentralization of public administration a step further by introducing the SIAF into municipalities. The communications network is being extended nationwide to all departmental centres accordingly.

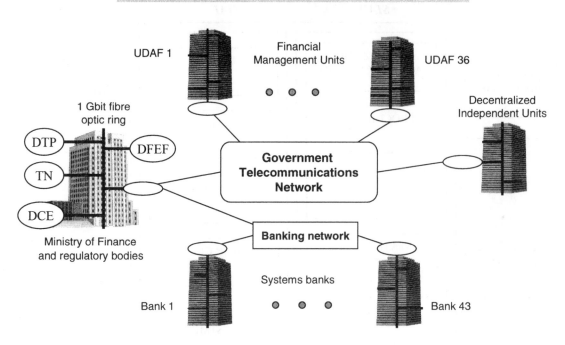

Government Financial Network

UDAF 1

Financial
Management Units

UDAF 36

Decentralized
Independent Units

1 Gbit fibre
optic ring

DTP

DFEF

TN

DCE

**Government
Telecommunications
Network**

Ministry of Finance
and regulatory bodies

Banking network

Systems banks

Bank 1

Bank 43

2.2.   Integrated administrative systems (SIAD)

As reforms in financial management were introduced, it was found that the ministries and government departments were very weak in terms of administrative capacity. This meant that the full application of the SIAF would be jeopardized unless financial programming was backed by appropriate programming of material and human resources in the various ministries.

An effort was therefore made to strengthen the ministries and government departments by providing the financial management units (UDAFs) with organizational handbooks and functions, subject to the rules of the Organizational Law of the Executive. The UDAFs were provided with job profiles and administrative procedures for their main functions. They were also given staff training, model organizational agreements, as well as computer and communications equipment with the necessary software.

Software was developed to operate the Integrated Administrative Systems (SIAD), covering procurement, storage and government asset systems, all integrated within the SIAF. The system starts with the procurement of an item by an administrative unit within the system; it ensures the administration of stores, using differing inventory evaluation systems and the establishment of maximum and minimum values; it ensures compatibility between store items and budget classifications, and inventory movements are reflected in budget and asset accounts. The procurement system provides for the monthly programming of purchases within the budget and registration in the SIAF on the basis of purchase orders for goods and contracts. The movements of inventoried goods are reflected in the administration of State assets and the accountability records of those in charge of their administration and maintenance.

2.3.   Tax administration system (SAT)

From 1999 onwards, the collection of domestic taxes and foreign trade dues by the Ministry of Finance was decentralized and transferred to a Tax Administration Supervisory Office (SAT). The systems developed for the SAT were conceptually and technologically coordinated with the SIAF. Treasury accounts have been opened at each of the public and private collecting banks; within 24 hours, information is received concerning tax collections from the SAT through the private banking communication network for automatic registration in the integrated SIAF accounting system. Within five days, the Bank of Guatemala receives the corresponding cash transfers, in accordance with the contracts signed with the banks.

2.4.   Human resource administration system (SINARH)

As the public sector's human resource management system in Guatemala is fairly outdated, a plan has been drafted to modernize it from 2001, based on a new Civil Service Act. The Ministry of Finance has already initiated a new design of the payroll settlement system to start the process.

2.5.   National public investment system (SNIP)

The General Planning Secretariat (SEGEPLAN) and the Ministry of Finance are jointly organizing the SNIP, for which a project information system is being developed as part of the SIAF, as well as new methodologies for the approval, administration, monitoring and evaluation of projects, in order to standardize procedures of the many public bodies participating in project management. In addition, a SNIP Bill is being drafted, defining the roles of ministries, secretariats, social funds, entities and other organizations that invest in the Guatemalan public sector, and the role of management bodies.

2.6. Project management system (SIGEPRO)

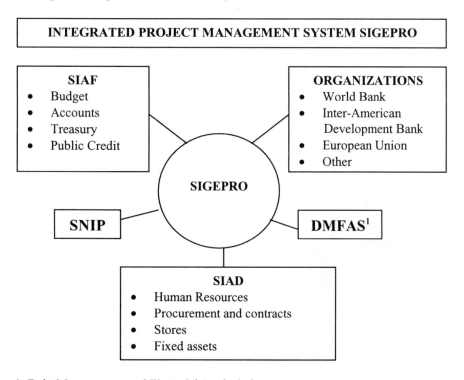

1: Debt Management and Financial Analysis System

SIGEPRO is a software for the administration of international projects, designed to meet a series of objectives common to the whole integrated system.

In the first place the SIGEPRO system will allow efficient administration of project resources arising from loans and donations, by executing the budget of the different investment components and categories, registering transactions in budget and asset accounts, and handling cash flows. As these tools are provided by the SIAF, all transactions will automatically be reflected in government accounts, while the necessary information output will be generated for international financing organizations (such as the WB, IDB, USAID, etc.) using their own methodologies. SIGEPRO is a multi-project, multi-currency system. It records loan and donation operations, thereby maintaining interconnections with the DMFAS and the SNIP, since most projects involve public investment.

Lastly, in order to improve project management, the SIAD provides procurement systems to monitor purchases, tenders and contracts, the administration of administrative personnel and consultants, and the handling of project inventories and fixed assets.

2.7.   Control systems

The development of administration and finance systems depends on strengthening control tools. The organization and procedures software and handbooks, according to which the systems operate, contain the legal rules and requirements needed to ensure conformity with legal norms and the principles followed by budget, accounting, treasury and administrative systems.

A further effort is being made to strengthen the Internal Audit Units (UDAIs) of the ministries and secretariats, providing them with equipment and training auditors in the handling of the new tools. The Comptroller General's office is also being restructured to adapt it to the new administrative changes and to enable it to develop modern external auditing tools.

3. Public credit system

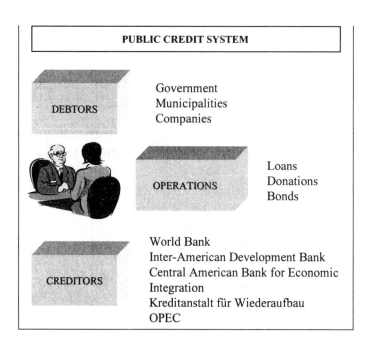

Within the framework of the SIAF, the Ministry of Finance has undertaken to strengthen the system of public credit. A Directorate of Public Credit is being set up to take charge of the integrated handling of external and internal public debt. Legislation is being revised to establish institutional responsibilities. Procedures are being overhauled to achieve greater efficiency in all processes related to the receipt of information concerning disbursements and to monitor the execution of loans and donations by the various project implementation units. At the same time, procedures involving the Bank of Guatemala are being revised to enable the Ministry of Finance to assume responsibility for the handling and completion of operations formerly delegated to the Bank.

UNCTAD's Debt Management and Financial Analysis System (DMFAS) is being introduced for the proper monitoring and registration of all operations. So far information concerning the external debt has been incorporated in the DMFAS and the same is being done with discounted debt. It is hoped to complete these changes by the second half of 2000 so as to incorporate donations thereafter.

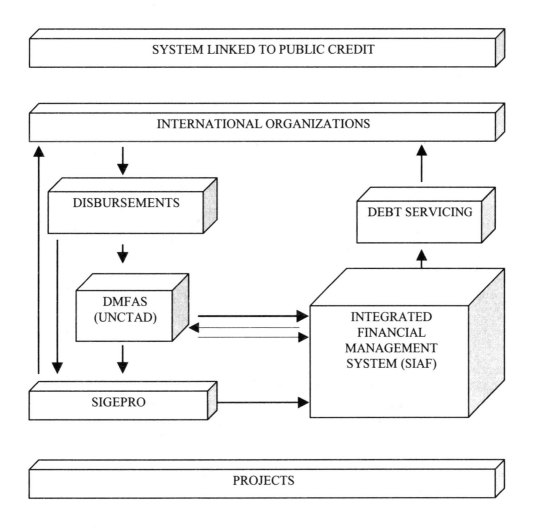

To complete the system, a further DEUDASIAF system is being developed, integrating the DMFAS and SIAF, which will automatically receive information concerning disbursements and the programming of maturities. In this way the DMFAS will become a significant support for the preparation of the General Income and Expenditure Budget and the quarterly and monthly execution programme. It will also generate data for the Multi-Annual Budget.

Within the integrated public management system, all systems are interrelated. Thus, when a disbursement occurs, the necessary resources are transferred to the projects and the information is captured in the DMFAS, either through the Internet or by fax, from the international organizations, and subsequently checked through bank transactions. The DMFAS automatically generates the accounting entries for the SIAF and at the same time informs the projects through the SIGEPRO.

The DMFAS also provides data on maturities, so that the Treasury can include them in payment schedules, which are then implemented through orders of the Bank of Guatemala. Payment data are provided by the SIAF and DMFAS, for the monitoring of individual loans.

At the same time as it registers budget execution, the SIGEPRO processes entries in the SIAF so that they are reflected in government accounts and informs the lender or donor international organizations.

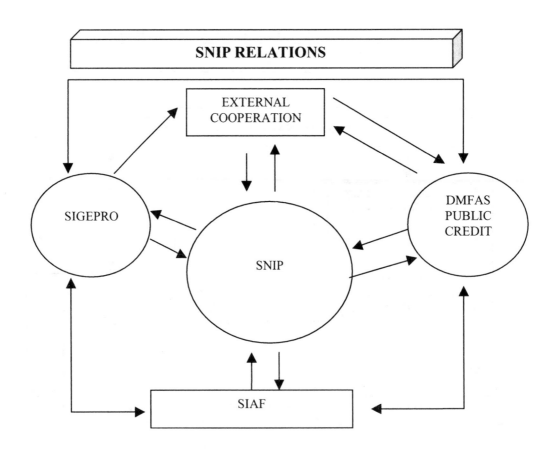

Through the SIGEPRO and SIAF, data concerning the execution of public investment-related projects are registered in the SNIP project monitoring system.

The DMFAS maintains close information exchange with all the systems: with the SIAF for the programming of disbursements and debt-servicing and subsequent execution thereof; with the SNIP because financing is generally involved in investment projects; and with the SIGEPRO for the execution of projects run by implementing units. In addition, it is a source and receiver of information concerning operations related to external cooperation.

THE ASTER PROJECT IN CÔTE D'IVOIRE

Christian Michel

1. Ministry of Foreign Affairs' stake in the project

(i) Partnership and transparency in public finances

In the various design phases, the countries concerned get together to validate both the information technology (IT) and the operational aspects: preliminary study, operational specifications, technical solution chosen.

ASTER should facilitate rapid access to all nationwide statistics, making it easier to assess the effects of public finances on the domestic economy and to plan investments when the State budget is drawn up.

(ii) Support for regional integration

The project proposed for Côte d'Ivoire is based on legal texts prepared in the West

---

Aster project

The objective of the Aster project (formerly called Integrated Financial Applications Programme-Public Accounting) is to design and develop a software package to manage the general accounting of the State and to monitor its expenditure and revenue auxiliary accounting. Currently, it is planned for six countries that signed an assistance agreement or asked to be involved from the beginning. The programme is now entering in its development phase and will be progressively implemented in the following countries: Benin, Burkina Faso, Côte d'Ivoire, Gabon, Mauritania and Senegal.

African Economic and Monetary Union (WAEMU). ASTER should, of course, be suitable for use by other legal and accounting systems, but it should certainly be a tool for promoting regional reforms, and thus supporting regional attempts to better harmonize budgetary policies.

(iii) Integrity of an IT system for public accounting

The government authorities should retain long-term economic and technical control over the software package; they have an exclusive right to use the software, and can make free use of the results of the services provided for in the contract. The intention is to ensure that French cooperation is independent of suppliers.

(iii) Facilitate the exchange of budgetary and accounting data

Installing the software should make it easier to:
- Develop an integrated accounting process, from the initial entries (in the networked terminals) to the centralized collection of national data, in order to produce the various public-finance performance indicators (including the State flow-of-funds table);
- Consolidate relationships with the officials who authorize expenditure, by:
    - Standardizing schedules;
    - Simplifying budgetary and accounting payments; and
    - Preparing for auditing operations.

For all these reasons, training is also a vital part of the process and should be included as a prerequisite for the success of the project (training both administrative and IT staff).

For each country, all these conditions are spelled out in an assistance agreement covering, among other things:

- Organization of the project;
- Description of the services to be provided: preliminary studies, supervision of installation, parameter-setting, validation, tests, training of trainers, top-level support;
- Each party's commitments: methodology, provision of staff, assistance to organizations in the country; and
- Each party's financial responsibilities.

2. Main features of the project

The ASTER project is akin to an institution and requires strong political will in each country, as well as long-term technical commitment. In this sense, it is a global undertaking; it is not, strictly speaking, an IT tool. The process should involve all concerned in the management of the project, particularly in defining a modern framework for State accounting procedures.

ASTER provides a structural framework: While each applicant country is free to set its own administrative rules, the project contains a minimum number of requirements that are essential to the functioning of the software:

- Not all the accountants can create new accounts: only one central actor can do this.
- The functions are based on the double-entry principle. The software can only be installed in the secondary accounting terminals in countries that use the single-entry system after a modern accounting system has been set up for the whole country.

ASTER technology: The tools used conform to the latest international IT norms and standards; the system is designed using the object-oriented approach, and making use of standard, reliable IT tools (Oracle database management system, Oracle development tools, UNIX and Windows NT operating systems and Internet technology).

Before ASTER is installed, a number of steps must be taken to ensure its optimal use, its effectiveness in managing public finances and its durability. This requirement involves revising legislative and regulatory provisions (directives on budget law, general regulations on public accounting, functional and organizational provisions, budgetary and accounting schedules) and modernizing the country's financial institutions in order to:

- Rationalize information or decision-making processes to produce a common system;
- Improve the reliability of overviews and published results; and
- Encourage multilateral supervision.

Experience with this kind of process has shown that at least two years of preparation are needed before this type of software can be installed.

3. Project design

3.1. Scope

The aim of the project is to handle the State's bookkeeping and to monitor the implementation of the budget, through:

- Bookkeeping for both centralized and non-centralized finance departments;
- Exchange of information among officials who authorize expenditure and other financial administrators; and
- Production of the documents needed to manage public finances.

3.2. Software features

- Origins: The software package grew out of a preliminary study carried out in Côte d'Ivoire (the pilot country) and in the four countries associated with the project from the start Burkina Faso, Gabon, Mauritania and Senegal.
- On the basis of this study, specifications were drawn up and provided a road map for the automation process. Thanks to the specifications, an adaptable high-performance IT tool can be supplied.
- Multiplatform: The software package is configured so as to comply with international norms and standards. This is essential given the diversity of countries, which, nevertheless, have a public accounting system as a common factor.
- It is flexible: In addition to the core product, there will be modules adaptable to the administrative arrangements of each country. It is, therefore, not a fixed software package, but one that allows each country to meet its different needs.
- It is multilingual.
- It sends and receives information: It should allow upstream and downstream links with other actors – officials authorizing expenditure, other financial administrators and public decision-makers.

3.3. The functional modules

The system has six functional modules:

(i) *The reference management module* brings together the elements for setting parameters shared by all the software modules: specialization by country, description of the network of finance departments and officials authorizing expenditure, authorizations, budgetary and accounting schedules and technical elements of the operation.

(ii) *The third-party management module* handles general data on creditors and debtors.

(iii) *The general accounting module* handles the bookkeeping: capture of accounting entries, transfers between finance departments, account statements and publication of accounts.

(iv) *The auxiliary accounting module* for expenditure and revenue records, budget forecasts and budget use, and credit controls.

(v) *The standard-exchange module* takes into account the exchange of data between actors: files received or to be sent, and storage of these exchanges.

(vi) *The packaging module* contains the systems added to the installation at different sites: automatic installation procedures, maintenance applications and associated data migration.

3.4.   Technical architecture proposed

- A central system – a transactional client-server system operating on a local area network;
- Two specialized sub-systems, comprising:
  (i)   The stand-alone work station corresponding to the finance departments connected to the main system. They comprise either a single work station or are connected to local area networks; and
  (ii) Distant computers (Web client) that can be used by officials to consult summary publications.

Conclusion

The ASTER project is a good example of project cooperation. Côte d'Ivoire is sufficiently advanced in its preparations to be able to host the new system in mid-2000.

It is a system downstream of debt management, as it collects global information on debt for inclusion in a State's overall accounts. From this point of view, ASTER perfectly complements the Debt Management and Financial Analysis System (DMFAS) developed by UNCTAD.

The project will gradually be extended beyond sub-Saharan Africa to cover geographical areas such as the Maghreb and Central and Eastern Europe.

PLANNING FOR DEBT MANAGEMENT: A COMPUTER-BASED DECISION SUPPORT TOOL FOR ANALYSING DEBT CAPACITY

Leonard P. Wales

1. Introduction

In 1992, Fairfax County in Virginia, the United States of America, faced a recession resulting in, among other negative effects, a diminution of its debt capacity. At that time the County's authorized and planned Five-year Capital Improvement Program (CIP) projected requirements for new debt of almost US$ 975 million through 1997. These requirements reflected capital needs for schools, roads, a new jail, parks, storm drainage and various other public improvements. Its existing debt was already over US$ 940 million, and debt service claimed 9 per cent of the general fund budget. The planned programme was projected to increase debt service requirements to well over 11 per cent of the budget if carried out as planned. It was believed that increasing levels of debt would jeopardize the County's coveted triple-A bond rating. As a result, long-standing County management principles and objectives were closely examined for continued relevance and effectiveness under the new fiscal realities.

Since 1975, Fairfax County's financial management has been governed by a set of firm principles, designed to ensure the long-term stability of its finances. These policies, known as the Ten Principles of Sound Financial Management, were developed as part of an effort to transform the county from a weak AA to a strong triple-A credit rating, in the words of its then financial adviser. In fact, since 1978, the leading rating agencies have granted Fairfax County the triple-A rating which is, the highest rating possible. This rating gives Fairfax County bonds an unusually high level of marketability, and enables the County to borrow for needed capital improvements at low rates of interest, thereby realizing significant savings in debt service. Among the County's financial management principles is a self-imposed limitation placed on net debt, and restricting the share of debt service in General Fund expenditures. At the time, net debt stood at 1.2 per cent of assessed value compared to a Board-established limit of 3 per cent. The crucial factor, however, was a 10 per cent limit established for debt service in order to ensure that sufficient resources were available for essential services such as schools and public safety.

In order to plan appropriately in this situation, and rationally address potential conflicts, a more effective decision support mechanism was required to blend the capital planning process and financial forecasting in such a way as to maximize the application of resources within the constraints of fiscal reality.

2. Planning

The County uses two planning systems for financial management governed by the Ten Principles:

- The Five-year Financial Forecast, which focuses on recurring tax revenues and operating expenditures; and
- The Five-year Capital Improvement Program.

During the growth years of the 1980s, only a loose association between the two was necessary. Management of bond sales was accomplished through analysis of cash flow requirements, and by matching projected debt service to projected revenues and expenditures. During this period, the financial forecast had always projected more than enough revenues to fund all operating requirements, pay-as-you-go capital needs and bond programmes so that the debt ratios were never approached. In light of the new fiscal situation of the 1990s, a new process was required to achieve closer coordination of the two plans.

Using the Ten Principles as the basis for the programme, the planning processes were merged to analyse cash flow patterns, match bond sale amounts to construction needs (a just-in-time method of planning sales), and balance debt levels with the current and projected revenue patterns.

3. The model

A personal computer model was developed to provide the decision support tool for this new process. Utilizing Lotus 123, a series of linked spreadsheets was developed by County staff (with much consultation of the user's guide) to calculate the ratios generated by various combinations of demographic, financial forecast and capital projects data. Primary inputs and resources included:

- Projected cash flow for authorized projects and planned sales (under the CIP);
- Projected new referendums (as part of the CIP);
- Five-year revenue and disbursement projections (financial forecast);
- Interest rate assumptions (variable).

The model itself calculates changes in debt service based on bond sales and interest rate projections and compares those calculations to disbursements as a simple ratio. The model is also capable of generating other valuable ratios, such as projected net debt as a percentage of market value, net debt per capita and net debt per capita as a percentage of per capita income, based on inputs from demographic and tax base projections. The primary product was a debt capacity projection (table 1), which starts with a display of the current planned programme of sales and the ratios generated by those sales (Lines A - D.) The chart then displays the adjustments to the current plan (plus or minus), necessary to achieve the desired target (Lines E - F.) During this first round of decisions, the model was programmed to calculate for the 10 per cent debt service limit. For any given projected pattern of disbursements and programmed sales, the model will calculate the minimum changes to sales necessary so that total debt service will not exceed 10 per cent.

The primary advantage of the model is the ease of calculation and flexibility offered by changing assumptions, and its adaptability to changes in policy or economic conditions.

4. The decision-support process

When applied against the projected economic conditions and the demands of new referendums, the model established that a total of over US$ 220 million of projected sales from fiscal year (FY) 1993 through 1997 would be necessary to eliminate or defer from the nearly

US$ 1 billion proposed five-year CIP, a decrease of nearly 25 per cent. This was based on a projected average annual revenue increase of 5.2 per cent. Reasonable manipulations of interest rate assumptions, and projections using more optimistic revenue projections failed to improve the picture significantly, or justify a programme in excess of the US$ 750 million five-year sales limit established by the Ten Principles in 1988. The assumptions finally agreed upon and used were consistent with the observed behaviour of the economy and reasonable economic forecasts.

In order to consider the options available for implementing such a large curtailment of the capital programme, a process was created to sort and prioritize among the competing demands. A team of County managers from the key financial, planning and public works departments met to prepare a report to the Board and set criteria with which to establish project priorities.

As a first step, the committee initiated a review of all projects then under way or under contract, determined the next logical stopping point for each (e.g. completion of design or land acquisition), and projected costs to that point. Assuming all projects were curtailed and deferred at the next logical stopping point, the committee then used the model to calculate the total value of projects which could be continued while remaining within the five-year target of US$ 750 million. This figure actually overshot the target of US$ 220 million, resulting in a reduction of US$ 291 million from the proposed plan. Armed with this figure, the committee then proposed four criteria with which to assess and prioritize project restoration up to the limit permitted – a total of US$ 71 million under this scenario. The criteria used included the following:

- Legal: Projects which are affected by current or potential legal action.
- Alleviating threatening conditions: Projects designed to protect property or persons. Federal/state commitments: Federal/state-granted projects funded by a combination of County bond funds and Federal/state matching funds, for which application has been made and commitments received.
- Maintaining expertise: Project activity sufficient to retain some County staff; and contract expertise to minimize loss of time, efficiency or effectiveness when programmes are recommenced.

When these criteria were applied to the list of potentially deferred projects, projects proposed for continuation included parks, transportation facilities and roads, storm drainage, human services facilities and public safety facilities. Cash flow from new referendums for transportation and schools was analysed and sales included. Any project additions to be restored would require additional deferrals to balance.

The econometric data, the financial forecast and the results of the model were presented to a newly-elected Board of Supervisors in January of 1992, along with staff recommendations. After two work sessions, at which additional data were presented and project priorities discussed, the Board adopted the staff recommendations with amendments. The tangible results have been that the County was able to trim over US$ 220 million of intended CIP projects, some of which had already received voter approval, while at the same time seeking new voter approval for US$ 130 million of new Transportation Improvements Bonds in 1992, and US$ 140 million of new School Bonds in 1993. Major projects, such as roads and transportation improvements, schools and a new jail, are continuing to move forward.

Management in this fashion has permitted a bond-funded capital construction programme totalling US$ 753 million in the five-year period, 1993-1997, to proceed despite the worst economic recession and curtailment of County revenues for the last 30 years. The stated priorities of the Board, to focus on school construction and renovation, transportation improvements and the construction of a new jail, were met.

5. Future applications

In each year since that historic decision, the debt capacity model has been used to reassess the County's debt position against the projected financial forecast. Each time the Board has upheld the Ten Principles of Financial Management as the policy basis for management of the County's debt. Except for minor adjustments, the plan established in 1992 has remained intact, and over US$ 130 million of authorized projects remain deferred, even in the face of tremendous political pressure to restore or increase allocations for pressing needs. In FY 1994, for example, in the face of continued lacklustre revenue performance, construction of the new jail was delayed for yet another year. However, the use of the model permitted other County priorities to be funded, including $204 million of new School bonds approved in 1995, the single largest bond question ever on a County ballot.

The model has also proved to be adaptable to changing economic conditions and policy emphasis. During the early 1990s, as the County worked its way through the recession, it was hoped that revenue growth would rebound to a level that could sustain a restored capital programme and an increasing demand for services as a result of population growth. Unfortunately, revenues did not rebound, as hoped, and remained relatively flat. The operating budget during this period was cut back, showing real cuts in 1993 and minimal growth thereafter, in line with revenue projections. The real estate market showed minimal to no growth in residential values and continued to show what eventually became six straight years of decline in commercial values. During this period a total of 1,512 jobs were lost, representing 13.5 per cent of the workforce.

However, this period was also one of continued vitality, as commitments to new facilities were honoured for human services, libraries, fire stations and public safety and 1,023 positions re-established for these high priority areas. A new cross-connecting county parkway was built, the regional mass transit rail system expanded within the County and a new regional commuter rail service instituted. The County was by no means in dire straits, but the effect of the recession was to slow or stop actual growth in services, while demand from new and ever diversifying population pressures continued to increase.

In the latter half of the 1990s extraordinary growth was expected in the school system, which accounts for 50 per cent of the County's general operating funds. Increased demand for juvenile and family services and new technology demands also were anticipated. There was also recognition that much routine maintenance, which was deferred early in the decade to balance the budget, could no longer be put off without jeopardizing the value and safety of the facilities. Transportation demands continued to increase as did normal use of all County services. In all these changes, the operating and capital budgets were inextricably linked.

Slow growth was reflected in the capital programme, as viewed through the model. The good news is that projected growth in disbursements, coupled with the completion of some major projects, primarily the parkway and jail mentioned earlier, has resulted in potential restoration of projects previously deferred, and accommodated potential new referendums for schools, transportation and other areas. It should be noted that the County has not had any new referendums for any area other than schools and transportation since 1990. The bad news is, according to the financial forecast, the County cannot afford the increase in debt service, even though the programme would fall well within the ratios. Specifically, the projected growth rate of debt service exceeds the projected growth rate in revenues, thereby directly competing with funds for needed services.

TEN PRINCIPLES OF SOUND FINANCIAL MANAGEMENT

1. Synchronize the Planning System with the Capital Improvement Program (CIP), and capital and operating budgets. Review land use plans at least every five years.
2. Reflect fiscal constraint in the Annual Budget, maintaining a managed reserve of not less than two percent of combined General Fund Disbursements.
3. Reduce appropriations and/or increase revenues to staff off any forthcoming deficit.
4. Ensure that the County's Net Debt as a percent of Assessed Value does not exceed three percent, and the Debt Service as a percent of Combined General Fund Disbursements does not exceed 10 percent. Bond sales shall not exceed US$ 750 million over a five-year period.
5. Maintain a Cash Management System, and continue to garner support from all facets of County government.
6. Employ management by objectives as in integral part of the budget process.
7. Continue to streamline operations and increase productivity and efficiency of County programs and staff.
8. Reduce redundancy and overlap in functional areas.
9. Keep "underlying" debt to an absolute minimum.
10. Continue to diversify the County's economic base.

Accordingly, as the Board of Supervisors deliberated the FY 1997 - 2001 CIP, a number of planning guidelines were adopted by the Board for the years 1998 - 2000. The primary principles adopted were that growth in debt service shall not exceed growth in revenues, and, perhaps more importantly, the planning horizon was extended from five to eight years. This permitted a larger view of capital needs and a more realistic projection of cash flow and sales requirements for multi-year projects. In addition, the eight-year planning horizon also corresponded to a sunset provision in Virginia law, which limits voter-approved debt authorization.

The County's innovation in integrating the financial and capital planning processes through the debt capacity model has been recognized by awards. As shown through constant and highly visible use, it has proven to be a flexible tool, adaptable to changing economic conditions and policy demands. With minor refinements and adaptations to new software, the model should continue to be useful for quite some time.

6. Programme detail (Figure 1)

A master spreadsheet was created, which receives inputs from the results of the financial forecast: demographic data such as population, per capital income and tax base data. Most of the calculations are based on simple formula relationships within the master spreadsheet. For example, debt service for each year of the projection is divided by the disbursements for that year and expressed as a simple percentage. More complex, however, are the calculations consolidating the debt service projections resulting from variable sales over five years. Starting with current debt service an underlying spreadsheet is constructed which records outstanding principal and interest payments for each year. The total for each year is extracted by the master spreadsheet as a part of the cell formulas.

Debt service schedules are constructed for each projected year, each in an underlying spreadsheet (up to five.) Sales data fed by the master spreadsheet are used by the underlying detail sheets to construct the principal and interest payments for each sale. In order to simplify the programme, the standard County serial pattern is used which is level principal over a 20-year term. The master spreadsheet also contains the interest rate assumption for each year, allowing the user to vary interest rates if desired. The debt service payments, which result in each year of the projection, are aggregated by the master spreadsheet and recorded as the total debt service for that year. Net debt is calculated in the same way and extracted from the detail sheets for display on the master spreadsheet.

Sales data is generated in two different ways. In a separate file, linked to the master spreadsheet through a desktop file, the results of the cash flow analysis are recorded. The cash flow analysis is generated through a series of bar charts (Figure 2) which show the engineers' estimates of expenditure for each project by quarter and type of expenditure (land acquisition, design, or construction). The totals are aggregated by purpose and recorded in a summary spreadsheet. Grand totals by year are the basis for the bond sale projections which in turn feed the master spreadsheet. Results from the master spreadsheet are fed back to a summary chart (table 1).

Another method for calculating sales is simply to enter the totals directly into the master spreadsheet. This may be necessary to generate "what if" options. A useful feature available in the spreadsheet programme called "Back Solver", allows the user to employ the programme to calculate sales by varying any other potential variable.

As already mentioned, the early calculations solved for the 10 per cent debt service limit through the simple formula: make cell <ratio> equal to 9.99 per cent by varying cell <sales>. Later, as economic circumstances changed, the formula was changed to focus on the rate of disbursement increase as the key variable.

The spreadsheets were developed by an average user of the programme with no special training. Diligent use of the user's guide and some experimentation over two or three afternoons produced the desired result. Numerous minor modifications in format and new links to minimize data entry have occurred through constant use. Future modifications may include electronic links to a new financial forecast model and cash flow graphics programmes. Maintenance is relatively simple, primarily through advancing column headers one year at the turn of the fiscal year. Much of that effort is minimized if generic years are used in the detail sheets. Changes to demographic data, tax data, and the results of actual sales also must be monitored, and the spreadsheet updated to reflect the most current information.

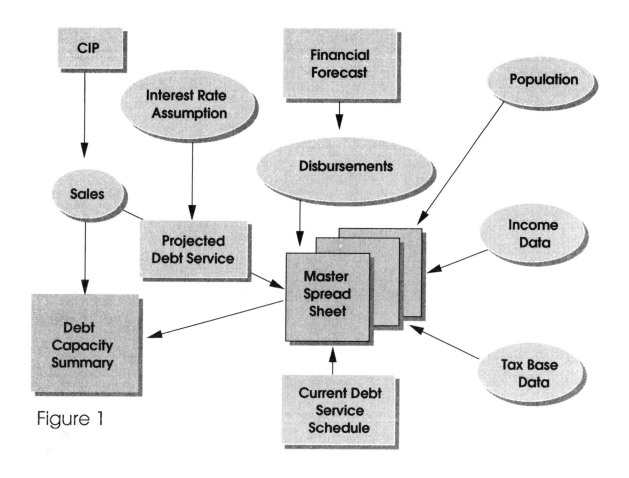

Figure 1

Sales Capacity Summary
(millions)

	Unissued	1992	1993	1994	1995	1996	1997	1993-1997 TOTAL	AUTH. REMAIN.
Sales Limit		$150.00	$150.00	$150.00	$150.00	$150.00	$150.00	$750.00	
County Total	519.345	56.00	163.24	126.76	87.11	17.50	4.22	398.83	64.5
Schools' Total	245.730	94.00	80.00	71.73	0.00	0.00	0.00	151.73	(0.0)
A SUBTOTAL	765.075	150.00	243.24	198.49	87.11	17.50	4.22	550.56	
				NEW REFERENDA					
Schools' Referenda	300.000	0.00	0.00	10.27	82.00	82.00	82.00	256.27	43.73
Parkway Referenda	117.000	0.00	22.84	44.54	36.25	8.10	5.27	117.00	0.00
METRO Referenda	100.000	0.00	0.00	0.00	4.61	25.68	19.59	49.88	50.12
B GRAND TOTAL	1,282.075	150.00	266.08	253.30	209.97	133.28	111.08	973.71	
			DEBT RATIOS CURRENT PROGRAM						
C Net Debt % of Market Value	3%	1.20%	1.70%	2.00%	2.12%	2.07%	1.83%		
D Debt Service as % of Gen Fund	10%	8.97%	9.50%	10.60%	11.18%	11.64%	11.35%		
			NECESSARY ADJUSTMENTS						
E Maximum Sales Permissible To Remain Within Ratios		150.00	170.00	150.00	150.00	135.00	148.00	753.00	
F Deferral Necessary		0.00	96.08	103.30	59.97	(1.72)	(36.92)	**220.71**	
Net Debt % of Market Value	3%	1.20%	1.55%	1.70%	1.75%	1.74%	1.54%		
Debt Service as % of Gen Fund	10%	8.97%	9.50%	9.85%	9.86%	9.99%	9.99%		
Operating Costs of New Facilities		0.00	3.79	25.73	22.29	$43.94			

Table 1

DEBT MANAGEMENT IN SUBNATIONAL GOVERNMENTS THE CASE OF ARGENTINA

Marcelo Tricario & Emilio Nastri

1. The circle of subnational public debt

1.1. Decentralization of spending

During the last 20 years there has been a growing tendency worldwide for central Governments to devolve their responsibilities to local and regional governments. About 70 countries in Latin America, Central Europe and other parts of the world, with more than five million inhabitants, have adopted decentralization policies.

Opinions differ with respect to the advantages and disadvantages of this process. There are those who maintain that decentralization promotes a more efficient allocation of resources for the provision of public services and, consequently, that it requires greater accountability; this forces subnational governments to be more responsible when entering into debt. Others, citing the symbolic case of the Brazilian crisis in 1999, argue that decentralization can have an adverse effect on a country's macroeconomic stability, as officials can use their new powers to borrow irresponsibly and use the debt as a means of pressuring the central Government into transferring more resources.

Despite the continuing debate about the necessary restrictions and the level of access to capital markets that should be granted to subnational governments, and the degree of participation of the central Government in the process, the trend towards more decentralization, during the last 10 years, has led to a significant increase in subnational governments' participation in the capital markets and in public finance.

In the particular case of Argentina, the provinces and municipalities have almost complete responsibility for public administration in the fields of education, security, justice and health, and concentrate 80 per cent of consolidated expenditure on those services. Consequently, the provincial public sector as a whole manages to spend about US$ 36 billion a year, which represents over 40 per cent of Argentina's total public expenditure. The year 1999 closed with an estimated deficit of around US$ 2.8 billion and a public debt of about US$ 18 billion, with maturities heavily concentrated over the following two years.

1.2. Impact on the fiscal accounts

In addition to decentralizing spending, in the last 10 years Argentina has been engaged in carrying out a series of structural reforms, basically designed to exclude those activities which are unconnected with the core responsibilities of local government, to enable it to function better. Together, these measures have given rise to a system of fiscal and financial arrangements that has made many of the reforms irreversible. Nevertheless, not all the subnational governments are in the same fiscal situation, since, in some jurisdictions, unresolved structural problems continue to exist. As a result, the fiscal situation in Argentina as a whole is not without its risks.

Accordingly, in analysing the fiscal accounts, the IMF follows a line that reflects the arithmetic of the capital markets by considering the country's global deficit, which is made up of three separate components: national, provincial and municipal. Thus, for example, the letter of intent and economic policy memorandum signed by the Argentine Government and the IMF in connection with the standby arrangement of February 2000 included, for the first time, guidelines for the provincial public sector deficit and binding growth targets for the public debt of the consolidated public sector, involving both the central and provincial governments.

Clearly, the fiscal deficit is all one, although from the institutional standpoint, in a federal system of government, the nation cannot interfere in the public accounts of the subnational governments, and nor can the IMF negotiate with them, since its own internal regulations prevent it from doing so. In short, the national Government can negotiate fiscal targets with the provinces, but only within the framework of voluntary agreements. The impact on the public finances can no longer be considered in isolation. The central and provincial governments are all in the same boat, and when one subnational entity has problems, it generates turbulence, with adverse effects on public credit as a whole. Thus no subnational government can finance itself reasonably in a country that is not financing itself.

If we also take into account the fact that the deficit is highly pro-cyclic – just as spending is pro-cyclic, because, when the fiscal deficit increases, so does the risk premium – then, from a long-term standpoint, it becomes essential to pursue two basic strategies:

(i)   create the conditions necessary to establish credibility; and
(ii)   hierarchize fiscal policy as an instrument of economic policy so as to offset the effects of endemic budgetary imbalances.

In this connection, Dillinger and Webb of the World Bank have made an analysis[1] of the fiscal behaviour of subnational governments in Argentina and Brazil during the 1990s. One of their basic conclusions is that if we want good fiscal behaviour, we must provide institutions that offer proper incentives.

1.3.   Financing through subnational treasury debt

In addition to decentralizing spending, it will be necessary to define the responsibility of each tier of government with regard to authorized expenditure, allocated resources and tax collection, a combination of which will determine the level of self-financing by each local government and the need for it to resort to other sources of financing to cover its costs and investments.

The case of Argentina is an example of "lack of fiscal correspondence" since, on average, the taxes raised by the provinces themselves barely cover 40 per cent of their expenditure (in the OECD member States, the coverage is over 70 per cent) and the provincial governments are not exercising strict fiscal responsibility, as their management of their expenditure appears to be largely detached from the effort and risk of collecting their own resources from their taxpayers.

---

[1] Dillinger W and Webb S. Fiscal Management in Federal Democracies (undated) . Policy Research Working Paper 2121: The World Bank, Washington DC. - www.worldbank.org/html/dec/Publications/Workpapers/home.html.

Within this context, in order to meet the Argentine provincial public sector's financing requirements in the year 2000, which amount to approximately US$ 6 billion, smooth access to sources of financing and less onerous loan redemption terms are essential. Thus, better administration of the public debt will make a definite contribution to improving borrowing conditions, especially in the more deeply committed jurisdictions which find themselves in a weak negotiating position.

1.4. The dilemma of centralized or decentralized decision-making and control of subnational government debt

It is not the main purpose of this study to determine the best model for controlling subnational debt; in fact, it is important to understand that there are various possibilities depending on each country's institutional organization.

There can be no doubt that decisions on subnational debt should be subject to controls. However, opinions differ as to which is the most appropriate method of control in each particular case, how the control should be exercised and by whom. For example, under a unitary system of government, the subnational governments do not have real autonomy of resources or expenditure, and it is therefore advisable that their debt be strictly controlled by the central Government, which is the ultimate guarantor of the fulfilment of their financial obligations. On the other hand, under a federal system of government, it is debatable whether a nation can regulate the borrowing capacity of the provinces, although in situations of crisis or imbalance, federal remedies are generally available for providing relief to subnational governments.

There are those who question the effectiveness of controls; for example, one of the conclusions of the Dillinger and Webb study is that the objective of fiscal discipline is better achieved by the central Government adopting a "neutral" policy, rather than a policy which makes it responsible for what the subnational governments are doing and for monitoring their debt and bailing them out when they run into trouble. The study describes how, in Brazil, the subnational debt was under the direct control of the Senate which was susceptible to political pressure, and how the controls which the federal executive tried to establish were ultimately evaded by the states.

Eggers[2] (1999), commenting on the study by Dillinger and Webb, notes that under a federal system of government, central paternalism could be counterproductive since it deters subnational governments from shouldering their responsibilities. Eggers also points out that, in general, the central Government cannot prevent subnational governments from obtaining access to all types of debt. At best, it can prevent access only to certain types of debt, such as that arranged through government securities or bank loans. In fact, it would always be possible to borrow in other ways, for example by giving undertakings to suppliers and contractors or guaranteeing third-party debts which, as a result of the principal defaulting, end up by reverting to the subnational government. In this case, controls would simply have the effect of worsening the quality of the debt.

Ter-Minassian[3] (1996) presents a broad panorama of the various methods of controlling the debt of regional and local governments in a wide range of industrialized and developing

---

[2]Eggers F. Control of subnational debt. The experience of Argentina and Brazil in the 1990s. *Revista ASAP No 34. December 1999.*

[3] Ter-Minassian T. Subnational government debt. Problems and international experience. PPAA/96/IMF working paper, International Monetary Fund, Washington DC, April 1996.

countries. She points out that the nature and coverage of these controls vary considerably depending on the history of the country, the relative power of the different levels of government, the macroeconomic and fiscal conditions and the state of development of the financial markets.

There are four main methods, which range from leaving almost everything to the discipline of the market, to direct control by the central Government over every public borrowing operation carried out by subnational government entities by way of intermediate policies, such as cooperation between the different levels of government in controlling debt and rule-based controls.

In the above-mentioned study, Ter-Minassian notes that central government control over the debt of subnational governments could be justified if:

(i)   Debt policy is linked with other macroeconomic and exchange rate policies;

(ii)   A unified method, which could result in better terms than a fragmented one, is used for raising loans;

(iii)   The deterioration of the credit rating of a subnational borrower might spread contagion and there is a risk of a default by one subnational government, affecting all the rest; or

(iv)   The lenders require an explicit guarantee from the central Government or, at the very least, are counting on an implicit guarantee.

Among the principal conclusions is a recommendation calling for greater transparency and the dissemination of information on the finances of subnational governments, increased cooperation between all levels of government with a view to slowing or reversing the growth of public debt, and the maintenance of effective political and intellectual leadership by the central Government, as a natural next step in the evolution of the central Government's traditional administrative controls in an increasingly decentralized world.

It is clear that, regardless of the different approaches described, when the data on the finances of subnational governments in developing countries are analysed, all these countries are found to be suffering from serious deficiencies in the coverage, quality and up-to-dateness of the debt information available. There can be no question that any method adopted should provide transparent and reliable information on the public debt, should solve the problem of information asymmetry, and should ensure that everyone in the same country speaks the same fiscal language.

1.5.   Proposals for achieving fiscal solvency in subnational government

In a federal country, progress towards transparency and fiscal responsibility on the part of Governments requires the establishment of agreed standards, approved and accepted by the parties involved and, of necessity, government austerity, which is indispensable if the political signal is to be reflected in the national accounts. What has been the common denominator in cases such as those of Italy and the United States, where the financial situation has been brought under control? Confidence, a serious policy, credible executants, a time horizon and certainty. A study of the experience of other countries clearly reveals that the search for the necessary agreement between the national and subnational governments mainly involves:

(i)   *The need to achieve fiscal balance*, which requires the provinces and municipalities to make progress with the adoption of a regulatory framework that places limits on the imbalances permissible.

(ii)   *The generation of anti-cyclical contingency funds* as a means of offsetting possible economic shocks and reducing the risk premium, given that expenditure does not necessarily increase at the same rate as income.

(iii)   *Greater transparency in public administration* and transformation of the management of the State to improve the quality of public services. This includes the need for a public information system covering such areas as finances, debt, procurement and the allocation of funds, based on the possibilities offered by advances in communications.

(iv)   *The organization of provincial public investment systems* which systematically evaluate investment projects, using internationally recommended methods, with a view to steering borrowing towards projects that yield a social return.

(v)   *The establishment of integrated financial information systems* to improve the quality and timeliness of information on resources, expenditure and public borrowing. In this connection, UNCTAD's Debt Management and Financial Analysis System (DMFAS)[4] or another equivalent information system, together with an appropriate regulatory and structural framework, could be transformed into a powerful tool at the service of fiscal policy and the management of subnational public debt.

All these factors, plus all the other initiatives that point in the same direction, will help to improve transparency in public administration, and ultimately make it easier for the public in general, its representatives in the legislature and the press to exercise control.

To sum up, economic growth and fiscal order, in keeping with the golden rule of financing all current expenditure out of current income, together with that other golden rule of public spending – a high degree of austerity on every front – require, inter alia, good debt management with the following principal objectives: first, the fulfilment of obligations and the reduction of financing costs and, second, the maintenance or extension of the average life of the obligations.

2.   The case of Argentina: the situation and the legislation adopted

2.1.   The public debt situation in the Argentine provinces

At the end of 1999, the consolidated debt stock of the 24 jurisdictions that make up the provincial public sector amounted to about $18 billion, or approximately 55 per cent of the total resources of the corresponding provinces for the same year, and could be broken down according to type of creditor and type of debt instrument as follows:

---

[4] DMFAS has been installed in more than 40 countries for the purpose of providing those facing large external debt balances with a tool for managing and organizing their debt and public finances.

Breakdown of provincial debt stock by type of instrument

(as a percentage of the global debt of the 24 provincial jurisdictions)

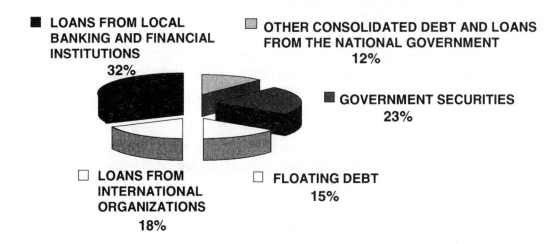

■ LOANS FROM LOCAL BANKING AND FINANCIAL INSTITUTIONS
32%

☐ OTHER CONSOLIDATED DEBT AND LOANS FROM THE NATIONAL GOVERNMENT
12%

■ GOVERNMENT SECURITIES
23%

☐ LOANS FROM INTERNATIONAL ORGANIZATIONS
18%

☐ FLOATING DEBT
15%

Source: Based on data compiled by the Regional Programming Sub-Secretariat of the Ministry of the Economy for the year 1999

In the year 2000, because of the concentration of due dates within a short period of time, the provincial governments will have to go out and seek approximately US$ 6 billion in financing, that is somewhat more than in the previous year. This will have a considerable impact on the local financial market, since it represents a significant proportion of the creditworthiness of the system.

2.2.   Principal components of the subnational public sector debt stock

This section describes the characteristics of the more common debt instruments that make up the public debt of the subnational governments.

Loans from local banking and financial institutions: According to the figures available, there is strong interest among jurisdictions in this type of debt, which accounts for about one third of the total. It takes the form of bank loans guaranteed by the legal assignment under the federal revenue-sharing scheme of taxes collected by the national Government and transferred to the provinces on a proportional basis in accordance with the laws in force. In general, these are three-to five-year loans at interest rates which vary according to the negotiating capacity of the province concerned. Agreements of this type are made with a large number of eligible banks and are based on a wide variety of loans with a complex legal and financial structure.

In most cases repayments of principal and interest payments are made under the "daily drip"[5] system. The fact that this is a variable process makes it impossible to calculate exactly when the debt will be completely paid off. In general, it is possible to observe an acceleration of

---

[5] Regular daily deduction of the percentages or fixed amounts transferred by the province to the creditor until the debt has been completely paid off. The deductions and transfers are made by Banco de la Nación Argentina as the payments agent for tax and revenue sharing resources.

the process leading to a decrease in the average term (1-3 years), which is causing serious reconciliation problems and making it difficult for the debtor to monitor the state of the loan. This is because the effective amount of federal revenue-sharing income allocated to each province depends on the levels of tax collection, is ultimately variable and remains closely linked with the debt stock. This type of guarantee is also used for loans from international organizations, for government security issues and as surety for third-party operations with, in some cases, different orders of priority or preference, depending on the terms of the various agreements with the creditors.

Government securities: the "provincial government securities" category has grown the most rapidly in recent years and now accounts for about 23 per cent of the total debt of the provincial jurisdictions. These operations have terms that range from 6 to 16 years (including grace periods) and generally pay a variable rate of interest.

Within the provincial securities category, there are two groups clearly differentiated with respect to the way in which they are placed on the market, namely, forced placement securities, (i.e. those issued compulsorily as a means of paying arrears of wages or debts owed to suppliers), and voluntary debt issues (placed by direct subscription, auction, sale on the securities markets, or through financial syndicates, for example for purchase by investors who are not obliged to accept them).

Some jurisdictions, such as, for example, the government of the City of Buenos Aires and the provinces of Buenos Aires and Mendoza, have issued securities without assigning specific provincial resources. In the event of default these would be backed by the Provinces' assets. On the other hand, most provincial issues have been based on the allocation of resources from the federal revenue-sharing regime or from other sources such as oil royalties.

Floating debt: The floating debt consists of obligations originating in arrears in payments to suppliers, contractors and employees or transfers not made to the municipalities. It differs from financial debt in having matured and not having a fixed due date. This type of debt is reaching significant levels for the provincial jurisdictions as a whole (about 15 per cent of the total).

Strictly speaking, until such time as a proper consolidation and/or refinancing mechanism is established, the floating debt will remain excluded from the classical definition of the use of public credit. Nevertheless, in many provinces, when large instalments of financial debt, generally guaranteed by federal-revenue sharing, fall due, they are often paid from these resources by delaying regular payments for a time and thus increasing the floating debt.

In this way, the floating debt is being transformed into a more or less non-transparent mechanism for increasing the public debt, since it evades the legal requirements relating to its composition, makes no provision for proper recording and is threatening to become one of the most expensive forms of debt. This is because it conceals price markups by suppliers and contractors who pass on their financial costs, and more, in the face of the repeated adoption of this practice by the Government.

Loans from international organizations: The provincial debt, corresponding to resources obtained through loans from international organizations such as the Inter-American Development Bank and International Bank for Reconstruction and Development, accounts for approximately 18 per cent of the total; it is showing a tendency to increase as compared with previous years. In general, these funds are being spent on infrastructure projects and on reform of the provincial accounts.

From the standpoint of the provincial administrations, there are two kinds of modalities for these loans. Less common are loans made directly to the jurisdiction by the international organization, generally with a national government guarantee. The more usual arrangement is a subsidiary agreement applicable to a number of eligible jurisdictions and signed by the provincial and national governments the latter assuming the obligation to the international organization.

In this latter case, the information on disbursements, repayments and loan conditions is handled by the central project implementation unit, which makes it difficult for the provinces to obtain access to precise information about the loans in which they are involved.

2.3.   Main Legislation adopted

Under the Constitution, Argentina is a country with a federal system of government in which the provinces retain all the powers not delegated expressly to the federal Government.

The right to control the provincial debt is not one of the functions delegated. Thus there is no legal way in which the federal Government can regulate the capacity of the provinces to enter into debt, although, in practice, it generally provides the assistance to a province threatened with financial collapse.

Nevertheless, in view of Argentina's fiscal deficit and debt crisis, and because of the commitments made to the IMF, a number of joint strategies designed to strengthen the fiscal policy of the governments are currently being put into effect. These include, in particular, the approval of a national fiscal solvency act which invites the provinces, to adopt similar provisions, and an act ratifying the federal agreement signed by the governors and the central Government, described below.

Fiscal Solvency Act (No 25.152): Promulgated in September 1999, this Act establishes the framework within which the powers of the national Government for administering public resources must fit. To this end, it lays down the following basic rules:

- Limits to be placed on the fiscal deficit (as a percentage of GDP) until financial balance is achieved in the year 2003;

- The real rate of growth of primary public spending not to be allowed to exceed the real rate of growth of GDP;

- Strict limits to be imposed on the maximum increase in the national debt as a function of the national non-financial public sector deficit and other variables;

- Creation of an anti-cyclical tax fund;

- Establishment of a series of guidelines for the reform of the State and an expenditure quality assessment programme.

In addition, the Act requires documentation produced within the national administration to be classed as public information, freely accessible to any interested institution or individual. It also requires the national executive to invite the provincial governments and the autonomous government of the City of Buenos Aires to adopt legislation consistent with its provisions.

Act ratifying the Federal Agreement (No 25.235): Promulgated in December 1999, this Act ratifies the agreement signed by the governors of the provinces and the central Government laying down guidelines for the implementation of measures designed to contribute to balanced national growth and to avoid the adverse effects on production and employment of a high level of global public sector debt.

To this end, it encourages the incorporation of the following principles in the national and/or provincial legislation to be adopted in the future:

(i)   Transparency of fiscal information;

(ii)   Ratification in the year 2000 of the new federal revenue-sharing act;

(iii)   Creation of an anti-cyclical fund financed from revenue-sharing resources, similar to that created by Act 25.152;

(iv)   Coordination of the public credit and provincial debt systems; and

(v)   Rationalization and improvement of interjurisdictional tax administration and establishment and strengthening of a federal fiscal authority.

In this connection, the federal Government, the provincial governors and the head of the government of the City of Buenos Aires agree to:

- Submit a federal-revenue sharing bill in which all the provinces assume greater responsibility for the determination and control of primary and secondary resource distribution criteria;

- Promote, in each jurisdiction, the passage of legislation that adopts principles similar to those laid down for the nation in the Fiscal Solvency Act (No 25.152) with a view to reducing the fiscal deficit, holding down public spending, establishing self-imposed limits on indebtedness and ensuring fiscal transparency.

- Establish procedures for facilitating the broad dissemination of their fiscal accounts, including the budget, its implementation, debt and debt service projections, using systems that employ the new technology provided by computer networks.

Within the framework of the Federal Agreement, in February 2000, the first specific agreements were concluded with the provinces of Tucumán, Tierra del Fuego, Catamarca and Río Negro. It is expected that agreements with other provinces will be signed in the course of the year. In these agreements, the provinces undertake to reduce their fiscal deficits and the national Government undertakes, through a trust fund, to negotiate banking sector loans to cover short-term obligations on terms more favourable than those available to the provinces individually. At the same time the central Government undertakes to establish a system of quarterly monitoring of the fulfilment of the undertakings given.

2.4.   National strategy for management of the public debt

The State strategy with respect to the management of the public debt was brought within the framework of the Government's financial administration reform programme and began to be implemented with the promulgation of Act No 24.156 at the end of 1992. In this context, at the beginning of 1993, the lack of accurate information on the public debt made it necessary to set up, as quickly as possible, a recording system that would provide reliable information about the nation's financial commitments and which, at the same time, would contribute to the due and timely fulfilment of its obligations to creditors.

Accordingly, at the end of 1993, with the assistance of the UNCTAD project on the creation of a debt registry and the strengthening of public debt management in the Argentine Republic, it was decided to install version 4.1 plus of the DMFAS in the National Public Credit Office, the agency in charge of the public credit system. Regular updating of DMFAS, together with the incorporation of the network processing modality, made it possible in 1996 and 1997, to develop a connection module linking DMFAS and the Integrated Financial Information System (SIDIF). This involved procedures relating to the servicing of the debt and the recording of the receipt of funds in connection with public credit operations.

On the basis of the experience acquired, and in view of the requests from some provinces stressing the need for reliable and transparent information on the debt assumed, a project for the installation of DMFAS in subnational administrations was drawn up and signed on 16 February 2000 with a view to improving the management of the public debt by local governments and strengthening the administration of their public finances. The installation of DMFAS in the provincial administrations calls for strategies of cooperation and coordination between the different levels of government. The strategies are designed to consolidate policies of fiscal discipline and transparency in the use of public resources by establishing common rules and exchanges of experience in financial administration in the particularly sensitive area of public debt management.

3.   Project for the installation of DMFAS in subnational administrations

3.1.   Aim of the project

The main aim of the project is to strengthen the ability of subnational governments to manage, record and administer the provincial and municipal public debt by installing, providing training in, and bringing into operation, the computerized DMFAS developed by UNCTAD, suitably adapted to the realities and needs of the governments concerned.

3.2.   The participants, their basic roles and responsibilities

Responsibilities of the Ministry of the Economy: These include: national project management; establishment of a framework agreement with UNCTAD; definition and coordination of framework agreements with subnational governments and project financing conditions; and maintenance of the central facilities of DMFAS Provincial.

Requirements to be met by each of the subnational governments involved: Establishment and/or designation of a special public credit working group and allocation of personnel suitable for providing training in operating and administering DMFAS; provision of suitable premises and operating conditions for the equipment; and agreement to create the conditions necessary for gathering the reliable debt information which the system requires.

Responsibilities of UNCTAD: Supplying of the system; development of the modifications necessary to adapt the system to the situation prevailing in the provinces; supervision of the preparation of special system manuals; provision of system updates; and general follow-up and technical support for the project.

Responsibilities of the project coordinator: General coordination of the project; general coordination of the installation and training operations in the provinces; and general coordination of the training programme in Buenos Aires.

Responsibilities of the working group: Installation of DMFAS and provision of training; analysis of the necessary adjustments to the system and coordination with UNCTAD on its development; technical assistance with the input of information into the system and its correct use; and direct help for the users in maintaining and operating DMFAS.

It is important to point out that the programme will be administered on a national implementation basis with the active participation of the United Nations Development Programme (UNDP) office in Buenos Aires, which guarantees the participating provinces transparency and internationally accepted standards for the administration of the assistance provided to each subnational government in implementating the project.

3.3.   Expected outcome

At the end of the project, the participating subnational governments will have at their disposal a technical team whose main task will be to manage, record and administer the public debt, supported by the National Directorate for Fiscal Coordination with the Provinces of the Ministry of the Economy and the technical expertise of the National Public Credit Office, backed by the DMFAS Group at UNCTAD.

With this in mind, it is considered that the main results expected to be achieved by the end of the project are as follows:

(i)   Strengthening of the capacity of subnational governments to manage, record and administer the public debt;

(ii)   Establishment in each jurisdiction of a technical group, department or office responsible for carrying out public credit-related tasks, with proper training in the operation and maintenance of DMFAS;

(iii)   Installation and commissioning of DMFAS, under the supervision of the offices mentioned in (ii);

(iv)   Incorporation in the database installed in each jurisdiction of particulars of the loans outstanding and debt service schedules;

(v)   Establishment within the National Directorate for Fiscal Coordination with the Provinces, in the Ministry of the Economy, of a group to provide support and technical assistance for subnational governments;

(vi)   Adaptation of DMFAS to the realities and needs of the subnational governments;

(vii)   Preparation of special DMFAS user manuals for provincial administrations; and

(viii)   Initial study of the feasibility of a link-up between DMFAS and the Provincial Financial Administration System.

At the same time, the use of the same debt management and administration tool in all the different jurisdictions will help to ensure greater transparency and standardization of the information on the subnational public sector debt. This will make it possible to improve the coordination and consolidation of provincial and national fiscal policies. In addition, it should be noted that the present project forms part of a series of fiscal policy and public resource administration measures and instruments. Insofar as these are consolidated, they will help to improve the perception and characterization of the credit risk, on the part of both the central Government and subnational governments, with a consequent improvement in financing costs and conditions.

3.4.   Description of the project

The project for the installation of DMFAS in the subnational administrations will be divided into five main phases or stages as described below:

(i)   *Setting up the project and detailed work programme*: This stage consists of negotiating and drawing up the necessary agreements with the participating provinces, establishing the infrastructure and a working team suitable for providing training in and installing DMFAS at headquarters and in each of the provinces, and developing and updating a detailed project work plan. The activities to be undertaken include recording, analysing and reporting on the situation in each province and preparing special manuals, adapted to the conditions in the provinces. The manuals will include definitions of common terms and explanations of the use of the system in conformity with the particular characteristics of the provinces and their legislation. This stage will also include a feasibility study of the development of a link-up between DMFAS and the Provincial Financial Administration System.

(ii)   *Training in DMFAS*: This stage covers all the training activities necessary for the proper installation of DMFAS in the provinces. It includes general training in public credit at project headquarters, training in database administration and training for the future DMFAS users in each province in the use of the system and the entry of debt information into the database.

(iii)   *Installation of DMFAS and input of information into the provincial debt database*: This stage involves the installation of DMFAS in designated computers, with a corresponding functionality test, together with the establishment of a debt database in each province. To this end, in each case it will be necessary to establish a cutoff date for the system, enter the loan balances and corresponding schedules, and identify the sources of information on individual transactions from the date in question to the present, in addition to reconciling the balances on the cutoff date with the respective creditors.

(iv)   *Localization of DMFAS*: This stage includes the adaptation of DMFAS to the particular characteristics and requirements of the provincial debt instruments and the incorporation of these modifications in to the information system. The main activities to be developed involve recording the particular terms of the provincial contracts, designing and programming the new functions, preparing the documentation, testing, and incorporating the modifications in the installations in each province.

(v)   ***Technical assistance***: This phase of the project comprises ongoing technical assistance for provincial users in aspects relating to public credit, in general, and DMFAS, in particular, and technical support for the working team provided by UNCTAD. This stage also includes the necessary updating of the special system manuals and the provision of new versions of DMFAS developed during the course of the project.

3.5.   Work plan

Schedule of activities (in months)

Results and activities	Entity responsible	1	2	3	4	5	6	7	8	9
Allocation of personnel and resources, headquarters	National coordinator	■								
Allocation of personnel and resources, provinces	Provinces	■								
Recording of situation in provinces	National coordinator	■								
Work programme and report, by province	National coordinator		■							
Preparation of special manuals	UNCTAD/work team		■							
General training at headquarters	National coordinator		■							
Technical DMFAS training in each province	Working team				■					
Training in the use of DMFAS and data input in each province	Working team					■				
Advanced training in each province	Working team								■	
Installation of DMFAS in each province	Working team					■				
Establishment of database	Provinces and working team					■	■	■	■	■
System adaptation survey	UNCTAD		■							
Global design for system adaptation	UNCTAD			■						
Programming of system adaptation	UNCTAD				■					
Testing and modifications to manuals	UNCTAD/work team					■				
Support for users in the provinces	Working team			■	■	■	■	■	■	■
Technical support for working team	UNCTAD	■	■	■	■	■	■	■	■	■
Updating manuals	UNCTAD/work team								■	■
Updating DMFAS versions	UNCTAD					■	■	■	■	■

3.6.   Project organization and cost estimates

Initially, the project has been designed for an overall period of nine months. It envisages the installation of DMFAS in three local governments, with the support of a central facility under the Ministry of the Economy. On the basis of the objectives and scope of the project, transparent, economical and efficient means of administering the resources allocated by the provincial administrations for achieving these objectives have been devised. Thus, in view of the fact that the debt problems of the various subnational governments are similar in nature, a shared-cost project that ensures the maximum possible economies of scale has been drawn up.

It is estimated that under the above-mentioned plan for the project, the overall cost per subnational government will be about US$ 75,000, not including the cost of the computer equipment and software licences.

References

1.	World Bank, Sipa, Moody's and DEVFIN Advisers. *How to Gain Access to the Capital Markets*. Manual for local and regional governments in Latin America and Central Europe.

2.	Dilliger W and Webb S. Fiscal management in federal democracies.
	Policy Research Working Paper 2121 (draft) The World Bank, Washington DC.
	www.worldbank.org/html/dec/Publications/Workpapers/home.html.

3.	Eggers F (1999). Control of subnational debt. The experience of Argentina and Brazil in the 1990s. *Revista ASAP* No 34, December.

4.	Ter-Minassian T (1996). Subnational government debt: Problems and international experience. Working paper, PPAA/96/IMF, International Monetary Fund, Washington DC, April.

Printed at United Nations, Geneva
GE.01-53138–December 2001–3,695

UNCTAD/GDS/DMFAS/MISC.23

United Nations publication
Sales No. E.01.II.D.17

ISBN 92-1-112528-6